Winning Badminton Doubles

Winning Badminton Doubles

JAKE DOWNEY

Photographs by Louis Ross

Adam & Charles Black · London

TO SARAH

First published 1984
by A & C Black (Publishers) Limited
35 Bedford Row, London WC1R 4JH

Downey, Jake
  Winning badminton doubles.
  1. Badminton (Game)–Doubles
  I. Title
  796.34'5   GV1007.5.D6
  ISBN 0-7136-2603-8
  ISBN 0-7136-2655-0 Pbk

Design and illustration: Douglas Martin Associates

Typeset by Armitage Typo/Graphics Limited, Huddersfield
Printed and bound in Great Britain by R.J.Acford,
Chichester

ISBN 0-7136-2655-0

Contents

Part Three: Performance

Part Four: Training and Practice

Preface

Winning Badminton Doubles has two main purposes: first, to explain clearly what goes on in doubles; second, to show you how to become a better doubles player and achieve more success in competition. This book is concerned with ladies' and men's doubles (level doubles) and mixed doubles. As far as I know there is no other book devoted solely to doubles play. One reason why such a book has not yet been published may be that there appear to be too many variables to include them all in one volume; this was the opinion of one of England's world class doubles players when I was discussing the project with him. He was right in suggesting that there are many variables, in the sense that there appear to be numerous situations with many moves possible in each situation; but in fact doubles looks more complex than it is. When you watch doubles it appears to be a frenzy of activity as the players constantly adjust their positions to hit the shuttle which hurtles across the net at speed, and it seems difficult to sort out what is going on and to distinguish the various patterns that occur in the game. Actually it is quite easy to do this. Doubles can be reduced to simple situations and patterns of play – when you read Part One of the book I am sure you will agree with me that this is so.

Part Two takes a closer look at the situations in level doubles and includes a chapter devoted exclusively to mixed doubles. In the situations examined in doubles I look at and discuss the positional play, the various attack and defence formations, the stroke-moves and the replies the players can make. Part Three explains what is entailed in your performance in the game with respect to skill, fitness and attitude. Finally, Part Four provides a wealth of practical information on how to develop certain aspects of your fitness, and suggests numerous exercises which you can select from in order to develop your flexibility, strength, speed, power and agility, and all of which relate specifically to badminton doubles. The last chapter deals exclusively with practice and includes a long list of practices designed specifically to improve your technical and tactical play in doubles.

I have written this book in such a way as to help you to follow the development of play in the game in simple stages. For that reason I would suggest that you read through the book from beginning to end to obtain a general idea of that development. After that you can 'dip in' anywhere to read about situations you might experience in play and for which you need some guidance. For those readers who prefer to be more selective, I would recommend reading Part One and Chapter 4 before looking at the other sections that interest you.

When using the book, please bear in mind these points:

1. I have assumed that all readers are right-handed players. Readers who are left-handed should reverse the descriptions when appropriate.

2. The noun 'man' and the pronoun 'he' are used for general discussion. All the comments about 'he' and 'man' in doubles play apply equally to women unless specific reference is made to male or female players, e.g. as in mixed doubles.

3. The following symbols have been used in the diagrams to designate the players and the shuttlecock:

   the attacking player

   the defending player

   represents the direction the player travels in the court

the length of the arrow indicates the distance the player travels

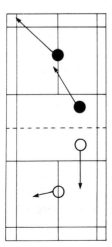

Example of players travelling while adjusting their positions in the court

The attacking side is in the top half of each diagram unless otherwise stated

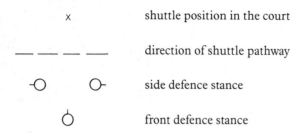

x   shuttle position in the court

— — — —   direction of shuttle pathway

side defence stance

front defence stance

The diagrams of the court positions have been drawn with the minimum of lines and symbols for the sake of clarity and on occasion have been supplemented with photographs.

I am pleased to add my thanks to friends who read through the text for me and made many helpful comments: Paul Whetnall, Sue Whetnall, Nora Perry, David Pegg, Eve Preston, David Eddy and Gillian Clark.

Part One

The Game

Chapter 1 The Structure of the Game

The purpose of this part of the book is to analyse the logical structure of the game in order to create a tactical framework for you and your partner to use. This framework will apply equally to ladies', men's and mixed doubles at whatever level you play the game. It can be used to decide what tactics to adopt and how you will combine and work as a pair in attack and defence to defeat the opponents and win the contest.

Tactics and the principle of attack

I am going to assume that we all know the different aspects of the game to some extent. We know that it includes the skills, the strokes, general movement and footwork. It includes tactics which we know are somehow related to the skills. Fitness too is related to the skills, and we also realise that certain attitudes play a large part in our performance. We admire those players who can concentrate and show determination in their efforts to win. We experience feelings of frustration, annoyance, fear, joy and excitement which may or may not help us to play better. Finally, most of us have a sense of what is correct behaviour in a game with another person and believe that fairness is highly desirable; we know this because we often discuss such things in conversations about the game and its players.

It is vital for all players and spectators to recognise and understand the connection between strokes and tactics. This is central to the game. If the connection is understood, players should be able to play more intelligently and with more imagination so as to create opportunities to win the contest. Likewise, spectators should appreciate to a greater extent the subtleties of play and the battle of wits between the two sides.

However, this is not to exclude the other aspects as unimportant. Indeed, they are very important, for if a player's attitude is not appropriate and his fitness is not up to the demands of the game then his strokes and tactical play can be affected. The

wrong attitude, fear or annoyance, can divert the player's thoughts from his opponents and the best means to beat them. Poor fitness can result in a tired body and affect the strokes and movement about the court, thus preventing the player from using his strokes effectively as tactical moves to defeat the opponents. If players cannot reach the shuttle and hit it accurately with control because of fatigue, then for all their skill and intelligence they will not possess the necessary instrument—a fit body—to carry out their plans; and it is most important that they should be able to carry out their plans, for tactics are the most essential part of the game—they give meaning to it.

Tactics cannot be physically seen; they are the underlying ideas which make sense of everything else that the players do during the game. They determine the extent to which all the other aspects are used and the way they relate to each other. Although without knowing tactics it is possible to enjoy the way players hit the shuttle, their athleticism and grace of movement, and to admire their competitive and sporting behaviour throughout the contest, it is not possible to know what they are trying to do or appreciate the sense of what they do. It is also impossible to judge what they do as right or wrong, good or bad, appropriate or inappropriate in relation to their partners, opponents and aim—to win the contest.

When a player smashes the shuttle to the midcourt and then travels into position to cover certain replies, he is applying tactics. Each time one player hits the shuttle he should be making a move to obtain a reply which will enable his side to make another move or end the rally. Tactics reflect the player's thinking—or lack of it. In choosing one particular tactic instead of some other, players should be guided by an underlying principle, the 'principle of attack': *at all times try to create a situation in which it is possible to make a scoring hit.* All the tactical moves are made towards this end, for this is the most important principle in the development of badminton as an attacking game. It provides the general strategic reasons, the rationale, for the use of any tactic.

If tactics are the moves in the game, then strokes are the means of making the moves. If the players apply the principle of attack in a game then the strokes cease to be only strokes and become 'stroke-moves'. The strokes and the moves become inseparable. Tactics do not exist without the strokes and the strokes are meaningless in the context of the game unless they carry out the tactics. The other components of the game, fitness and attitude, become important solely because they are necessary to ensure that players can maintain their chosen tactics throughout the duration of the contest. If one player is lacking in physical strength or firmness of character, then he and his partner might be forced to change their tactics during the game. For example, a pair could not choose tactics designed to speed up the game or out-hit the opponents if one or both partners were lacking in strength and agility, determination and adventurousness. The choice of tactics depends on skill to make the moves, and fitness and the right sort of attitude to keep up the work and maintain the pressure throughout. A doubles pair must be able to carry out the tactics which it adopts in accordance with the 'principle of attack'.

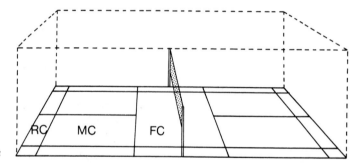

Fig. 1a

The situations in the game

These can be identified quite easily. Fig. 1a shows how the court is divided into three main areas: the rearcourt (RC), midcourt (MC) and the forecourt (FC). These areas provide the location for all the situations which occur in the game. As the court is rectangular and divided by a net 5ft (1.5m) high it is possible to establish a specific number of situations in each area. This is done by taking the position of the shuttle in the court, relative to the height of the net and the player about to hit it. The shuttle is either high or low in the court. In a high position the shuttle is above net height and can be hit in a downward direction; in a low position the shuttle is below net height and must be hit in an upward direction. These positions will vary from very low (near the ground) to very high (the highest point a player can reach to hit the shuttle). Midway between these two positions, at approximately net height, the shuttle can be hit on a horizontal pathway (see fig. 1b).

Fig. 1b

The basic situations are:

Rearcourt situations: the stroke-moves are made from high or low positions at the sides and the centre of the rearcourt.

Midcourt situations: the stroke-moves are made from high or low positions at the side and centre of the midcourt.

Forecourt situations: the stroke-moves are made from the sides and the centre. The shuttle positions will be clearly above net height, just below or above the net, and near the ground.

The moves in the game

Each time one partner hits the shuttle he makes a move which alters the present situation and creates a new one for both his side and the opponents. The new situation will be to the advantage of one side or the other, or to the advantage of neither side—a sort of *status quo*. During each rally many different situations will occur as each side creates new ones, and if we study these we can obtain much useful information. In each situation a number of moves are logically possible. For example, imagine that the shuttle is high in your right rearcourt. From there it can be hit in various directions with more or less force to different places in your opponents' court (see figs. 2 and 3). Though certain moves are

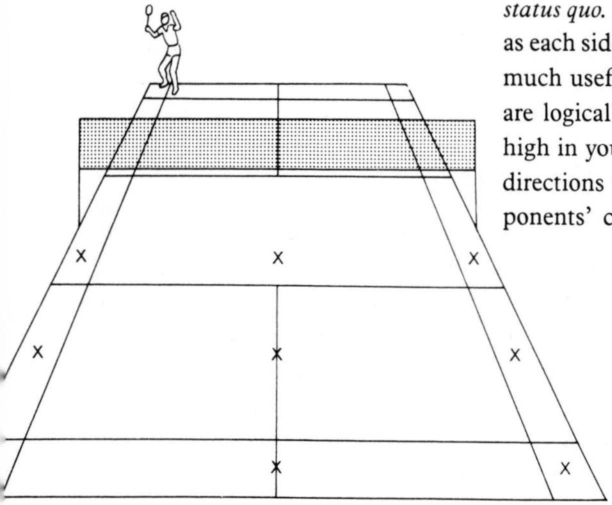

Fig. 2

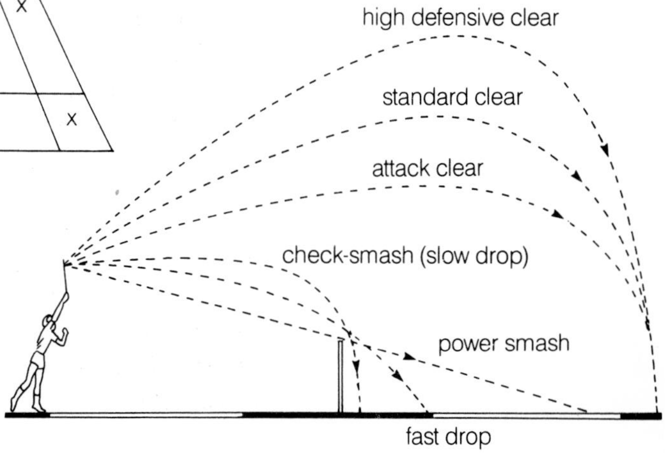

high defensive clear

standard clear

attack clear

check-smash (slow drop)

power smash

Fig. 3

fast drop

logically possible, not all of them would be appropriate in the situation. For example, it would be silly to play a slow drop shot from the rearcourt with the opponents waiting in a forward defensive base (see page 72). A sensible move would be to smash to force a lift for the partner to attack from the forecourt, or to hit an attack clear to get the shuttle behind the opponents and force a late reply—that is, if the player can hit an attack-clear, which might be difficult for an inexperienced player. The suitability of a certain move in a situation partly depends on the ability of the players to perform various strokes, for players need technical skill to be able to execute the full range of strokes in a given situation; if that skill is lacking then the number of moves they can make will be limited and that might prove advantageous to their opponents. Players who are limited in any way can now do something about it: the charts on pages 20-27 describe all the situations and the stroke-moves players need to learn.

The logical structure of the game

This is summarised in the diagram below.

The *situations* that obtain are determined by reference to the nature of the game: the court shape and space, the net height, the equipment used, the rules, the human limitations of the players, and the position of the shuttle in the court.

The *moves logically possible* are determined by reference to the type of situation from which they are played.

The *moves appropriate* are decided by reference to the 'principle of attack' and a consideration of the positions and the ability of the opponents.

The *moves actually possible* depend on the ability of the player hitting the shuttle.

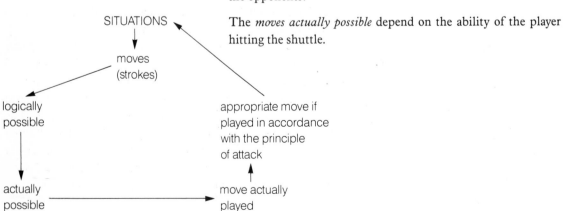

The *move actually played* in a situation will only be appropriate if the player judges the situation correctly on the basis of the facts he knows about the opponents, and then makes a move in accordance with the 'principle of attack' to end the rally or create a situation which enhances his side's chances of winning the rally.

The *framework* is the sum total of all the parts of the game. It is determined by the nature of the game and can be no different unless there are changes in those factors which make up the game. The framework is illustrated in the charts which follow.

Chapter 2 The Framework

In the following pages the framework is presented in chart form, divided into three main sections: rearcourt, midcourt and forecourt situations. All the stroke-moves in each situation are shown and explained in the three charts. When studying them, read across the columns from left to right, beginning from the *shuttle position* which determines the type of situation the players are in. It has been assumed that all the players are of equal ability and play an all-court game, so no allowance has been made at this stage for differences between players of the same sex, or between men and women, children and adults. This makes it possible to create a complete framework within which different forms of the game and the way it is played can be studied and compared, for example, men's, ladies' and mixed doubles from club to international level. Eventually you will find it quite easy to compare the tactics, and hence the differences and similarities between the world champions and the local club pair.

The charts represent a picture of all that goes on in the game. Imagine a doubles situation you have experienced and reflected upon. Did you play the right stroke-move? Did you both position yourselves to cover the opponents' replies? How should you have responded when the opponents made a certain reply? The answers to these and other questions you might want to ask about the game can be found by referring to the charts. If you look at them carefully you will gain a good understanding of doubles tactics before reading in more detail about attack and defence in Part Two.

Rearcourt situations

SHUTTLE POSITION	PARTNER'S POSITION	STROKE-MOVES	DIRECTION	INTENTION
1. High (at sides or centre and in front of player: see figs. 4, 5, 6)	Attacking stance in MC, 4-6 ft (1.21-1.82m) behind the T, on or to right or left of centre line relative to position of shuttle (see figs. 4, 5, 6)	1. Power smash to MC or RC 2. Fast sliced smash	Straight—centre—x-court to space or at opponent; steep or shallow trajectory	To hit the ground or fo a lift or weak reply
		3. Fast drop to FC or MC	To centre or sides	To force a steep lift
		4. Check-smash to FC	Straight or to centre	To force opponents to scramble and obtain a weak lift
		5. Attack clear to RC	To sides or centre	To catch opponents wrongly balanced and force a late or weak re
		6. Standard clear	To sides or centre	To push opponents de into the RC (particular weak smasher) and enable you to attack t reply
2. High in RC/MC (at sides or centre and in front of player) see figs. 20, 21, 22	Attacking stance on or just behind service line, in front of partner and slightly to one side of 'line of fire'	1. Power smash	Straight—at opponent's body	To hit opponent or for weak reply (the play t place down a narrow channel with the focu one opponent)
	Attacking stance behind T in MC; position adjusted relative to position of shuttle	2. Fast sliced smash	Straight or to centre — x-court	To hit the ground or fo a lift
		3. Fast drop	Sides or to centre	To force a lift
		4. Check-smash	Straight or to centre	To catch opponents wrongly balanced, ca them to scramble and make a weak reply
		5. Attack clear	To sides or centre	To get shuttle behind opponents and force a weak reply

OPPONENT'S POSSIBLE REPLIES	YOUR PARTNER'S ACTION	YOUR ACTION
1. Block to FC	Travel into FC to attack shuttle	Travel to MC to cover partner
2. Push to MC	Travel sideways to attack shuttle	Travel to adjacent half of court near centre line and level with partner into sides attack position in MC
3. Drive to MC or RC	Travel sideways to attack shuttle	
4. Whip to RC	Jump sideways or up to attack shuttle	Travel to centre MC prepared to adjust position for sides attack or front man near T
5. Lob to RC	Adjust position in MC relative to shuttle position in RC	Travel to RC to attack shuttle
1. Net reply to FC	Travel into FC to attack shuttle	Travel to MC to cover partner
2. Lob to RC	Adjust position in MC to new position in RC	Travel to RC to attack shuttle
1. Smash to MC/RC	Travel into MC to take up sides defence position	Travel to MC to take up sides defence position
2. Drop to FC	Travel into FC if shuttle in his half of court and to the centre by agreement	Same as for partner
3. Clear to RC	Travel to attack shuttle in own RC; take up attacking stance behind T if shuttle is in partner's RC	Same as for partner
1. Block to FC	Attack shuttle in FC	Remain in MC behind partner ready to attack any replies that get past partner
2. Push to MC	Attack shuttle in FC	
x-court returns and the drive, whip and lob are possible if smash is weak or opponent has strong defence, in which case the smasher's partner would stand further back behind the T and in a position to cover the x-court reply	Attack 'drive' in MC Attack 'whip' by jumping to intercept in MC	
	If lobbed, readjust position in MC relative to shuttle position in RC	Travel to RC to attack shuttle
1. Block to FC	Attack shuttle in FC	Travel to centre MC behind partner ready to attack any replies that get past partner
2. Push to MC	Travel to attack shuttle	
3. Whip to RC	Jump to attack shuttle	
4. Lob to RC	Adjust position in MC relative to shuttle position in RC	Travel to RC to get into the smash position
1. Net reply	Attack shuttle in FC	Travel to centre MC behind partner ready to attack any replies to MC and RC
2. Lob to RC	Adjust position in MC relative to shuttle position in RC	Travel to RC to attack shuttle
1. Net reply	Attack shuttle in FC	Travel to centre MC to cover partner
2. Lob to RC	Adjust position in MC relative to shuttle position in RC	Travel to RC to attack shuttle
1. Smash	Adjust position in MC to defend – ready to travel to the FC for the drop shot and RC to attack the clear	Recover and travel to MC to defend – ready to travel to the FC for the drop shot and RC to attack the clear
2. Drop		
3. Clear		

Rearcourt situations

SHUTTLE POSITION	PARTNER'S POSITION	STROKE-MOVES	DIRECTION	INTENTION
3. High (at sides or centre) (see figs. 4, 5, 6)	Attacking stance in MC, 4-6 ft behind T on or to side of centre line relative to position of shuttle, ready to threaten any reply to FC	1. Jump power smash 2. Jump sliced smash	Straight—centre—x-court	To send shuttle on a s[...] trajectory to get belo[...] the opponent's defen[...] and force a steep lift
4. High in RC/MC (at sides or centre) (see figs. 20, 21, 22)	Attacking stance on or just behind service line, in front of partner and slightly to one side of 'line of fire', ready to threaten any reply to FC	1. Jump power smash 2. Jump sliced smash	Straight—at opponent's body—centre	To send shuttle on a s[...] trajectory to get belo[...] the opponents' defen[...] and force a weak or s[...] lift
5. High in RC/MC (at sides or centre and to the rear of player)	Attacking stance in MC behind T relative to the shuttle position. Watching partner to see if he can hit an effective stroke-move. Ready to intercept the x-court reply used if his partner is off balance on landing and slow to recover	1. Backward jump smash (flat or sliced)	Straight—or to centre	To force a lift
		2. Backward jump dink-smash	To centre or x-court	To obtain a steep trajectory. To surpris[...] opponents and force [...]
		3. Backward jump fast drop shot	To centre or x-court	To force a lift
		4. Backward jump attack clear 5. Backward jump standard clear	To centre or sides To centre or sides	To get shuttle behind opponents To manoeuvre oppone[...] into RC
6. High (at sides or centre and to the rear of player)	Attacking stance in MC behind the T relative to the shuttle position, watching partner and the shuttle	High defensive clear to RC	Straight or to centre	To get out of trouble a[...] to make time to take [...] defensive position. To drop the shuttle vertically in the RC making it more difficu[...] for the opponent to tir[...] his smash.
7. Low (level with or to the rear of players)	In own MC near centre line, watching partner to see what stroke-move he plays	1. Clear to RC	Straight or to centre	To send opponents de[...] into RC and make tim[...] recover
		2. Drive to MC	Straight or to centre	To neutralise the situa[...]
		3. Drop to FC	Straight or to centre	To force a lift

OPPONENT'S POSSIBLE REPLIES	YOUR PARTNER'S ACTION	YOUR ACTION
1. Block to FC	Travel into FC to attack shuttle	Travel to centre MC to cover partner
2. Lob to RC	Adjust position in MC relative to shuttle position in RC	Return to attack shuttle
1. Block to FC	Travel into FC to attack shuttle	Travel to centre MC to cover partner
2. Lob to RC	Adjust position in MC relative to shuttle position in RC	Return to RC to attack shuttle
1. Block to FC	Travel into FC to attack shuttle	Travel to MC to cover partner
2. Push or drive to MC – RC	Travel sideways to attack shuttle	Travel to MC near centre, level with partner
3. Whip to RC	Jump to intercept and attack shuttle	Travel back to RC or take up 'front man' position relative to shuttle position
4. Lob to RC	Adjust position in MC relative to shuttle position	Return to RC to attack shuttle
1. Block to FC	Travel into FC to attack shuttle	Travel to MC to cover partner
2. Lob to RC	Adjust position in MC relative to shuttle position	Return to RC to attack shuttle
1. Net reply to FC	Travel into FC to attack shuttle	Travel to MC to cover partner
2. Lob to RC	Adjust position in MC relative to shuttle position	Return to RC to attack shuttle
1. Smash 2. Drop 3. Clear	Adjust position in MC to defend, ready to travel to FC for the drop shot and RC to attack the clear	Recover and return to MC into sides defence, ready to travel to FC for drop shot and RC to attack the clear
1. Smash 2. Drop 3. Clear	Adjust position in MC to defend, ready to travel to FC for the drop shot and RC to attack the clear	Recover and get into balance; return to MC into sides defence with partner to cover replies to FC, MC, RC
1. Smash 2. Drop 3. Clear	Adjust position in MC to defend against the smash, ready to attack the drop shot or the clear	Travel to MC and join partner in sides defence formation
1. Drive to MC or RC 2. Block to FC 3. Lob to RC	Take up attacking stance in own side of MC ready to travel to FC or RC on own section of court	Travel to MC to attack replies, ready to cover FC and RC in own section of court
1. Hit down in FC	Take up a defensive stance	Travel to MC to defend
2. Net reply in FC	Take up an attacking stance	Travel to MC ready to attack FC reply
3. Lob to RC	Travel to RC to attack if shuttle in own section of court	Return to RC to attack shuttle in own half of court

Midcourt situations

SHUTTLE POSITION	PARTNER'S POSITION	STROKE-MOVES	DIRECTION	INTENTION
1. High (at sides or centre: see figs. 27, 28, 29)	Attacking stance in centre of adjacent half of court, near or away from centre line relative to shuttle position	1. Power smash to MC/RC 2. Fast sliced smash 3. Side arm slash **Note:** These stroke-moves can be performed with jumps to steepen the trajectory of flight of shuttle; other stroke moves (drop and clear) could be used but no real advantage to be gained in this situation when a powerful attack can take place	To centre – sides – at opponent, steep or shallow trajectory	To hit ground or oppor or force a weak reply
2. High (at sides or centre and to the rear of the player) shuttle travelling upwards quickly on a shallow arc after a flick serve, whip or attack clear	Attacking stance, watching partner and adjusting position on own side of court relative to shuttle position and probable stroke-moves of partner. Ready to cover all replies to own side of court and also partner's FC if he cannot recover quickly	1. Backwards and/or sideways jump smash (power or slice)	To centre or sides	To hit ground or opponent, or force a w reply and steep lift
3. Net height (after drive or shallow smash)	Attacking stance in MC ready to counter hit against speed or travel to FC or RC	1. Drive to MC/RC	Straight – x-court or to to centre	To hit opponent or forc error or weak reply
		2. Push to MC		To cause shuttle to fall below net height or for a lift
		3. Whip to RC		To get shuttle past opponent
		4. Drop to FC		To force a lift
4. Low (after the smash)	Attacking stance ready to cover replies to his side of the court and centre	1. Block to FC	To sides or centre	To place shuttle away from front man and for a lift
		2. Push to MC	To sides or centre	To get shuttle past fron man or force a lift
		3. Whip to RC	To corners	To reduce opponents' recovery time–get it p. them–force a weak re
		4. Lob to RC	To sides or centre	To send opponent back RC
5. Low (after a fast drop or low reply to MC)	Attacking stance, watching the play	Prepare to hit the shuttle early as you approach it and	To sides or centre	In both moves the opponents are caused wait or commit themselves before the shuttle is hit
		1. 'Hold and drop' – prepare as if to hit shuttle to RC but then check racket head speed and drop to FC		1. To check opponent make him pause and s be late for the reply–o make his weight go backwards and then h shuttle into FC
		2. 'Hold and flick' – prepare as if to hit to FC but then flick the shuttle over opponent's head into RC		2. To check opponent make his weight come forwards and then flick the shuttle over his hea to the RC

OPPONENT'S POSSIBLE REPLIES	YOUR PARTNER'S ACTION	YOUR ACTION
1. Block to FC 2. Push to MC 3. Drive to MC/RC 4. Whip to RC 5. Lob to RC	Attacking stance in MC ready to travel to attack all replies in his side of court and to centre by agreement with partner	Recover from the smash and travel into position to attack all replies to your side of court and centre by agreement with partner
	Note: There is a variation on these tactics when one player decides to cover all RC situations and the other, the FC situations, each player taking a distinct role as rear man or front man according to relative strengths and weaknesses. See discussion on doubles formations.	
1. Block to FC 2. Push to MC 3.· Drive to MC/RC 4. Whip to RC 5. Lob to RC		
Counter drive—push, whip, drop	Travel to all replies in his section of court and centre by agreement. Defend against the smash.	Travel to all replies in your section of court and centre by agreement
Push, drop, lob, whip		
Smash, slash, drop, clear		
Net kill, net reply; lift to RC		
Hit down if above net; if below, net reply to FC or lift to RC	Attacking stance ready to travel to all replies in his section of court	As for partner in own side of court
Reply to FC or MC; lift to RC		
Slash, drop, clear	Defensive or attacking stance in MC	
Smash, drop, clear	Sides defensive stance in MC	
FC attack: opponent can hit down to MC—drop to FC—lift to RC	Attacking stance ready to defend on travel to all replies in his section of court and centre by agreement	As for partner in your own side of court
1. Smash	Take up a sides attacking or defensive stance	
2. Clear	Travel to RC to attack shuttle	
3. Drop	Travel to FC to attack shuttle	

Midcourt situations

SHUTTLE POSITION	PARTNER'S POSITION	STROKE-MOVES	DIRECTION	INTENTION
6. Low (in MC/FC area)	Attacking stance behind you, astride centre line in MC	1. Low serve to FC	To centre or sides	To force opponent to li
		2. Flick serve to MC/RC	To centre or sides	To catch opponent ou and force a weak reply
		3. Drive serve	To centre or sides	To surprise opponent a force a weak reply
		4. High serve to MC/RC	To centre or sides	To manoeuvre an opponent to RC
7. Low (after opponent's reply to the low serve)	Attacking stance in FC positioned relative to the shuttle position and ready to threaten a FC reply	1. Low return to FC	To sides	To hit shuttle away fro opposing front man an force a lift
		2. Push to MC	Straight or x-court	To get shuttle past fro man and force a lift
		3. Whip to RC	To centre or sides	To get shuttle past opponents. Force a w reply
		4. Lob to RC	To centre or sides	To move opponent to F

Forecourt situations

SHUTTLE POSITION	PARTNER'S POSITION	STROKE-MOVES	DIRECTION	INTENTION
1. Above net height, travelling upwards from the serve or block to the smash or as a low return to FC or MC; or as a drive or whip from MC	Attacking stance in centre MC ready to attack any replies to MC or RC	1. Slash to MC or RC	Downward or at opponent	To hit ground or oppon
		2. Brush shot or dab to MC or RC	At or away from opponent	To hit ground or opponent, restrict his movements and force weak reply or a lift
		3. Push to MC or RC		
		4. Check-smash to FC	To centre or sides	To force a lift
		5. Block (to a fast shuttle)		
2. Near the top of the net, just below net height at the sides or the centre	Attacking stance in centre MC ready to attack any replies to MC or RC	1. 'Tumbler' or 'Spinner'	Straight or to centre	To force the opponent lift or mishit the shuttle
		2. Tap to FC or RC	To centre or sides	To control a rotating shuttle, force a lift or move opponent to RC
		3. Whip to RC	To centre or sides	To get shuttle behind opponents and force a late or weak reply
3. Low (close to the net and near to the ground after net reply or drop shot)	Attacking stance in MC covering any replies to MC or RC	1. 'Hairpin' drop	Straight or angled across the net	To 'crawl' the shuttle o the net and force the opponent to lift—or ma an error
		2. High clear	To centre or sides	To move opponent's de into RC, drop shuttle vertically and make it difficult for opponent t time the hit

OPPONENT'S POSSIBLE REPLIES	YOUR PARTNER'S ACTION	YOUR ACTION
Net reply to FC; hit down to FC or MC; lift to RC	Ready to attack replies to MC and travel to attack shuttle in RC	Attack replies to FC and ready to adjust position for replies to MC and RC
Smash, drop, clear	Take up attacking or defensive stance in MC according to efficacy of serve; 'sides' with partner	Take up defensive or attacking stand in MC; 'sides' with partner
Slash; tap to FC or MC; block to FC; lob to RC	Ready to attack replies to MC and RC	Ready to attack replies to FC and to adjust position for replies to MC and RC
Smash, drop, clear	Take up a sides defence formation in MC with partner	Take up a sides defence formation with partner
Hit down to FC or MC; net reply; lift to RC	Threaten replies to FC and force a lift	Attack any reply to MC or RC
Drop to FC; push, drive to MC; whip, lob to RC	Withdraw from FC and take up an attacking stance in MC; travel to shuttle	Take up the attacking stance; travel to attack replies in your section of court
Smash, drop, clear	Withdraw to sides defence in MC	Adjust to sides defence in MC
Smash, drop, clear		

OPPONENT'S POSSIBLE REPLIES	YOUR PARTNER'S ACTION	YOUR ACTION
'Dig up' or 'snatch' back shuttle	Attack any shuttle in MC or RC	1. Recover to attacking stance on edge of FC and attack any replies to FC
Block to FC; whip or lob to RC	Remain in MC for FC rally; travel to attack shuttle in RC	2. Withdraw to MC behind T and adjust position relative to shuttle position in RC
Push to MC; drop to FC; whip or lob to RC	Remain in MC ready to attack replies to MC and travel to attack shuttle in RC	
Net reply or lift to RC		

1. Net reply to FC	1. Remain in MC ready to attack	Step forwards and attack shuttle
2. Lob to RC	2. Travel to RC to attack shuttle	Withdraw to MC behind T and adjust position relative to shuttle position
1. Net reply to FC	1. Remain in MC ready to attack	1. Step forward, and attack shuttle
2. Lob to RC	2. Travel to RC to attack shuttle	2. Withdraw behind T and adjust position
3. Smash, drop, clear	3. Adjust position to sides defence	3. Adjust position to sides defence
Smash, drop, clear	Adjust position to sides defence	Adjust position to sides defence

1. Hit down from above net	Take up defensive stance and try to anticipate the direction	Curse oneself for a poor shot and hope partner can retrieve the situation. Stay out of partner's way and recover after his reply
2. Net reply from below net into FC	Remain in attacking stance in MC	Attack shuttle
3. Lift to RC	Travel to RC to attack shuttle	Withdraw to MC behind T and adjust position relative to shuttle position
Smash, drop, clear	Adjust position in MC and take up a sides defensive formation with partner	Withdraw from FC and take up a sides defensive formation with partner

Chapter 3 Comments on the Framework

The contents of the charts

The charts contain all the factors that you must take into account in each situation. The *shuttle position* determines the situation. The 'principle of attack' accounts for all the other factors, that is, where the players position themselves and the stroke-moves they select.

The *partner's position,* that is the position of the partner of the player about to hit the shuttle, is most important. He has to take up a position to cover the opponents' possible replies before he knows which reply the opponents will make to his partner's move. Until his partner hits the shuttle he cannot know what to expect. This is where the principle of attack is useful. He will assume that his partner will prepare to make what is generally recognised as the most attacking move in the situation. Consequently, it is usual to expect the opponents to prepare to guard against this threat to them, ready to make one of the possible replies in that situation. If the shuttle is high in the rearcourt, the partner will position himself to cover the possible replies to the smash. And because doubles is a game where there are two players to control the space, the partner will only need to position himself to cover the replies to a certain section of the court. In the charts the 'partner's position' described is always that which exists before the shuttle is struck.

The *stroke-moves* listed are the effective ones taken from those which are logically possible. In each situation some of the moves are appropriate, others are not. The appropriateness of a move is determined by the principle of attack. With some thought and practical experience you should quite easily be able to work out all the moves possible and appropriate in a situation. When you play, you should be able to judge what alternative moves are open to your side in any given situation, and consequently what sort of situation you will create when making a specific move. If you play intelligently you will avoid creating a situation to your disadvantage.

The *direction* in which the shuttle is hit is also important, as is the trajectory of the shuttle. Both are factors which can make quite a difference in maintaining the attack. For example, you might smash the shuttle very hard to the centre of the court, usually an intelligent placement which narrows the angle of return and allows the front man more opportunity to intercept the reply. But you might hit the shuttle on a shallow trajectory which the opponents drive back horizontally across the net at speed, neutralising the situation and increasing their chances of gaining the attack. In this case a shuttle hit with less force, to make it fall more steeply, or a jump smash to achieve the same effect, would have been more appropriate and in accordance with the principle of attack. Yet on another occasion an opponent who is prepared to defend against a steep smash can be surprised by a shallow smash aimed directly at his chest. The possibility of a weak reply would enable the front player to attack the shuttle in the forecourt and attempt to hit a winner.

The *intention* behind each stroke-move is obvious. Whether or not you succeed in your intention depends on how alert the opponents are and how well they execute the replies possible in the new situation you will have created with your stroke-move.

The *opponents' possible replies* to the most attacking move your side can make will determine where your partner positions himself and where you recover to position yourself after making the stroke-move.

Your partner's action and *your action* simply refer to what you do as or when the opponents make their reply. If you have been watching the opponents while they prepare to make their reply you will get some clues as to what sort of reply you are likely to receive. One of you will travel to attack the shuttle while the other adjusts his position to cover the replies to your stroke-move, and so on until the rally ends.

Rearcourt situations

Situation 1   *Shuttle position.* One player travels to the rearcourt, takes up the smash position and prepares to hit the shuttle from a high position (see plate 1).

Partner's position. Partner takes up an attacking stance in the midcourt approximately 4-6ft (1.2-1.8m) behind the T, ready to

Plate 1. Front and back attacking formation.

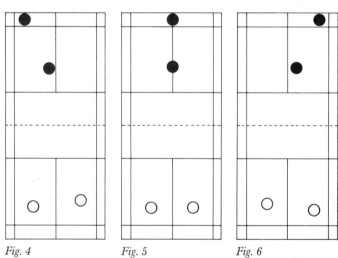

Fig. 4   *Fig. 5*   *Fig. 6*

threaten the replies to the smash (see figs. 4-6 and plate 1). This is known as the 'front and back' doubles attack formation.

Stroke-moves. The column in the chart describes the strokes you can use as moves in the situation. The first four listed stroke-moves are seen as moves which maintain the attack. They all originate from a balanced smash position on the floor or in the air (see plate 2), which is itself tactical, since even before the shuttle is struck the opponents anticipate the threat and take up defensive stances (see plate 1). This is known as the 'sides defence' formation. The opponents should know that you can hit a power smash for if they do not they might not take up defensive stances,

Plate 2. Stefan Karlsson off the ground in a balanced smash position.

Fig. 7   Fig. 8

in which case your alternative moves might not be as effective in achieving the result or obtaining the replies you want. The first four stroke-moves, being downward hits, deny your opponents the chance to make a scoring hit. If they are successful they obtain a lifted reply with your side waiting to attack. After making any of these four moves the hitter should travel forwards towards the centre of the rearcourt/midcourt area to cover the lob or whip to the rearcourt. At the same time he should be ready to travel into the midcourt to hit any shuttle that gets past his partner, or to cover his partner if he has to travel into the forecourt to attack the shuttle (see figs. 7-8).

The fifth move, the attack clear, is used as a variation on the smash. It is not often used in good men's doubles because any good player would immediately seize the opportunity to jump up and smash the shuttle. It is, however, extremely useful as a move in top ladies' doubles. Ladies are less explosive in accelerating to travel and jump backwards to smash; if they do reach the shuttle their smash is less powerful than the men's and less of a threat to an alert defence. Women are usually relatively stronger in defending against the speed of the shuttle than in generating speed.

The attack clear and the sixth move, the standard clear, are very useful at a lower level of doubles. Both moves place the opponent in the rearcourt where the smash is less effective against a good defence. Often a doubles pair can give the opponents the opportunity to smash in order to attack and drive the shuttle back at

speed. They counter-attack the smash, thus changing defence into attack.

After the clear from the rearcourt, the rearcourt player should
travel to the midcourt, in his own side of the court, to take up a
sides position with his partner who, as front man, should move
over into the adjacent side of the court to make room for his rear
man partner (see figs. 9-11).

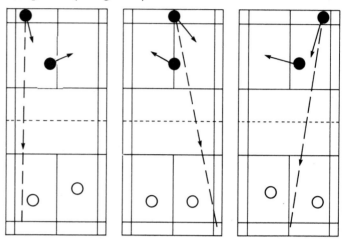

Figs. 9-11

The opponent's possible replies. If you consider the replies to the
power smash or to any fast downward hit to the midcourt, it
becomes clear why the front man stands in the midcourt, about
4-6ft (1.2-1.8m) behind the T and relative to the place from which
the partner hits the shuttle. Not only must the front man take
responsibility for the replies to the forecourt; he must also try to
intercept pushes and drives aimed straight or cross-court to the
midcourt and rearcourt (see figs. 12-14). The earlier he can in-

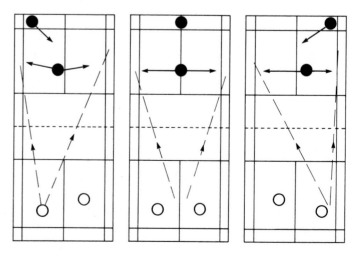

Figs. 12-14

tercept the shuttle the higher it is and the more chance there is of maintaining the attack. Once the shuttle gets past him from a drive or a push it may begin to fall below net height and cause the rear man to hit upwards, thus losing the attack.

It is for this reason that players differ in how close they stand to the centre line on each side of the court. There are good reasons for these variations, as figs. 15-17 show. In fig. 15 it is assumed

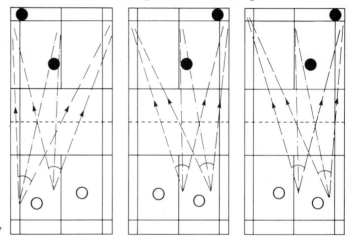

Figs. 15-17

that the rear man will smash straight or to the centre of the court between the defenders. The job of the front man is to cover the block replies to the forecourt sides or centre, and the pushes or drives to the sides. He takes up a position to divide the angle of possible returns between straight and cross-court replies, for replies from the centre or side of the opponents' court. He adjusts his position so that he is square on to the hitter. Cross-court replies have to pass through his range of reach so that he finds he can intercept replies to his backhand side. He is almost equidistant from each forecourt reply but inclined slightly towards the forehand corner, towards which the shuttle travels the shortest distance, and away from the backhand forecourt towards which the shuttle travels its longest distance: if it is hit there he has more time to reach it to make his reply.

In figs. 16 and 17 players vary their front position. In fig. 16 the front man is positioned to divide the angle of possible returns from the side or centre, in a position similar to that in fig. 15. In taking up that position the right-handed player exposes a gap down the backhand side of the court which he cannot cover adequately; he often has to leave the shuttle to his rear man, who must come forwards and hit a falling shuttle upwards from below net height. The fact that the front man is right-handed with his racket arm on the right side of his body makes it difficult to close this gap if he stands close to the centre line – unless, of course, he has a very good backhand smash for shuttles which have gone past him on the backhand side. However, to reach behind him to hit a shuttle runs contrary to a sensible rule applying to the front man: *do not* attempt to hit shuttles which have got past you unless you can ensure that you hit them downwards. To overcome this weakness down the backhand side, some players close the gap. They place themselves further over in the backhand court so that both the front man and the rear man are positioned in the same side of the court (see fig. 17). This position does expose the forehand side of the court for a cross-court reply; but as the front man is right-handed the reply would have to be quite wide to travel beyond his outstretched reach. He is in a good position to intercept the cross-court reply and attack the shuttle with his stronger forehand strokes. If the rear man's smash is to the centre he must quickly adjust his position and travel to the centre mid-court, on the centre line, to cover all the replies.

Sometimes the rear man smashes cross-court. Usually the front man is aware of this move of his partner's or, if not, should be informed about it. If it occurs the front man should adjust his position once more to the replies he might expect in the new situation. Such a tactic is often planned and accepted by both partners as part of their general play and usually both are ready for it, and know what to do when it happens.

The alternative downward stroke-moves, the fast drop and the check-smash, fall quickly into the forecourt, too steep and too near the net for the opponents to drive or push the shuttle horizontally past the front man. The replies are a lob to the rear-court and a net reply to the forecourt. The front man, positioned as he is outside the forecourt, can watch his opponents for clues about their possible reply. Immediately he sees that a net reply is being made he can travel forward quickly into the forecourt to attack the shuttle as it crosses the net. As he does so the rear man travels forward to the midcourt to cover his front man in case the opponents should succeed in hitting the shuttle past him to the midcourt (see fig. 18). If the opponents lob the shuttle to the rear-court then both front man and rear man can adjust their positions relative to the new situations (see fig. 19).

The opponents' replies to the attack clear and/or the standard clear are the same as for any shuttle which is positioned high in the rearcourt. Hence, the rear man would travel forwards after

Fig. 18　　　*Fig. 19*

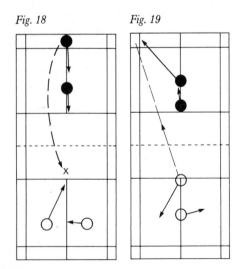

making the clear, and his front man would move across to the adjacent court – both taking up a sides defence formation. The stances in this formation may vary according to the effectiveness of the clear. If the opponents have travelled quickly into a balanced smash position, and are able to smash effectively, the defenders should adopt defensive stances (see plate 3). If the attack clear move succeeds in getting behind the opponents, the defenders might adopt attacking stances (see plate 4). They

Plate 3. Tjun Tjun and Wahjudi take up defensive stances ready to receive the smash.

Plate 4. Kondo and Takada defending in attacking stances, set to attack a weak smash.

would calculate that the opponents could not smash with power or steeply, and any other move the opponents did make would be open to attack. So the 'defenders' stand side by side ready to attack.

Situation 2   *Shuttle position.* On this occasion the shuttle is inside the midcourt near to the long service line for doubles. The player in position to hit the shuttle is now nearer the net (see figs. 20-22). The front partner's position varies slightly in this situation, depending on the stroke-move used. If the rear man has a strong power smash then the front man can stand almost directly in front of

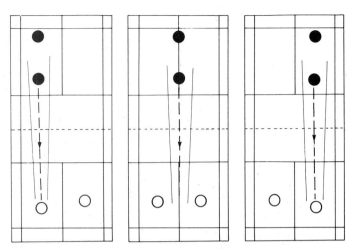

Figs. 20-22

him on the same side of the court (see page 61). It is the power of the smash which enables the players to take up such a 'front and back' formation. From inside the midcourt/rearcourt area, a powerful smash hit directly at the opponent or to his backhand side is extremely difficult to hit cross-court. The usual reply is straight to the forecourt or high towards the rearcourt. The attacking side can focus all its attention on the one defender and keep him pinned down in a narrow channel (see fig. 20). The side maintains the attack until either the front man or the rear man forces an error or hits a winner.

I was told of the experience of an English player who suffered the attack of the brilliant doubles pair, Tjun Tjun and Wahjudi of Indonesia. The occasion was the first round of the All England doubles championships. The player told me that he was hit in the chest and arms so often by their fierce attack that the following morning he felt as if his body was covered in small bruises.

Of course, if the defenders have an equally strong defence and can hit cross-court replies to the smash then the front man would have to adjust his position to cover the cross-court reply as he does in fig. 53, page 61.

Situation 3   The *shuttle position* is high in the rearcourt. The front man takes up his usual position in the midcourt relative to the shuttle position and ready to attack any replies to the downward hits.

The *stroke-moves* used here are: the jump, power or sliced smash.

The *intention* is to hit the shuttle on a steep trajectory and compel the defenders to contact the shuttle near the ground, thus preventing such replies as the drive, push or whip. Left with only the block to the forecourt or the lob to the rearcourt to contend with, the front man can approach the net to threaten and the rear man can approach the midcourt to attack any weak returns. Should the defenders block the smash or give a weak lift to the midcourt/rearcourt area, the 'front and back' attackers would adopt the channel attack shown in fig. 20. If the defenders lob the shuttle high to the rearcourt the attackers would withdraw from the net and adjust their positions accordingly.

Situation 4   The *shuttle position* is inside the midcourt/rearcourt area as in situation 2. The front man positions himself directly in front of his rear man in the channel attack formation. At this stage he will not know whether his partner intends to jump unless he is watching him. The stroke-moves used are the power or sliced smash, hit very steeply to restrict the replies to a block and a lob. When the front man realises that the smash is very steep (he will see his opponents prepare to defend for a low shuttle), he will travel forwards to crowd the net and threaten the block to the forecourt. His rear man will take up a position in the midcourt directly behind him. Should the defenders lob the shuttle to the rearcourt both attackers will adjust their positions relative to the shuttle position.

Situation 5   This situation is slightly different. Here the shuttle has been hit to the rearcourt and is behind the player attempting to hit it. It may be directly behind him or slightly to the right or left of him. The rear man is compelled to jump backwards to get behind the shuttle. Unless he can do this to some extent, he will be unable to hit downwards. If he can get right behind the shuttle he will be able to hit it with full force, e.g. a power smash. If he cannot, he can still achieve a downward hit by using less arm movement and applying less force. His main problem then is speed of recovery. In jumping backwards he hits the shuttle during his flight through the air. After hitting it he continues to travel through the air until he lands. He must get into balance, change direction and accelerate quickly forwards to recover into position to cover the replies. Often, how hard he hits the shuttle is determined by how quickly he knows he can recover before the opponents make their reply. If he hits it too hard and cannot recover quickly the speed of the shuttle can be counter-productive. The opponents may make an early reply and get the shuttle below net height in the midcourt or catch him out of position and so gain the attack. For the same reason he would not attempt an attack clear in this situation; for his opponents, seeing his difficulty, would take up sides attack stances (see plate 4), ready to attack high or weak returns. From such stances they could easily revert to defensive stances if they thought he could hit the shuttle with full force.

His *partner's position* is in the midcourt behind the T and relative to the shuttle position. It is important that the front man watches his rear partner while he prepares to attack the shuttle. He can then judge his rear man's difficulty, if any, and adjust his position to cover more of the opponents' replies. He might, for example, move more to one side to cover the cross-court reply and yet still be ready to do his own job in the forecourt (see fig. 23). It is the task of his rear man to control his smash and ensure that it goes downwards, the steeper the better. Trajectory, not speed and power, counts on this occasion.

The *stroke-moves* used during the jump are:

1. The power or sliced smash hit straight or to the centre to reduce the angle of return. The power of the smash is determined by the speed of recovery and the trajectory necessary to aid recovery. The sliced smash (a glancing blow) diverts some of the force and helps to make the shuttle fall quickly and steeply.

2. The dink-smash. This is a wristy action in which the player jumps up with outstretched arm and, using his hand mainly, brings the racket head over the top of the shuttle to tap it down very steeply into the opposite court. In the 1960s it was used with great effect by Finn Kobbero, thought by many to be the greatest doubles player of all time. In the modern game, Thomas Kihlstrom uses it to surprise opponents and force a lift if he cannot get behind the shuttle to hit it hard (see plate 5).

The *direction* can be to any part of the court. Hit cross-court, it can surprise the opponents by catching them defending on the wrong side. They might have their rackets ready for a smash towards one side of their bodies and the shuttle is hit towards the other side (see fig. 24). The switch in direction can catch them out and cause them to give a weak reply for the front man to attack. Alternatively, they might be late reaching it and have to lift it on a steep trajectory, so giving the opportunity for a smash. The usual replies to a steep trajectory smash, especially if the shuttle is hit with less force, are the low return to the forecourt and the lob to the rearcourt.

On each occasion the front man would travel forwards to threaten the reply to the forecourt whilst his rear man would

Plate 5. Thomas Kihlstrom performs a dink smash.

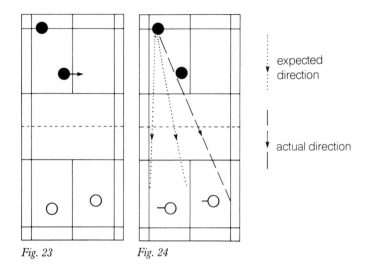

Fig. 23   *Fig. 24*

recover quickly and get into position behind him in the midcourt.

The front man would adjust his position very quickly once he realised his partner had switched the direction to cross-court. Such a switch should not be a surprise to him if he knows how his partner plays and if he has been looking behind him to follow the play. He will expect the cross-court move and be prepared to respond immediately. It is on such occasions that good teamwork and understanding between players is most apparent. All doubles pairs could practise this sort of stroke-move, once aware of it as a possible move in the game. Later I shall explain how to use the charts to select situations for practice and how to practise.

The fourth and fifth moves are the attack clear and the standard clear. It is easier to hit upwards than downwards when one is jumping backwards with the shuttle to the rear. Rather than reply with a weaker downward hit some players would choose to hit the shuttle up to the rearcourt. The attack clear will be more effective than the standard clear for, if successful, it will place the opponents under pressure with the shuttle behind them. The risk here is that if the stroke-move is not executed accurately, the opponents are given an easy chance to attack before the other side is ready to defend. The standard clear is hit on a higher trajectory and will give the player more time to recover after his landing from the jump. Though the opponents gain the attack from the rearcourt, the other side has time to recover into position to defend.

The *direction* of the attack clear should be straight or to the centre. There is little to be gained from attempting a cross-court attack clear to the rearcourt when under pressure.

Immediately after hitting the shuttle the player should travel forwards to the midcourt to take up a sides defence formation with his front partner, who will have moved over to the adjacent court. Both defenders are now ready to cover the opponents' possible replies, i.e. the smash to the midcourt, clear to the rearcourt and the drop to the forecourt.

Situation 6 This is similar, in some respects, to the fifth situation. The shuttle has got behind the rear man. It is so far behind him that he cannot possibly hit down or recover quickly from a standard clear. He is caught out, off balance, fighting to gain control and in haste. His partner in the midcourt watches him.

The *stroke-move* he uses is the high defensive clear (see fig. 3). It is *directed* straight or to the centre and aimed to fall steeply in the rearcourt. His *intention* is to make time to allow himself to recover into a balanced position in the midcourt, and also to give his opponents the least favourable situation in which to attack. A vertically falling shuttle in the rearcourt is not the easiest of shots to time accurately, nor will the probable smash be as effective from deep in the rearcourt against a balanced alert defence.

After making the move he recovers into a sides defence formation next to his partner. Both players are now ready to cover all the replies from the opponents' rearcourt.

Situation 7 The *shuttle position* is low and level with or to the rear of the player. This situation does not normally occur in good standard ladies' and men's doubles. When it does occur in level doubles (ladies' and men's) it is usually because the rear player has hit a flat (horizontal) smash from the rearcourt corner, straight down the side. The opponents will have whipped or driven the shuttle cross-court past the front man too quickly for him to intercept it. Consequently the rear player must now rush across to the opposite corner of his rearcourt and try to retrieve the situation he has helped to create. This can happen also if the rear man smashes cross-court without concern for the trajectory of the shuttle: the opponents simply push or drive the shuttle down the line to the rearcourt; the front man cannot intercept and the rear man must again retrieve the situation he has brought about. In these examples the rear man has performed inappropriate moves; they are instances of unintelligent play by the attacking side, making it easy for the defenders to create such a situation and regain the attack.

In mixed doubles this situation often occurs. It can happen, as

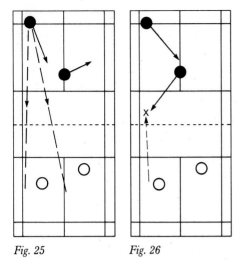

Fig. 25   *Fig. 26*

in the previous example, if the man smashes flat straight or cross-court and allow the opponents to counter-attack and hit the shuttle quickly to the empty rearcourt corner – an example of poor play by the man, who does not create a situation to the advantage of his side. Situation 7 also comes about as a result of skilful play by one side, who manage to draw the man forwards out of position and then hit the shuttle quickly to the vacant space in the corner of the rearcourt, with the result that the man is sometimes late arriving there.

The *partner's position* is in the midcourt near the centre line, watching to see what stroke-move his rear player will use. The *stroke-moves* used are the clear, drive and drop, hit straight or to the centre. After the move the player travels forwards quickly to his side of the midcourt whilst his partner moves across to his own side of the court (see fig. 25). Both players are in the midcourt ready to defend against the smash, fast replies to the midcourt and any replies to the forecourt or rearcourt. Each player looks after his own side of the court, unless the rear man is slow to recover after hitting the drop to the forecourt or the drive to the midcourt. If the opponents make a straight reply to the forecourt, the front player might go into his partner's side of the court to make a stroke-move, in which case the rear man would travel into the centre midcourt to cover him (see fig. 26).

Midcourt situations

Situation 1 The *shuttle position* is high in the midcourt. The player is in balance and ready to attack – a great opportunity to win the rally with an outright winner or, if not, immediately after the opponents' reply.

The *partner is positioned* in the adjacent midcourt near or away from the centre line relative to the shuttle position (see figs. 27-29). Both players adopt a forward attacking stance while they position themselves in a sides attack formation (see plate 6).

The *stroke-moves* used are all strong attacking moves in accordance with the principle of attack; the power smash, sliced smash and a side-arm slash. They are performed with or without jumping.

The *direction* does not really matter, though an intelligent player might aim the shuttle to ensure that the opponents can make only a weak reply if they do manage to return the shuttle. For example, he could aim it at the weaker defender, or at some

Plate 6. Chandra and Christian in sides attack positions.

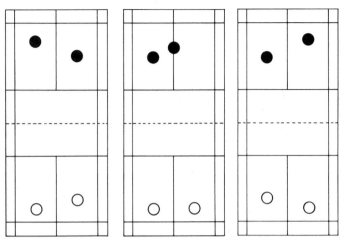

Fig. 27   *Fig. 28*   *Fig. 29*

part of the body or space on the weaker side. As both attackers are positioned in a sides attack formation the replies to a cross-court smash are covered and ready to be attacked.

The *opponents' replies* are quite basic in this situation. They can block the smash to the forecourt, drive or push it to the mid-court, or whip or lob it to the rearcourt.

The attacking side must be ready to cover all replies to the forecourt, midcourt and rearcourt. Replies to the centre are taken as agreed between the two players. Some pairs agree that the player who would hit the shuttle on his forehand side should play the centre stroke-move (see fig. 30). Others agree that the best placed player should hit the shuttle. Players should discuss the matter and agree that one or other takes replies to the centre, or that they will respond intuitively in the situation. Players who have no policy in this situation will find they have a tactical weakness in their game.

The *positions* after the smash do not change. Both players continue in an attacking stance ready to travel to any replies.

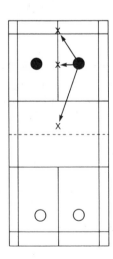

Fig. 30

Situation 2   This is similar in some respects. The *shuttle is high*, the dif-ference being that the player has to jump backwards or sideways to hit the shuttle. The partner watches the jump and *positions* himself in the midcourt on his own side of the court, relative to the shuttle position and the probable stroke-moves of the oppo-nent (see figs. 31-33). He is ready to cover all the replies to his own side of the court and also to his partner's forecourt if he does not recover quickly. The *stroke-moves* in this situation should all

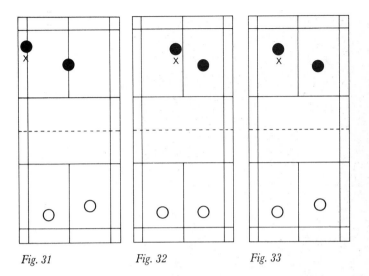

Fig. 31   Fig. 32   Fig. 33

be downward hits, the smash being the most appropriate move in accordance with the principle of attack.

The other aspects of the situation – intention, opponents' replies and the player's actions – are similar to situation 1.

Situation 3 The *shuttle position* is at net height or thereabouts. This is the most evenly balanced situation for both sides during a rally. The players on both sides are in a sides attack formation in the midcourt.

The first *stroke-move* is the drive to the midcourt/rearcourt area. The player replies to speed with speed. He counter-hits against the opponents, hitting the shuttle at them or between them. The intention is to hit the opponent, or force a mis-hit or a weak reply. All the players have to be on the alert to counter the speed, or for a different stroke-move, e.g. a quick block to the forecourt or a whip to the rearcourt.

The second *stroke-move* is the *push,* used when the shuttle is too far below net height to drive it without causing it to travel upwards and so give the opponents the chance to hit it down. The push is a softer shot, the shuttle travels less quickly through the air and falls towards the midcourt as it skims the net. The intention behind the stroke-move is to force the opponents to lift.

The *whip* is used in an attempt to hit the shuttle in a shallow arc over the opponents' heads, behind them into the rearcourt. The shuttle is hit to rise quickly upwards and catch the opponents by surprise. The risk is that they are ready to intercept it and attack. If so, you and your partner must adopt a sides defence formation and get ready to defend against the smash, the drop to the forecourt or the clear to the rearcourt.

The fourth *stroke-move* is the *drop* to the forecourt. In this case the speed is taken off the shuttle so that it is returned to fall into the forecourt and so force the opponents to lift. If successful, your side must be ready to attack any net reply to the forecourt or the rearcourt.

Situation 4   The *shuttle position* is low after the smash. Your partner is positioned next to you on his side of the court, in a sides defence formation relative to the previous shuttle position in the opponents' court. In this defensive formation both of you should be approximately equidistant from the smasher prior to his stroke-move. If he smashes from his forehand or backhand court the player diagonally opposite will be nearer the net. When he smashes from the centre both defenders are level with each other (see figs. 34-36).

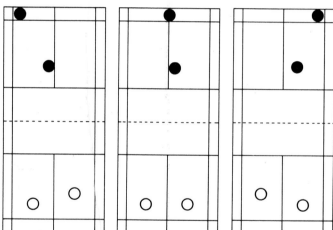

Figs. 34-36

The *stroke-moves* you use in reply to the smash are those which will increase your chances of gaining the attack. The block to the forecourt directed to the sides away from the front player will achieve this if you succeed in getting the shuttle below net level before the opposing front player can hit it. Then, if you threaten his reply quickly, you may force him to make a weak net reply in the forecourt or lift to the rearcourt. If your opponent manages to hit the shuttle from above net level you will need to be ready to defend against his attack.

The push to the midcourt sides, away from the front man, is designed to get the shuttle below net level in the midcourt. If successful, the *opponents' replies* will be a return to the forecourt or midcourt, or a lift to the rearcourt. You are both ready to attack the replies from below net level and take up sides attack stances to do so. The next stroke-move, the whip, is used to counter-hit at speed – to hit the shuttle over the opponents' heads to their rearcourt. This move reduces their recovery time and may cause a mis-hit or a weak reply, especially if you catch them out of position. The lob to the rearcourt, directed to the sides or centre, places the opponents away from the net, giving you an easier situation in which to defend against the smash. The *opponents' possible replies* to the whip and the lob are the smash, drop, or clear, in which case you must take up a sides defence formation ready to defend against the smash and travel to the drop and the clear on your respective sides of the court.

Situation 5 The *shuttle position* is low after a fast drop or low reply to the forecourt/midcourt area (see fig. 37). Your *partner is positioned* in

Fig. 37

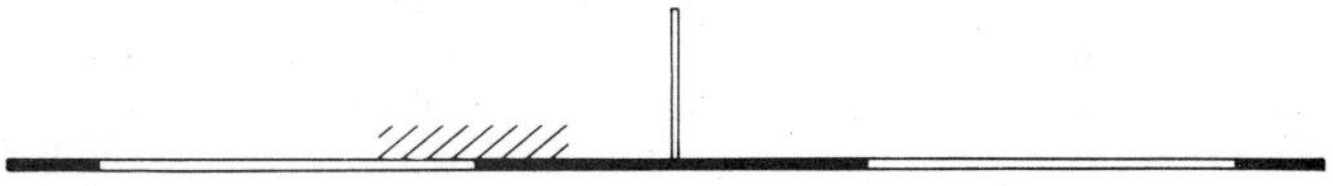

MC/FC area

an attacking stance on his side of the court, watching the play. The opponents are positioned in a sides attack formation in the midcourt, ready to attack your replies. In this situation your *stroke-move* requires some deception to create space in which to hit the shuttle and create time for it to get there before an opponent. You want to delay the opponent's attack. You intend to try to make him remain in position and not anticipate your reply, or anticipate the wrong reply. You will look as if you are going to play one stroke-move, and then play another to deceive one opponent.

1. You prepare as if to play a net reply and then as his weight comes forward in anticipation you flick the shuttle over his head to the rearcourt (a similar type of action to the flick serve).

2. You prepare as if to whip the shuttle over his head and then, as his weight goes backwards, you check the racket speed and stroke the shuttle gently over the net into the forecourt.

The *opponents' replies* are to attack and hit down if the shuttle is above net height into the forecourt, or play a net reply or lift to the rearcourt, if the shuttle is below net height. If you see that your opponent is going to hit the shuttle from below net height then you must both adjust your positions and adopt sides attack stances, ready to attack any replies to your respective sides of the court. If the opponents are about to attack from above net height in the forecourt then you must quickly get ready to defend.

Their replies to the lift to the rearcourt are the smash, drop or clear. If the rear man looks as if he is in a good position to smash, you should both take up a sides defence formation. If the shuttle is behind the rear man, and he looks as if he cannot smash effectively, then take up a sides attack formation.

Situation 6   The situation here is the opening move of the rally: the serve. The *shuttle position* is low in the forecourt/midcourt area. Your *partner is positioned* directly behind you in the midcourt, with feet astride the centre line. The opponent is positioned to attack the serve, i.e. the lift to his forecourt or rearcourt. His partner is positioned in their midcourt next to the centre line, ready to cover him when he makes his reply to the serve. Both pairs are positioned in the 'front and back' attacking formation (see plate 7).

Plate 7. Serving and receiving positions as Delfs serves to Chandra.

The *stroke-moves* are as follows:

1. The low serve to the forecourt; *directed* to the sides or centre with the *intention* to force the opponent to lift the shuttle. The *opponent's possible replies* are to travel towards the net to hit down the shuttle if it is above net height, play a net reply to the forecourt or lift to the rearcourt if the shuttle is below net height. Your rear man is ready to attack replies to the midcourt and travel back to attack replies to the rearcourt.

    After the serve you should immediately step forwards and take up an attacking stance ready to threaten any replies to the forecourt. If the opponent lifts to the rearcourt, adjust your position in the midcourt behind the T relative to the position of the shuttle in the rearcourt.

2. The flick serve is used to surprise the opponent, catch him with his weight moving forwards and so wrongly balanced to travel backwards quickly. The server prepares as if to serve short, draws the opponent forwards onto his front foot and then flicks the shuttle over his head towards the rearcourt. The intention is to cause the opponent to be late getting there and to make an error or a weak reply. Often a good flick serve results in an outright winner. The *opponent's replies,* if he can get into position quickly, are the smash, drop or clear.

    After your serve, withdraw to the midcourt or edge of the forecourt ready to defend or attack, depending on how effective you think his reply might be.

3. The drive serve is used to surprise the opponent with speed and cause him to make an error or a weak reply. It is usually directed to the backhand side to prevent the opponent returning it with a powerful hit. The *opponent's replies* are to block the shuttle to the forecourt, tap it (from his backhand side) and slash it (from his forehand side) down to the midcourt, or tap it up to the rearcourt.

    After the serve your partner is ready in the midcourt to attack any replies to the midcourt and rearcourt, while you should be ready to cover replies to the forecourt and any to the midcourt that you can safely intercept.

4. The high serve. This is not often used in good standard doubles for it presents the receiver with an easy chance to smash from the midcourt/rearcourt area. It can be used quite effectively at the lower levels of play against a player with a poor smash, i.e. one who does not hit the shuttle very hard or hits it too flat, thus allowing the opponents to counter-attack. It is also effective in mixed doubles in manoeuvring the lady

to the rearcourt, so reversing the positions of the lady and the man.

Immediately after the serve, withdraw to the midcourt and adjust your positions to the sides defence formation.

Situation 7   The *shuttle position* is low, immediately after the opponent has attacked the low serve or a front man's net reply, and hit the shuttle past the front man down to the sides or centre of the midcourt. Your partner (the front man) withdraws to the edge of the forecourt relative to the position of the shuttle in the midcourt. He is ready to cover any forecourt replies to your move if you return the shuttle to the forecourt or try to push it to the midcourt.

Note: The difficulty here is that this situation arises because the opponent has attacked so quickly and there is not much time for the front man to adjust his position to defend. In fact, the opponent might aim the shuttle at the front man who would find it difficult, if not impossible, to return the shuttle. The usual response is for the front man to crouch quickly, or sway to one side and allow the shuttle to fly past him for his rear man to return (see plate 8).

Plate 8. Christian sways aside to allow Chandra to make the reply.

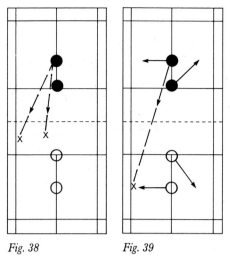

Fig. 38   Fig. 39

Your *stroke-moves* are:

1. A low return to the forecourt away from the opposing front man or to the centre if appropriate (see fig. 38). The *intention* is to force a lift. If successful, your partner – still positioned on the edge of the forecourt – will threaten any replies to the forecourt while you cover replies to the midcourt and rearcourt. If the opponent lifts to the rearcourt you would both withdraw to take up the appropriate 'front and back' formation.

2. The push to the midcourt past the opposing front man is used to obtain a lift and allows your front man to withdraw to the midcourt to join you in a sides attack formation. You adjust your position to occupy the adjacent court to your partner (see fig. 39). Both of you are now ready to cover all replies in your own section of the court.

3. The whip is used to get the shuttle past the opponents, over their heads into the rearcourt. The *intention* is to reduce their recovery time and force an error or a weak reply.

4. The lob will force the opponents into their rear court. The replies to the whip and the lob are the smash, drop and clear. Both you and your partner adjust your positions accordingly to a sides defence formation in the midcourt.

Forecourt situations

Situation 1   The *shuttle position* is above net height, having travelled upwards from a low return. Your *partner is positioned* in the midcourt, covering you and ready to attack any replies to the midcourt or rearcourt. Your *stroke-moves* vary in relation to how high the shuttle is above the net and how much space and time you have to perform your stroke. Your main *intention* is to hit a winner or force a weak reply. The stroke-moves you use to achieve this are:

1. The 'slash' – the strongest hit and the best chance of making the kill – the outright winner.

2. The 'brush-shot' (a glancing blow) or the 'dab' are also effective in making the kill when the shuttle is very close to the net.

3. The 'push' is used when the shuttle is slightly away from the net and at net height or just below. If the shuttle is too low it is not possible to hit the shuttle downwards effectively. The softer 'push' shot causes the shuttle to fall quickly once it crosses the net.

4. The 'check-dab' and
5. The 'block' to a fast shuttle take the speed off the shuttle and result in it falling close to the net.

Your *partner remains positioned* in the midcourt to attack any replies that get past you. After your stroke-move you should recover and take up an attacking stance on the edge of the forecourt. If the opponents lift to the rearcourt, you should withdraw to the midcourt behind the T, relative to the shuttle position in the rearcourt. Even if you believe that you have hit an outright winner, develop the habit of withdrawing to the edge of the forecourt ready to threaten any replies. *In badminton it is a wise policy to assume that the opponent will return the shuttle.* Follow it and you will rarely be surprised when they do retrieve the 'impossible' shuttle. Relax only when you see the shuttle hit the floor.

Situation 2   The *shuttle position* is near the top of the net and below net height. Your *partner is positioned* in the midcourt ready to cover you and attack any midcourt and rearcourt replies to your stroke-move. Your main *intention* is to force the opponents to lift, hence your most attacking stroke-move in the situation is a net reply; the stroke-move you use is either a 'tumbler' or a 'spinner'. The *opponents' possible replies* are a net reply or a 'lift' to the rearcourt. If your stroke-move is successful, be ready to step forwards to attack the net reply or, if they lob, withdraw to the midcourt behind the T relative to the position of the shuttle in the rearcourt. Alternative stroke-moves are:

1. The 'tap' to the forecourt or rearcourt. This is used to control a rotating shuttle without making an error. The racket face strikes the shuttle so quickly with the rebound effect of the tapping action that the rotation of the shuttle does not affect the performance of the stroke. The *opponents' possible replies* are to hit down if the shuttle is above net height; or a net reply to the forecourt, or a lift to the rearcourt if the shuttle is below net height.

    You should be ready to sway aside if the opponent hits down and let your rear man attempt to make a reply. Otherwise, attack the net reply. Adjust your position in the midcourt for the lift to your rearcourt—ready to attack as front man.

    If you tap the shuttle up high to the rearcourt, then withdraw from the forecourt and take up a sides defence formation next to your partner.

2. The whip to the rearcourt also places you in the defensive situation. Withdraw from the forecourt and take up a sides defence formation with your partner in the midcourt.

   The general rule in this situation is that you should withdraw straight from the forecourt into the midcourt of the side of the court you are in. Your rear partner can see you withdraw from the net and simply moves over into the adjacent side court (see fig. 40). If you are in the centre forecourt then take your choice of midcourt–whichever feels best, unless you have agreed otherwise with your partner.

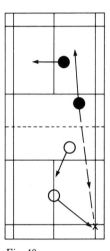

Fig. 40

Situation 3 The *shuttle position* is low in the forecourt, near the ground and close to the net. Your *partner is positioned* in the midcourt covering you and ready to attack any replies to the midcourt or rearcourt. You have two choices of *stroke-move* in this situation:

1. The hairpin drop which can be hit straight or angled across the net (see figs. 41 & 42). The *intention* is to force the opponent to lift the shuttle for your side to attack. It is, however, a very risky move to attempt with the opponent waiting poised to attack in the forecourt. If successful you will gain a lift and the attack.

2. The alternative stroke-move is to lob the shuttle high into the rearcourt. The opponents gain the attack but with less chance of hitting an immediate winner. The high lob gives you time to withdraw to the midcourt ready to defend against the attack.

Fig. 41

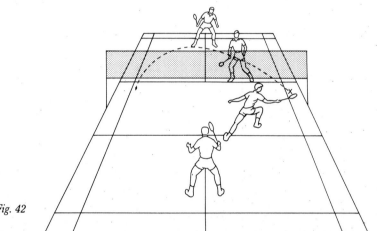

Fig. 42

Comment

The detailed explanation of the situations described in the charts provides the foundation for the rest of the book. We can now study the game situations in more depth and examine how the players position themselves to combine as a pair to defeat their opponents. The next part of the book is concerned solely with playing level doubles (ladies' and men's) and mixed doubles.

Part Two

Playing Doubles

Chapter 4 Ladies' and Men's Doubles

Introduction

The only way to learn to play doubles is to 'have a go' and play. If you have read the charts, looked at the 'attack and defence' formations, and considered the functions of the players and the stroke-moves you can make, you should have a good idea by now of the extent of what goes on in doubles.

It is obvious that the world class player will be able to do much more than the club player. Nevertheless, all players will find themselves, almost invariably, in one of the situations listed in the charts. In that situation they have a choice of stroke-moves to use. The highly skilled player may be able to perform all the stroke-moves; the club player might be more limited in what he can do, but can still make an appropriate move–one in accordance with the principle of attack. For example, in rearcourt situation 5 (see above in the charts) the highly skilled player would jump backwards, smash and recover quickly into position. The club player might not be able to smash when the shuttle is behind him, yet he might be able to hit a clear to the rearcourt, a sensible move in that situation, since it would manoeuvre his opponent into the rearcourt and still allow him time to recover to cover his opponent's replies. The opponents would gain the attack but might be unlikely to smash through the defence from the rearcourt.

It is always possible to make an intelligent move in a situation if you know what sort of situation you are in and what stroke-moves are possible and appropriate. At first this might appear difficult because it seems as if there are so many stroke-moves possible in each situation. But this is not so, for all the stroke-moves listed can be reduced to three basic ones. These are:

1. To hit the shuttle past the opponents, above their heads or down the sides, to the rearcourt. This move manoeuvres the opponents out of position and away from the net. The further away from the net, the less effective is the attack.

2. To hit the shuttle into the forecourt. This move draws the opponent out of position and forces him to hit the shuttle upwards, so giving you the chance to attack.

3. To hit the shuttle down or flat (horizontally) towards the midcourt. This forces the opponent to hit the shuttle upwards, or to make a weak reply or an error. Alternatively, it might hit the ground for an outright winner.

The strokes required to make these basic moves are explained in the glossary. They are:

To the rearcourt: the overhead clear, underarm lob, the whip, flick serve and high serve.

To the midcourt: the smash, net kill, the push and the drive.

To the forecourt: the overhead dropshot, the block and net replies.

The different stroke-moves are variations on these basic strokes. The stroke-move can be varied by altering the trajectory, distance, direction and the amount of force used, e.g. by giving the shuttle a full blow, as in the power smash; or a glancing blow, as in the sliced smash or 'tumbler.'

Any player who wants to reach a high standard must improve his technical skill so that he can perform most of the stroke-moves. It certainly helps if one does possess a range of stroke-moves to use in a particular situation. The most important factor, however, is not how many stroke-moves you can carry out, but when they are used. A player with a limited number of stroke-moves can play winning doubles by making intelligent use of those he can perform.

The full list of stroke-moves is given in the charts for reference, but what concerns us now is how players might make use of them in the various forms of doubles. Let us first look at level doubles (ladies' and men's doubles) in detail and then go on to discuss in depth the various aspects of mixed doubles.

There are few differences of any significance between ladies' and men's doubles. Women are as capable as men in learning and performing all the stroke-moves in a given situation. In general, men might defeat women in a game at the same level of play, e.g. a club doubles; but a county or regional ladies' pair might easily defeat a club standard men's pair. In fact, part of the practice of the 1975 England Uber Cup team was to play against a men's county side; invariably the women used to win the match. Quality is relative to the level at which men and women play; at the higher levels of play men are usually faster and stronger than women, though not necessarily more skilful or intelligent in their choice and performance of stroke-moves. Consequently, the discussion which follows applies equally to women and men unless there is something specific to be said about one or the other.

Doubles formations in attack and defence

If you have read through the charts carefully and studied the figures in chapter 3 you should have a good idea of how a doubles pair can combine and use stroke-moves to defeat their opponents. The charts are constructed on the basis that the players are of equal ability and play an all court game; they are equally at ease and effective at attack and defence in the rearcourt, midcourt and forecourt. Two such players are potentially the perfect pair – provided they are intelligent in their use of stroke-moves; and to be so they must always play in accordance with the *principle of attack*. However, in actual play it is not usual for both players to be of equal ability in all parts of the court. Players differ in their abilities. They possess different strengths and weaknesses. A good pair will combine to make the most of their strengths and reduce their weaknesses, and this results in differences in the ways players position themselves on the court and use stroke-moves in attacking and defensive situations.

In this chapter I want to look at different types of formation in attack and defence, and the different uses of stroke-moves in rearcourt, midcourt and forecourt situations.

ATTACK FORMATIONS
Rearcourt situations

Front and back attack formations

In this formation one player assumes responsibility for the front of the court, and the other player assumes responsibility for the rear of the court behind the front player. Hence one player is in the front and one player is at the back. I shall refer to them as the front player and the rear player, or as front man/front lady and rear man/rear lady. There are several variations on this basic formation, as follows.

Variation 1
(See figs. 43-45.) The rear player is positioned deep in the rearcourt ready to smash; his position is decided for him by the position of the shuttle. The opponents position themselves to defend

against the strongest threat in this situation—the smash; their positions are influenced by the principle of attack. The only player not accounted for is the partner of the attacker in the rearcourt. Where does he stand? There are several possible answers to this question, each of which result in a different variation. When we have looked at each in turn you can decide with your partner which one you will adopt.

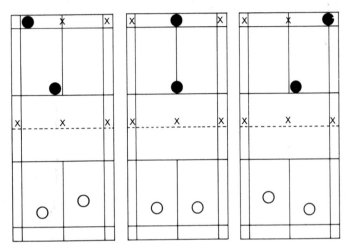

Figs. 43-45

In this first variation the front player stands in the forecourt on or close to the service line near the T. He takes up this position in order to cover any replies to the forecourt from his partner's smash or drop shot. The forecourt is his sole responsibility. The pair decide on this for several reasons.

1. Because the opponents choose to or can only reply to the smash with a block to the forecourt or a lob to the rearcourt, and to the drop shot with a net reply or lob; in which case this is sensible positioning. The front man is close to the net to attack all replies to the forecourt; the rear man would cover the lob to the rearcourt and weak lobs to the midcourt. This is an ideal attacking formation for the limited replies of the opponents.

2. The opponents now use more replies but the front man still looks after the forecourt and leaves anything else to his rear man. The opponents may use the drive and the push, to hit the shuttle past the front man to the midcourt (see figs. 46-48). In this instance the front man would allow many shuttles to go past him to the midcourt, only intercepting those which he could hit safely and with good effect, i.e. to hit a winner or block to the forecourt to gain a lift. If he

allows the shuttle to go past him to the midcourt, his rear man has to change direction and travel quickly into position to hit the shuttle which, by now, could be below net height (see fig. 48). This would mean that the attacking side had now lost the attack and must lift the shuttle, unless the rear man is able to hit a horizontal push or drive, in which case the sides would become equally balanced. In hitting the shuttle past the front man the defenders have achieved a neutral situation – both sides manoeuvring for the attack.

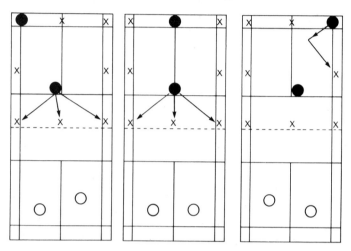

Figs. 46-48

Variation 2

This variation is used in modern doubles as described in the charts (see figs. 4-6) in rearcourt situation 1. In it the pair work hard to maintain the attack against pushes and drives to the midcourt. The front man positions himself in the midcourt ready to intercept replies to the midcourt as well as assume responsibility for all replies to the forecourt (see fig. 49). The rear man covers all replies behind his front man in the midcourt/rearcourt area (see fig. 50).

When a pair adopt this formation, with the front man ready to attack replies to the midcourt, the game becomes more dynamic. The front man has to work particularly hard and possess much explosive power and gymnastic/athletic ability. He must be prepared to be adventurous in committing himself to 'having a go' at an interception in order to maintain the attack. The rear man has to be alert and quick to cover the midcourt and the forecourt should his front man travel out of position in his attempt to attack the shuttle. To play as a pair in this way requires

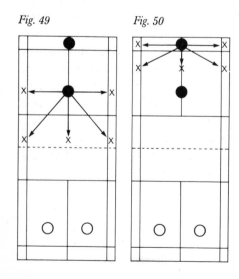

Fig. 49   *Fig. 50*

much work under pressure in practice and in the explosive type of fitness training exercises. (Practices and training are discussed in chapters 9 and 10).

Variation 3

This is the 'channel' attacking formation, adopted when the shuttle is in the midcourt/rearcourt area (see fig. 51). This shuttle position allows a player with a powerful smash to hit the shuttle very hard and ensure that it is still travelling fast when it reaches the opponent. This makes it more difficult for the opponent to defend and to play a full range of replies, particularly on the backhand side. A defender is often doing well to block the shuttle. To clear it to the rearcourt is quite difficult. To angle the shuttle cross-court away from the front player is even more difficult. Usually the most a defender can do is play a straight reply–the block, push or lob. The attacking side, therefore, attacks one opponent only. They keep him pinned down while they hit at him until he succumbs to the pressure and hits a weak reply, if any. They play down a narrow 'channel'. Should the defender manage to hit the shuttle cross-court into the midcourt/rearcourt area, the attackers switch to the other side of the court and continue with their channel attack (see fig. 52). If the opponent does manage to return the shuttle to the rearcourt, the attacking side revert to variation 2 (see figs. 49, 50).

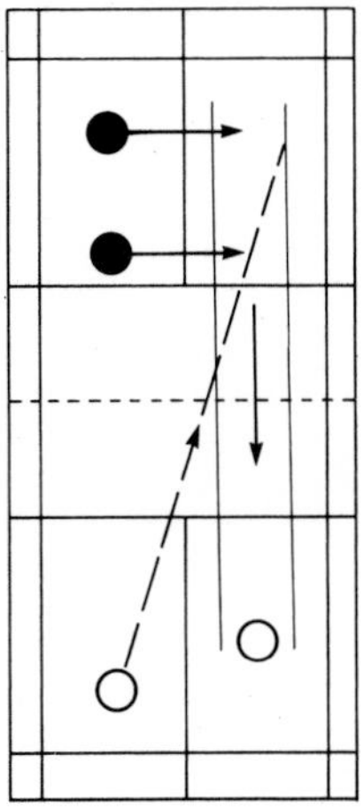

Variation 4

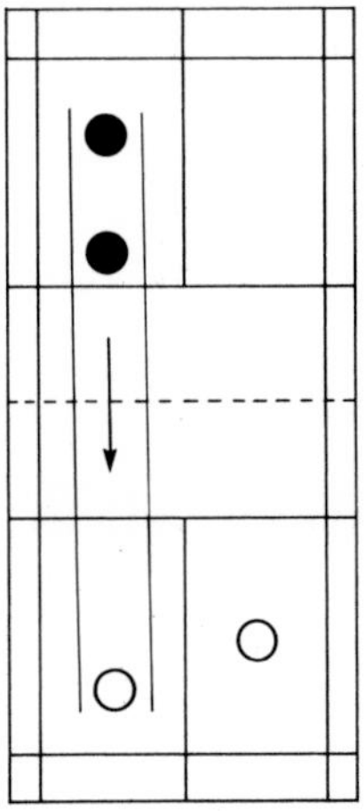

The 'wedge' attack is adopted when the rear man has a strong smash from the midcourt/rearcourt area and the defender has a strong defence and can direct the shuttle cross-court with control and accuracy. In this situation the front man must position himself to cover the cross-court reply. He should position himself to one side of his rear man, behind the T, near the centre of the midcourt. There he can cover any cross-court reply to the midcourt or rearcourt, yet is still able to attack in the forecourt (see fig. 53). In this formation both players focus the attack on one opponent only. If the opponent does manage to lob the shuttle to the rearcourt, the attackers revert to the usual rearcourt front and back attacking formation (see fig. 49).

Fig. 51

Fig. 52

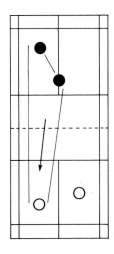

Fig. 53

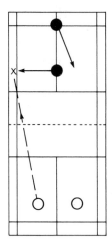

Fig. 54

Plate 9. Wu Dixi and Lin Ying engage in a fast MC rally with Li Lingwei and Hai Aiping.

Midcourt situations

Sides attack This is a development from the rearcourt situation variation 2 above. We can assume the front man has jumped across from his central midcourt position to attack a shuttle travelling down the side line towards the midcourt/rearcourt (see fig. 54). His partner, the rear man, immediately travels forwards into the midcourt to take up a position level with him and ready to cover the replies in his own section of the court. The game takes the form of half-court singles with each player responsible for his own side of the court. This often becomes a *neutral situation* with both sides 'slugging' away at each other like a couple of boxers (see plate 9).

As the shuttle is at net height or just above or below, the players will try to hit it at each other, skimming the net at speed. They will try to force the lift by hitting it with a slightly angled racket face to slice it and cause it to fall as it crosses the net; or, by taking some of the speed off, to make it fall short of the opponents.If that does not obtain a lift, the change of pace of the slower shuttle may cause the opponents to mistime their reply and so make an error.

Throughout the rally the players adopt attacking stances ready to hit and counter-hit at speed. The result is a very fast rally with the shuttle hurtling to and fro across the net. Once one side obtains a lift there is a new development. The sides attack changes very rapidly into some form of front and back attack formation in the rearcourt or midcourt/rearcourt. This can develop in the following way. The opponents may whip or lob the shuttle to the rearcourt or midcourt/rearcourt. Immediately the player on that side of the court travels backwards into position to attack the shuttle in the rearcourt. His partner adjusts his position and becomes the front man relative to the shuttle position and the doubles formation they usually adopt in that situation (see figs. 55-57).

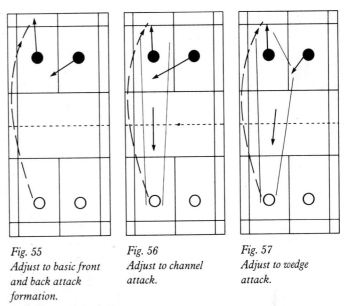

Fig. 55
*Adjust to basic front
and back attack
formation.*

Fig. 56
*Adjust to channel
attack.*

Fig. 57
*Adjust to wedge
attack.*

Forecourt situations

Front and back attack formations

An attack in the forecourt can develop from any one of the following: rearcourt front and back attack, sides, channel and wedge attack formations. The attack can be attempted in two types of forecourt situations: first, when the shuttle is above net height, and second, when the shuttle is just below net height.

1. Above net height

From the rearcourt or midcourt attack, the opponents may block the shuttle into the forecourt or attempt to drive it to the midcourt. Whatever the type of reply, it is assumed that the front man or the sides attack partner travels into the forecourt to hit down at the opponent from nearer the net. The nearer the net he is when hitting the shuttle down, the more chance there is of hitting a winner. His partner immediately travels to the midcourt to take up a position as rear man (see figs. 58-61). The rear man takes up this centre midcourt position because he has more replies to cover, even though his front man is close enough to the net to hit a possible winner. The front man should maintain the pressure on the opponent and commit himself to go for the winner. Such a commitment may take him even closer to the net and eventually out of the game for an instant—too late to recover to cover any replies should his opponents manage to return the shuttle. It is for this reason that the rear man positions himself in the centre midcourt ready to cover all the replies to the sides of

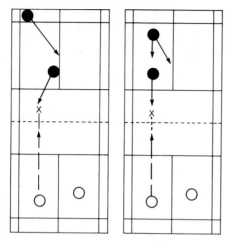

Fig. 58   Fig. 59

Rear man retains
channel attack or
positions himself in
centre MC.

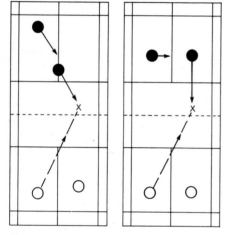

Fig. 60   Fig. 61

the forecourt and midcourt and anywhere in the rearcourt. He must be ready to travel to all replies which get past his front man and, in this respect, the whole court is open to his opponents.

Some pairs may be able to retain the channel attack formation if the front man is on the edge of the forecourt and in balance whilst hitting downwards at one opponent (see fig. 59); but once the front man commits himself to going for a winning hit off the top of the net, the rear man should take up the central midcourt position.

2. *Below net height*

The front man may have to travel into the forecourt because the opponents have made a good block return to the smash or drive. They have succeeded in getting the shuttle below net level in the forecourt. One of the opponents (usually the one on the same side of the court as the shuttle) will follow the shuttle and travel into the forecourt to threaten any replies and force a lift. The front man must travel forwards quickly to make his move, before the shuttle falls too far below net height. He cannot hit down and he wants to avoid the lob to the rearcourt. He decides to play a spinner or tumbler or any other tight net reply, with the intention of preventing his opponent from hitting down and forcing him to lift the shuttle.

In this situation the rear men of the two front players should travel to their respective centre midcourts to cover any replies which are hit past their front men. Fig. 62 illustrates the players adjusting their positions from sides attack formation to front and back formation for an attack in the forecourt when the shuttle is below net level. Should a front man lob the shuttle to the rearcourt the players revert to the appropriate attacking formation in the new situation.

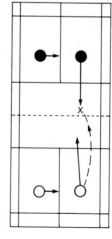

Fig. 62

DEFENCE FORMATIONS

Throughout I have referred to the defence as the 'sides defence' formation, and have mentioned that the defenders should be equidistant from the player set to smash in the rearcourt. This positioning results in one player being more forward, relative to the net, on his side of the court than his partner, when the attack is from the side of the opponents' rearcourt (see figs. 63-65). All

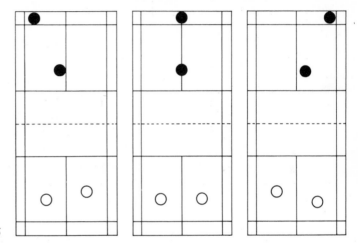

Figs. 63-65

the figures so far have illustrated this defensive formation with the players positioned in the midcourt, for it is a general rule, with few exceptions, that the players will adopt this sides defence formation. It is a sensible one to adopt since each player assumes responsibility for his own side of the court against an attack. Each has a certain spatial area to look after and positions himself to do so, relative to the position of the shuttle in the opponents' court, the type of stroke-move the attacker might use, and his own ability to make certain replies to that stroke-move.

Ways of defending

Players differ in how they prepare to defend against the smash. Some choose to defend while standing slightly 'side-on' to the probable smash, ready to cover shots to one side of the body only (see plate 10); this 'side-on defence' differs from 'front defence' in which the players prepare to defend against shots to either side of the body, as in singles play. In defence the player must be prepared to attack the shuttle. He must adopt a fighting attitude which is reflected in his stance (see plate 11). In this alert stance

Plate 10. Talbot and Stuart take up side-on defence stances.

Fig. 66

he is ready to counter-hit the smash with whatever reply might be appropriate, and to explode from his position to reach any shuttle hit to the rearcourt or forecourt.

The primary task of the defenders is to prevent the shuttle from hitting the ground. Consequently, they adopt one way of defending to perform this task: the side-on defence to cover the area of the court to their right or their left, or the front defence to cover both sides. For example, fig. 66 shows the players defending against the smash to the side or the centre. One player takes a side-on stance to cover the side line while his partner does the same to cover the centre (the area behind his partner). The defender in the left court must also cover the cross-court smash; however, as the shuttle will have further to travel he will have more time (if he is alert) to adjust his stance to hit it. In fig. 67 the players defend against the straight smash to the backhand side. In fig. 68 the players have a problem. If they adopt a side-on stance and turn inwards to defend against the straight smash, they expose the sides of the court.

There used to be a general rule in doubles play that the attacker should smash straight or to the centre, between the opponents. This policy was adopted to enable the front player to cover the replies more easily. Cross-court smashing was not recommended unless the attacker was in the midcourt and had a very good

Plate 11. Tjun Tjun and Wahjudi adopt a fighting attitude in defence.

chance of hitting an outright winner. Consequently, it was not expected that the defenders would be exposed to the cross-court smash (see fig. 69). However, as the game has developed the cross-court smash has become a sensible stroke-move to use, particularly from the midcourt/rearcourt area with the development of sides attack, in which there is the added emphasis of the smash at the opponent, rather than at the space around him. These days the defender is more likely to see himself as an attacking player

Fig. 67   Fig. 68

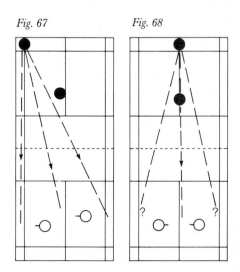

Fig. 69   Fig. 70

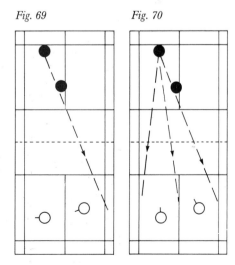

Plate 12. Tjun Tjun and Wahjudi take up front-on defence stances.

ready to cover his own half of the court whether the smash is aimed at him, or to either side of him, so he adopts a stance which enables him to 'attack'—the 'front defence' stance. Here he is square on to the attacker (see plate 12), like a goalkeeper or catcher, ready to receive the shuttle anywhere around his body. The racket is held in front, the racket head up and equidistant from his right and left side since he must be ready to adjust his position quickly. This change in attitude has led to a different method of hitting the shuttle. In the 1950s and early 1960s the racket was heavier, being made of wood or a wooden head with a metal shaft, and players tended to swing at the shuttle, which they could do in the side-on defence stance. In the later 1960s and the 1970s new, lighter materials led to the construction of lighter, whippier rackets. It has become much easier for any player to generate racket head speed with a 'flick of the wrist', and consequently players can now face the attacker and hit the shuttle ahead of their bodies with the minimum of movement. It is not necessary to prepare to defend against one side.

Not only has the technique of defending improved; there has also been an increase in the range of replies the defender can make. Hence the players shown in fig. 70 would turn to face the attacker, ready to defend on both sides of the body. This does, however, create a small problem to do with which player replies from the centre, which is discussed earlier (see page 42).

Attacking the smash

A good pair of 'attacking' defenders will attempt to attack the smash to make a reply which will force the opponents to lift the shuttle or give a weak reply. The block to the net will achieve a lift if it is successful as a move. The whip cross-court, past the front man and away from the rear man, might achieve the same result. Usually, it is the drive or push down the sides which proves the most attacking move, since here the shuttle skims the net and cannot be hit downwards. These two stroke-moves neutralise the situation and allow the players to engage in a slugging match until one side gains the initiative (see page 62).

The earlier the defenders attack the smash, the better the chance of gaining the attack. Therefore it helps to face the smasher in the 'front defence' stance. The racket head is held higher than the hand, in the 'attack' position. From this position the stroke-move is performed with a quick flick of the racket head

Plate 13. Wahjudi about to make a low defence reply to the smash.

Plate 14. Atsuko Tokuda plays a high defence reply to the smash.

to hit the shuttle from below. At the point of impact the racket face hits the shuttle when the racket head is level with or just below the level of the hand. This is called 'low defence' (see plate 13). Some players are more adventurous in their determination to attack the shuttle and adopt a 'high defence' (see plate 14). This type of defence is usually seen in mixed doubles and level doubles in the 'diagonal defence' formation: one player is more forward than his partner in the forecourt or midcourt (see figs. 74, 75 below). In 'high defence' the racket head is held almost directly above the hand to hit the shuttle, with the player squatting to lower his trunk to place himself below the shuttle. In this stance he is able to attack the shuttle quite easily and in some cases even smash it back at the opponents. It can be a risky stance to adopt, particularly if the smasher jumps to smash and hits the shuttle down on a steep trajectory which gets below the high defence; this defence, if used intelligently, can catch the attackers by surprise and change the defensive situation quickly into an attacking one. It is certainly a form of defence which the lady must use in mixed doubles, in order to attack the cross-court smash and place the opposing man under pressure.

The form of defence any player adopts is a matter of choice, with respect to what he considers most appropriate in the particular situation. It is something you can decide when you have examined and thought about the different types of positional play in doubles.

POSITIONAL PLAY

There are three basic court positions using sides defence. These are centre, deep and forward defence. There is also a variation, diagonal defence, which is a combination of (a) forward and centre defence, or (b) centre and deep defence. These are explained below.

1. Centre defence

The defending pair position themselves in the centre midcourt in a sides defence formation. This position is adopted when the attack is taking place from the rearcourt, with the attacking pair in balance ready to smash, drop or clear with ease (see plate 15).

The strongest threat is the power smash, against which the sides defence formation is positioned to defend. The defenders are also well positioned to travel to the forecourt for any drop shot, and to the rearcourt to reply to the standard or attack clear.

This is a comfortable position to adopt relative to the smash; they are well positioned to adjust to different trajectories and directions of the smash. An alert defending player should have time to make effective replies to a smash to his feet, or a flat smash to his body (see fig. 71).

2. Deep defence The defending pair position themselves deeper in the midcourt and nearer the rear court (see fig. 72 and plate 16). There are several reasons why a pair might decide on 'deep' defence:

1. To defend against an attacker positioned in the midcourt/rearcourt. He is nearer the net and his smash will be that much more effective. If the defenders positioned themselves in the midcourt they would have less time to see the shuttle and to perform a stroke-move in reply to a powerful smash – particularly as it could be aimed at the head, trunk, legs, or the sides. It would be extremely difficult to attack such a smash and drive it back across the net; it is more likely that the defender would just about manage to block the shuttle to the forecourt. The chances of making a weak reply to a powerful midcourt smash are increased if the defender positions himself in the midcourt. He might remain there to defend against an attacker in the midcourt/rearcourt who is known to have a weak smash, but that is not so here. Consequently, it is more sensible to reduce the chance of error, of making a weak reply, or of the opponent hitting a winner, by withdrawing to deep defence. There, the players have more time and space to make an effective reply to the smash.

There is a risk in doing this. In withdrawing from the net into deep defence the forecourt is exposed for a check-smash or a fast drop shot. This is something defenders must be ready for, and if they are alert they should reach the shuttle to retaliate with a net reply to the forecourt or a high lob to the rearcourt. The latter move would enable them to return to their centre defence with a better chance of attacking the smash from the rearcourt.

2. The second reason for adopting a deep defence is if the opponents have been using the attack clear move successfully. This happens often in ladies' doubles, and in men's doubles at the lower levels of play. The attack clear is usually successful in obtaining a weak reply because the defenders are slow in leaving the defensive stance and travelling to the rearcourt.

Some players are quicker and more at ease in running forwards than backwards. A pair who are caught out with attack clears when in centre defence might easily benefit by adopting a deep defence position, as a counter-tactic. From here they can cover

Plate 15. Yoshiko Yonekura and Tokuda take up centre defence positions.

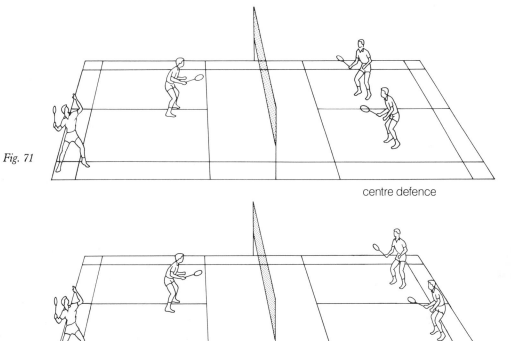

Fig. 71

centre defence

Fig. 72

deep defence

Plate 16. Tjun Tjun and Wahjudi take up deep defence positions.

the smash and the clear, although they do expose themselves to the check-smash or fast drop to the forecourt. In this situation, either of these is preferable to the attack clear which gets behind them.

3. Forward defence   The defending pair position themselves further forwards ready to attack the smash (see fig. 73). This can be a risky tactic to adopt,

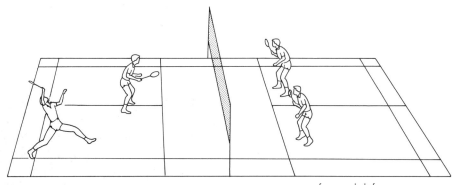

Fig. 73

forward defence

for it leaves the smasher free to hit the shuttle to the open rear-court and also gives less time to see the shuttle and reply to the smash when the opponent is balanced in the rearcourt. For these reasons it is not common practice except in certain situations. It can be used when:

1.   The shuttle has been hit behind the opponents and the rear man is late to hit the smash. Immediately both defenders travel forwards and adopt a forward defence.
2.   The rear man is known to have a weak smash and cannot hit the shuttle fast enough to trouble the defenders.
3.   The opponent is known to have a flat smash, i.e. he cannot hit down on a steep trajectory.
4.   The defenders are very quick and have a strong defence.

There are two factors to consider here. First, it is not a good policy to adopt the forward defence too early. If the opponent sees the position being taken up before he has committed himself to hitting the shuttle he might easily hit an attack clear to catch out the defenders. It is only advisable to travel into position once the attacker begins to perform his stroke-move, and not before then. Second, as the defenders are closer to the net they will contact the shuttle at a higher point in the air. It is customary, therefore, to adopt a defensive stance with the racket held high, i.e. high defence.

4. 'Diagonal' defence

A variation on the basic deep, centre and forward defence is to combine two of these within the one formation. The result is a diagonal defensive formation with one player further ahead than his partner and in a position to attack the shuttle from above rather than below. In this combination the forward player covers the cross-court smash. The pair might agree that the forward player could be allowed to be adventurous in attacking the shuttle. The two types of diagonal defence are:

1. One player in forward defence and his partner in centre defence (see fig. 74).
2. One player in centre defence and his partner in deep defence (see fig. 75).

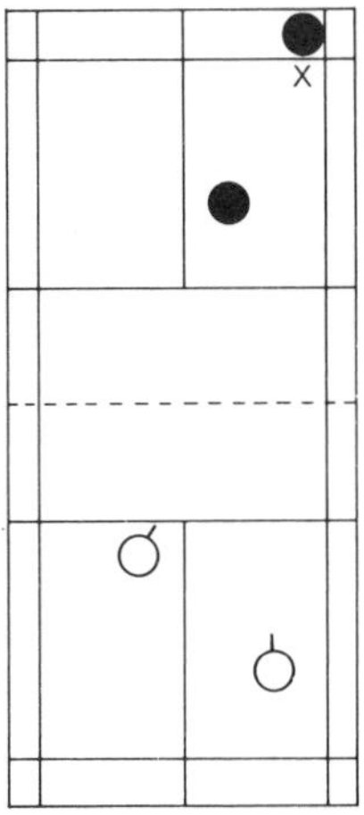

Fig. 74
In this situation the player in forward defence covers the x-court smash and defends with his racket head held high (above his hand).

The partner in centre defence covers the straight smash in the usual defence stance (see plate 17).

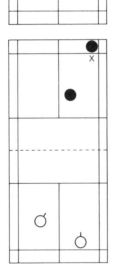

Fig. 75
In this situation the player in forward defence also covers the x-court smash but defends with his racket held in the attack position ready for high or low defence. His partner covers the straight smash, racket in the attack position and more ready for low defence (see plate 18).

Plate 17. A typical mixed doubles diagonal defence formation – the lady in forward defence ready to cover the x-court smash and her partner in centre defence covering the straight smash.

Summary

The framework in which the game is played makes it possible to identify and isolate the situations. In these situations certain stroke-moves are possible, some of which are on occasion more appropriate than others, if applied in accordance with the principle of attack. Knowing this, it has become possible to examine the different positions (the doubles formation) that the players adopt to make and reply to stroke-moves in order to win the rally. So far, no consideration has been given to the strengths and weaknesses of the individual players. Yet this is most important, for individual differences can and usually do effect where and how a player positions himself, and the stroke-moves he chooses to play in a given situation. Chapter 5 examines the work of the individual player in action.

Plate 18. Diagonal defence comprising deep defence and centre defence positions.

Chapter 5 The Work of the Players in Attack

Plate 19. Finn Kobbero poised to strike in the FC while Hammergaard Hanson watches from behind.

It has been assumed until now that both players are of equal ability in playing an all-court game, i.e. in the rearcourt, midcourt and forecourt. In practice this is quite rare, for it is often the case that one player is stronger in the rearcourt than forecourt, or *vice-versa*. Consequently, when a pair are in attack they will try to ensure that one particular player will remain in the rearcourt and the other in the forecourt. In the 1960s the great doubles pair of Finn Kobbero and J. Hammergaard Hansen played with Kobbero 'sitting' up front in the forecourt, killing any loose or weak replies to Hansen's smash. In the 1970s Hadinata Christian and Ade Chandra played with Christian mainly in the front and Chandra smashing from the rear. However, their compatriots Tjun Tjun and J. Wahjudi, who dominated the doubles scene from 1974 to 1980, played an all-court game, though Tjun Tjun would often dominate in the forecourt. The best exponents of the all-court game were the Swedish pairs, Thomas Kihlstrom and Bengt Froman in 1976, and Thomas Kihlstrom and Stefan Karlsson in 1983. All these players (see plates 19-22) combined into great pairs and adopted a style of play which best suited their individual strengths and preferences.

It is always a matter of contention which doubles pair were the best, and which style of play is most successful. In my opinion the all-court game is most effective because such a pair attack at speed all the time, whatever the situation; they never let up. Perhaps it is because such a game demands so much from the players in maintaining constant pressure on the opponents that so few pairs attempt to play this way; to do so requires a very high level of skill in handling the racket, very fast reflexes, good imagination and anticipation and a high standard of athletic/gymnastic ability. Thomas Kihlstrom possesses these attributes combined with much experience of top-class play. On the occasions when he has found a partner of equal ability at the time, he has won the All England Doubles championship.

Plate 20. *Ade Chandra plays the shuttle that manages to get past Hadinata Christian.*

Plate 21. *Wahjudi makes an adventurous interception while Tjun Tjun keeps alert for the reply.*

Plate 22. *Thomas Kihlstrom watches carefully as Stefan Karlsson returns the smash.*

We can gain more understanding of how players form successful partnerships if we examine the various ways in which they combine and make use of their abilities in the different attacking situations.

The functions of the players

In any attacking formation the players can perform two related functions. Each can adopt the role of 'hit-player' or 'set-up player'. The job of the hit-player is to hit winners or keep the pressure on the opponents; the job of the set-up player is to create the opportunity for the hit-player to hit a winner.

The all-court players of equal ability will each perform both functions; in general, however, most pairs contain one player who is mainly the hit-player or the set-up player. Either one can operate in the rearcourt, midcourt or forecourt. The rear player in the rearcourt or midcourt functioning as set-up player will attempt to create an opening for the front player to hit a winner. Or, the front player, if he is the set-up player, will create the opening for his rear player to hit a winner.

In such a partnership, it would still be expected that either player would take on the other's function should it be necessary, or should the opportunity arise. For example, a front hit-player unable to hit a winner might block the shuttle into the forecourt or push it down to the midcourt to force a lift which he or his partner (the rear set-up player) can hit for a winner.

The rear hit-player

This player requires a powerful smash, hit with control and accuracy. He/she must be strong with the good local muscular endurance which is required to keep smashing hard with consistency. He/she must be alert, agile, quick off the mark and able to jump upwards, sideways or backwards to smash the shuttle. Strength, good balance and power are needed to land lightly and to recover quickly to travel into position to cover any replies that get past the front player.

The front hit-player

The front hit-player needs quick reflexes, a high level of agility and a very fast racket hand, able to generate force quickly with the minimum of racket head movement. He should possess power and be able to use it to accelerate quickly from his front position to intercept and attack shuttles driven across the net at speed, or whipped upwards within his reach. Speed of recovery is most important for he must commit himself fully to the attack when the chance arises to hit a winner. He must be adventurous and prepared to take risks. His job is to keep the pressure on the opponents and hit the winner whenever possible.

The rear set-up player This player must possess a range of stroke-moves from high and low positions. He should be able to vary the speed and trajectory of the shuttle. He needs good control of the racket face to vary the direction of the shuttle and catch the opponents wrongly balanced. He should be able to mix smashes with drop shots performed with some deception. He must be patient and prepared to work to create the opening. Imagination and deception are a feature of his play.

When the shuttle is low he needs control, accuracy and deception to create a situation which forces the opponents to lift, or to prevent them attacking his reply. He must be ready at all times to cover his front player's adventurous attacks to the net for, once committed, it is unlikely that the front player will recover in time to cover the replies hit away from him at the sides or over his head.

The front set-up player The front set-up player must possess good racket control, a fine touch and a feel for the shuttle for he will need to play blocks, net replies, pushes to the forecourt and midcourt, and to slow the speed of the shuttle when necessary. He must be quick and alert, with good balance to intercept the opponents' replies. Additionally, he should be able to hit a winner off any weak replies. He should appear as a threat to the opponents, forcing them to lift rather than hit a reply to the forecourt or midcourt. In general, he will not attempt to hit a winner. He is not required to be adventurous and take chances. He requires patience, concentration and a good tactical mind to enable him to 'read' the game, anticipate the opponents' replies and make sure that he misses no opportunity to create an opening for his partner, the hit-player to his rear.

Comments In any doubles partnership the players combine to play for each other, relative to the function each performs best. This applies equally to ladies', men's and mixed doubles. In all these forms of doubles the players will function predominantly either as hit-players or set-up players, and sometimes as both.

It is unlikely that a pair could succeed at any level if both players were set-up players; certainly not against a pair that combined two hit-players, or one hit-player and one set-up player. They might succeed if their opponents were also set-up players, though such a contest would, in many respects, be like a game of soccer or basketball in which both teams passed the ball around without any player taking a shot at the goal or basket. Games are won by scoring points and to score points at least one member of the side has to attempt regular shots at the goal; and to do that the pair require a hit-player. I know that it is possible just to keep the shuttle in play, not try to hit a winner and yet still win on the opponents' mistakes. Such a policy could be a deliberate strategy for part of the game on occasions. But in general such a policy, if applied regularly, would result in very dull negative badminton. It certainly would not be compatible with the dynamic positive play required for winning doubles.

The players in attack and defence

After having discussed the functions of the players in attack, we can look at what happens in the attack and defence in specific situations.

Although there are a number of stroke-moves and replies logically possible in any situation, players will select their stroke-moves and replies to suit their style of play. An attacking pair with the hit-player at the front and a set-up player at the rear will use different stroke-moves from a pair with the hit-player at the rear and the set-up player at the front.

The defenders should endeavour to adapt their replies to the type of attack they meet. They will not want to give the hit-player a chance to hit winners, and should feel less threatened by a set-up player who might be less forceful though more creative.

The following examples illustrate situations in which different forms of attack and possible defences to the attack can take place. In addition, there is some discussion on how to weaken the positional play of the attacking pair – for example, by manoeuvring a front hit-player to the rear and a rear hit-player to the front, where both may be less effective in their new positions; we would then want to know how the players can manoeuvre their way back into their usual positions, where they are more effective. What sort of transition moves can they play in order to return to their strongest positions in an attacking formation?

Specific situations have been extracted from the charts. One side is on the attack, which results in the related situation in which the other side defends. In example 1 below, the attack occurs in a rearcourt situation and the defence in a potential midcourt situation. It is 'potential' because the defenders expect to receive the smash. The attacker, however, may hit the shuttle to the forecourt or rearcourt which would alter the situation in which the defenders make their reply stroke-move.

Example 1.

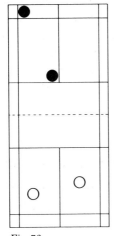

Fig. 76

The attack – rearcourt situation

The attackers are positioned in a front and back formation with the front player standing on or next to the T (see fig. 76). He is positioned to cover replies to the forecourt. The front player can function as hit-player or set-up player but only to the block or net reply to the forecourt and the occasional weak push or drive he can manage to intercept; he is not really in a position to intercept many fast returns to the sides. By standing so near to the forecourt he exposes his side to the push and drive to the midcourt. If his opponents succeed in hitting the shuttle past him to the midcourt, which they are likely to do, his rear player must travel forwards to hit the falling shuttle from below net height. In the situation illustrated in fig. 76 both front and rear players must be prepared to operate as hit-player and set-up player. Against a reasonable defence it is unlikely that the smash from the rearcourt will be a winning hit; nor is it likely that it will force a weak reply which the front man can kill. The first task, then, is to create an opening for the rear or front player to attempt a winner. Thus the rear player might employ a variety of smashes, of varying speeds, directions and trajectories to obtain a weak reply to the midcourt or to the forecourt, where his partner might hit a block reply, an angled net reply or a spinner to obtain another lift for his rear partner. If the rear player can smash from the midcourt, he can begin to use more power – go for a winner or pressure the opponents into giving a further weak reply, which will allow him or his front player to function as a hit-player and end the rally.

The defence – midcourt situation

The defenders are 'safe' if they keep the rear player deep in the rearcourt using high lobs or fast whips to do so. This policy is one of *passive defence*, i.e. defence for the sake of defence. It does not pose any threat to the opponents. If continued it should usually result in the opponents making a winning move. I say 'usually' because I was once a spectator at a doubles match between a world-class Indonesian doubles pair and a pair of ex-international

England players, at the All England championships. The indonesians were defending and adopted a policy of passive defence, returning each smash with a high lob to the rearcourt. After ten continuous smashes the crowd began to chant the count, 'Eleven, twelve, thirteen' and so on. After about twenty smashes the English player rapidly tired and his smashes became weaker and weaker until the Indonesians, grinning good-humouredly at the spectacle, switched to the attack and ended the rally quickly. Such a situation is not likely to occur at the present period when England's doubles pairs are ranked amongst the best in the world; but it does show that sometimes a policy of defence can be the best strategy against a weaker attack, to soften up the attack before counter-attacking.

In general, if the defenders want to gain the attack they must adopt a policy of *active defence,* i.e. counter-attack and try to neutralise the situation or force a lift. They can block the shuttle away from the opposing front player and get it below net level, so forcing him to lift to the forecourt or rearcourt. They can push or drive the shuttle past the front player so that it falls quickly below net level in the midcourt and forces the rear player to travel forwards to make the reply, which could be either a return push or drive or a net reply, which creates a neutral situation (see fig. 54); or a lift to the rearcourt, which presents the defenders with the chance to attack.

Example 2

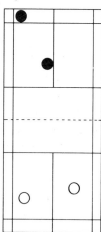

Fig. 77

The attack – rearcourt situation

In this situation the front player is positioned to cover the replies to the forecourt and midcourt, and to intercept the cross-court reply (see fig. 77). He can function as a set-up player or hit-player depending on which role he prefers. It is assumed that he can perform as a hit-player should a strong possibility of doing so occur. If he operates as the set-up player his rear partner must operate as the hit-player. In the rearcourt situation illustrated, the rear man may have to vary his smash and use the drop shot to obtain a reply which enables him to attack from nearer the net. His front player should be ready to intercept, blocking the opponents' replies and angling them down into the forecourt whenever possible. Any early interception before the opponents have fully recovered will assist his rear player to maintain the attack.

If the front player is a hit-player, his rear player will again have to vary his smash and drop – particularly the steepness of the smash and drop – to force the opponents to hit *up* towards the

Plate 23. Mike Tredgett attacks in the FC.

front player rather than *at* him. The flatter smash from the rear-court is sometimes to the advantage of the opponents. The shuttle can be angled away from the front player with a quick block, or hit quickly to skim the net and fall into the midcourt. The front player should attack the reply to the forecourt with his racket head held up, ready to hit down whenever possible (see plate 23). If he cannot hit down he will play a tumbler to force a mis-hit or a weak lift for his rear player to make a move to enable him (the front player) to attack and hit a winner. In the midcourt he must be ready to leap sideways to slash, drive or push the opponents' replies. If he is unable to hit the shuttle hard, he will tap it downwards towards the centre midcourt or to the centre forecourt, each time recovering very quickly to travel into position to threaten and attack all replies to the forecourt and midcourt. His theme is 'hit and move', 'hit and move'.

The defence – midcourt situation

The defenders should be ready for any variation in the type of attack, depending on whether the attackers function as set-up or hit-players.

1. Rear set-up player with front hit-player

When the rear attacker is the set-up player and his front player is the hit-player, the defenders should appreciate that the rear player will be inclined to create opportunities for his front player to hit the winner. The defenders' main task is to keep the shuttle away from the front hit-player unless they obtain an easy chance of forcing a lift from a reply to the forecourt. They must be patient and alert to receiving steep smashes and drop shots, and the occasional attack clear if they anticipate too soon. If they cannot counter-attack then they must keep the rear attacker pinned down deep in his rearcourt. Good length is important on any lob replies to the rearcourt, with sufficient height to give them time to recover into balanced defensive stances. *Too many defenders hit shallow lobs when under pressure and do not allow themselves sufficient time to recover into position.* When returning a steep angled smash or a fast drop to the forecourt, it is most important that the shuttle is returned to the rearcourt with height and length to make such time. It is obvious that the attacker will smash whether the shuttle is returned on a high trajectory or a shallow one. The essential factor is time to recover into defence (see fig. 78). As soon as the opportunity arises, e.g. a flatter smash, they should attack, by hitting the shuttle down the lines to skim the

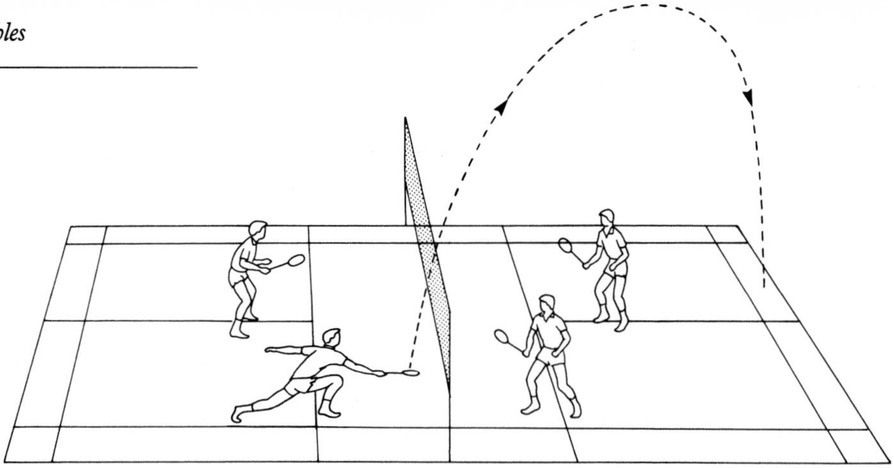

Fig. 78

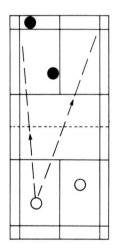

Fig. 79
Drive to MC past
front man; whip to
RC over front man's
head.

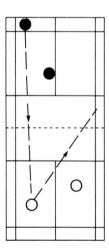

Fig. 80
Quick angled block to
the smash.

net past the front opponent, or by whipping it over the front hit-player's head to the rearcourt, away from the opposing rear set-up player. Additionally here, the quick angled block to the flatter fast smash will often succeed in getting the shuttle below net level in the forecourt before the opposing front hit-player can attack it (see figs. 79-80).

In this situation the defenders could use a diagonal defence with the forward defender edging near the forecourt, particularly if they have first managed to whip the shuttle away from the rear player in the rearcourt. If he is off-balance when making his stroke-move there arises a good chance of taking a forward defence base.

The front-player, as the hit-player, poses a constant threat in the midcourt and forecourt. He will attempt to hit the shuttle at them or between them to maintain the pressure until he gets the chance to hit a winner. The defenders must adopt an alert fighting stance with the racket ready to counter-hit at speed. Good balance and quick reflexes are essential, for they must be ready to travel quickly into the forecourt to reply to the front player's set-up shots if he has been unable to hit them. It helps if the defenders can use deception to wrongfoot the front hit-player and entice him to go one way while they hit the shuttle the other way – see discussion on deception in the Appendix, pp. 207-10.

2. Rear hit-player and front set-up player
It is quite obvious here that it is most important that the defenders give the rear hit-player few opportunities to attack. A good length is essential to reduce the force of his power smash on the arrival of the shuttle in their midcourt. They must try to keep him on the move, not allowing him to get into a well-balanced position before hitting the smash. For example, they could play high deep lobs when they are under pressure to keep him pinned

down deep in his rearcourt, or whip the shuttle on a flatter arc to the corners of the rearcourt, either away from him or to the place he is travelling away from. In this way he is not allowed to settle and will be less forceful in his attack. The shallow, less forceful smash must be attacked with pushes or drives past the front player to the sides of the midcourt. These moves will draw the rear man forwards and may result in a lift or a flat reply which can be attacked.

The front set-up player will be more inclined to intercept the reply and play for a lift rather than attack the defenders, unless there is an easy chance for the kill at the net. Consequently the defenders have more freedom to make replies to the forecourt than with a hit-player opposing them as the front player. Although the defenders must be ready for a variety of stroke-moves from the opposing front player they will be less threatening to an alert defence. It would be easier to engage in a net rally with the front player, to challenge him for the attack.

Comment It is important that the defenders understand the tactical basis of the attacking side's stroke-moves. To do that they need to appreciate the different use of stroke-moves depending on whether the front or rear opponent is the set-up player or hit-player.

Example 3 *The attack – midcourt situation*
Channel attack
The intention in this attack is to focus on one defender and attack him until he weakens under the pressure. When possible the attack is directed at the weaker defender. It is assumed that the defender is unable to direct the shuttle cross-court away from the attackers: either his technique is not good enough or the attack is too powerful (see fig. 51 above).

In this form of attack both the rear and the front players are all-court players performing as hit-players. One softer shot from the attackers during the rally would allow the defender to hit the shuttle deep into the rearcourt and escape from the situation, so the attackers must keep the pressure on. Speed is essential. They should aim at various parts of the defender's body until finally he makes an error or gives a weak reply – at which the attackers go for the kill.

The defence – midcourt situation
Only one defender is in action here, though his partner must be ready to take part in the rally at any time should the attackers switch their attention to him. It should be stressed here that the

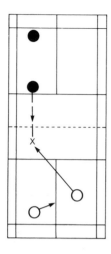

Fig. 81
Channel attack – plays drop shot to deep defender. Partner travels into FC whilst deep defender travels to MC.

Fig. 82
Front defender lobs shuttle to RC. Players adjust positions in attack and defence.

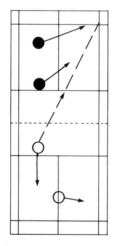

Fig. 83
Wedge attack.

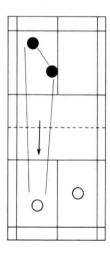

player not actually engaged in a rally should always keep alert and ready to become engaged.

The defender under attack must attempt to lob the shuttle to the rearcourt or counter-hit at speed. This is difficult when the attackers are hitting down at him. What can he do? He can make time and space by withdrawing into deep defence and hopefully whip the shuttle cross-court or high to the rearcourt; but if he withdraws he exposes his forecourt to the dropshot, and if that reply is played he or his partner must be ready to explode forwards to hit the shuttle. If they are ready and quick, it would be possible to lob the shuttle deep into the rearcourt and relieve some of the pressure (see figs. 81, 82).

Example 4 *The attack – midcourt situation*
Wedge attack

In this form of attack the front player, as hit-player, positions himself to cover the cross-court reply (see fig. 83). This formation will develop when:

1. Both attackers are hit-players and the defenders have a very strong defence which can contend with the speed of the shuttle to direct it cross-court away from the attackers.
2. When the rear attacker is a set-up player and does not possess a strong smash, so allowing the defender to hit a cross-court reply. The main objective is to attack the one defender with speed and try to prevent him hitting a controlled lob or whip to the rearcourt. The attackers keep the pressure on him until he makes an error or gives a weak reply which they can hit for a winner. If both attackers are hit-players, either one will try for the winner. If only the front man is a hit-player, he will try to gain control of the rally, with his rear partner ready to maintain the pressure by hitting down any shuttles that get past his front player. If the rear player is a hit-player and the front player a set-up player then the rear player will try to hit the winner. His front player will try to keep the pressure on the defender by crowding him, i.e. hitting the shuttle quickly at his body or to one side, giving him little time or space to perform a stroke-move. Softer hits, which allow the defender to lob the shuttle to the rearcourt or counter-attack with flat hits across the net, are to be avoided.

The defence – midcourt situation
The defender's task is to hit the shuttle above the front man to the rearcourt, or push it to the forecourt or midcourt and force him to

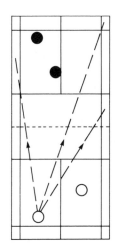

Fig. 84
The replies to the
attack.

lift. It is assumed here that the shuttle is too low in the midcourt for the defender to counter-attack with a drive to neutralise the situation.

The defender who is the target for the attack could now take up a deep defensive base to give himself time to perform a stroke-move. Or if he is a strong defender he could (see fig. 84):

1. Whip the shuttle high to the rearcourt away from the rear player and over the head of the front player.
2. Push the shuttle straight to the forecourt or midcourt between the front player and rear player.
3. Angle the shuttle quickly cross-court to the opposing front player's forecourt. The 'target' defender's partner should be ready to cover the opposing front player's replies if he should switch the attack to make him the new target defender; or if he replies to the cross-court move to his forecourt with a forecourt reply or a lift to the rearcourt (see figs. 85, 86).

   Note: If the attacking rear player is a front set-up player manoeuvred out of position then the defenders should try to keep him there and push him deeper into the rearcourt. The best stroke-move to achieve this is the lob or the whip, to the area of the rearcourt covered by the rear player.

If the attackers are in their strongest positions then the defenders can try to manoeuvre the front player to the rearcourt. There are several ways they could achieve this.

1. A flat reply to the midcourt towards the rear player would draw him forwards to make a reply. His reply could be returned with a move to the rearcourt over the head of his partner, who should have adjusted his position slightly to the side to cover such a stroke-move. The partner will have to travel backwards into the rearcourt to hit the shuttle, and the rear hit-player will have to travel into the midcourt to function as the front player. Their positions will have been reversed (see figs. 87, 88). The attackers maintain the attack but now have the problem of making a transition move to return to their favoured positions in the attacking formation.

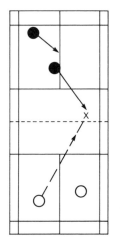

Fig. 85
Defenders x-court
reply to FC. Attackers
adjust positions.

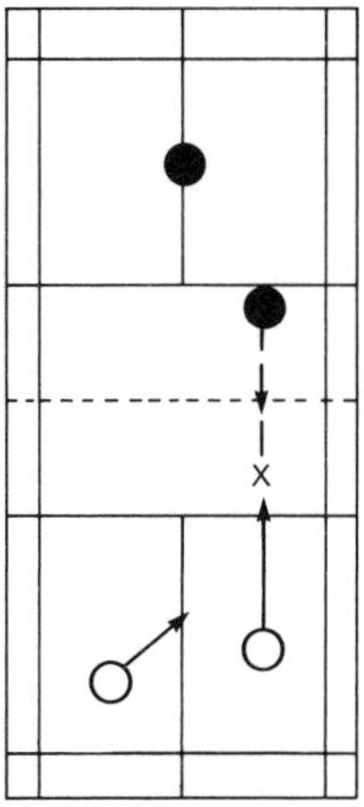

Fig. 86
Attacker plays a net
reply. Defenders adjust
positions.

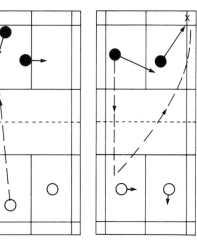

Fig. 87 (left)
Defender pushes flat reply to MC
towards rear player. Rear player
travels forwards as partner moves
into sides attack position.

Fig. 88 (right)
Attacker hits flat drive. Defender
lobs x-court reply to opposite RC.
* Players adjust positions in*
attack and defence. The attack
positions have been reversed.

Example 5

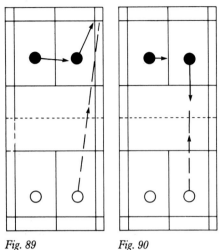

Fig. 89   *Fig. 90*

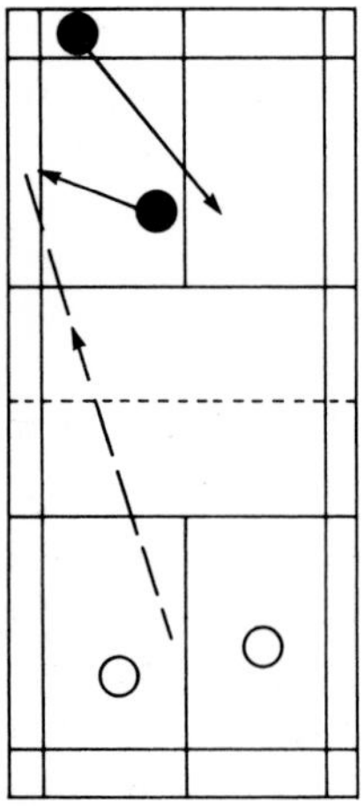

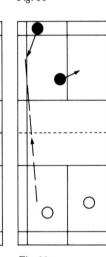

Fig. 91
Front attacker
intercepts the reply.
Rear man adjusts
position to sides
attack.

Fig. 92
Rear player intercepts
the reply. Front player
adjusts position to
sides attack.

Sides attack – midcourt situation

This is a typical attacking formation for two all-court hit-players. Each player occupies his section of the court and plays as if he were a singles player, with the responsibility for all replies to his side of the court. Immediately a sides attacker has to travel to the forecourt or rearcourt to make a reply, his partner adjusts his position in the centre midcourt relative to the shuttle position. The formation then changes from sides attack to front and back attack (see figs. 89, 90).

Sides attack usually occurs when the defenders push, drive or whip the shuttle, at net height or above, to the sides of the midcourt. Then, either the front player travels across to intercept the shuttle while his rear partner travels forwards to take up a position level with him in the other section of the midcourt, or the rear player has to travel forwards to hit a shuttle which has got past his front player, in which case the front player adjusts his position in the midcourt to be level with his partner (see figs. 91, 92). The attackers must now keep the pressure on the opponents and do so by hitting fast shuttles, which skim the net and are aimed at the opponent's body or the space between them. The intention is to force the opponents to make an error or lift the shuttle in the forecourt, midcourt or rearcourt.

The defence – midcourt situation

The defence are under pressure but in a situation where they too can apply pressure. They are not defenders any longer, but attackers. The drive, push or whip to the midcourt has created a neutral situation where both sides are more equally balanced. Both sides now engage in a slugging match, counter-hitting the shuttle at speed to and fro across the net until one side lifts. Immediately this occurs the other side should seize the attack and hit down. If one side does decide to lob to the rearcourt or drop to the forecourt, they should select the space carefully. If the opponents comprise a front hit-player and a rear set-up player, the obvious tactic is to drop to the forecourt of the rear set-up player and manoeuvre him to the front; or you could lob to the rearcourt of the front hit-player and manoeuvre him to the rear of the court. For any defenders, the flat return (drive or push) to the sides of the midcourt is a necessary first move in manoeuvring the opponents into sides positions in order to neutralise the situation or reverse the court positions of the opponents.

To bring a rear player forward or manoeuvre a front player to the rearcourt will take two stroke-moves (see figs. 93-95).

1. The push to the side midcourt.
2. The drop to the forecourt or the lob to the rearcourt.

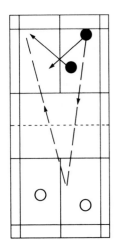

reversing positions
from the attack in
the rearcourt

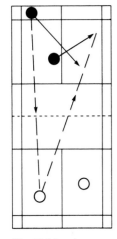

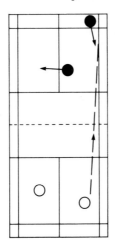

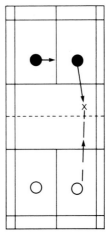

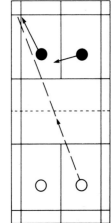

Fig. 93
1. Defenders drive to MC which draws rear man forwards from front and back attack formation to sides attack formation.

Fig. 94
2. Defenders block to FC. Attackers change from sides attack to front and back FC positions.

Fig. 95
3. Defenders lob to RC. Attackers change from MC sides to front and back RC attack formation.

Example 6   *All-court attack*

The all-court attacking game is the usual pattern of play when both players are equally skilful in operating as hit or set-up players. Either player will only set-up a chance for his partner if he is unable to perform as a hit-player.

There is much reversing of positions in the play of this pair. One player will always be trying to anticipate replies and attack the shuttle while his partner immediately adjusts his position to cover him (see figs. 96, 97). Each expects this of the other. Each allows the other the freedom to be adventurous; this is a dominant feature of their play. There is little margin for error in the game for it is not based on caution or patience, it is based on speed, for through speed they apply pressure on the opponents. When the all-court players are in full swing, they are exciting, dynamic and often unbeatable. When they are not, they can run into all sorts of difficulties and be surprisingly beaten.

It is quite usual to see the player sprinting into position in the forecourt, leaping forwards to meet the block or push reply while in full flight (see fig. 97). Thomas Kihlstrom and Stefan Karlsson are quite exceptional at switching positions, leaping for-

Fig. 96 (above)
1. Rear man smashes to centre MC.
2. Defender whips the shuttle x-court to MC/RC.
3. Front man jumps back to intercept and attack.
4. Rear man comes forwards to operate as front man.

Fig. 97 (below)
1. Rear man smashes at defender.
2. Defender whips shuttle x-court to backhand MC/RC.
3. Front man leaps backwards to smash.
4. Rear man sprints forwards towards channel attack position in FC.

wards to intercept replies and capable of hitting the shuttle in any of several directions while in mid-flight. In plate 24 you can see Karlsson angling the shuttle in the opposite direction from his jump.

Much of the dominance of the all-court attacking game is based on having control of the midcourt; hence the sides attack formation is adopted as much as possible. Unless the pair have pinned down one opponent in a channel or wedge attack situation, it is usual for either player to travel into the forecourt or rearcourt, hit the shuttle and return towards their own side of the midcourt into sides attack positions (see figs. 98a-d).

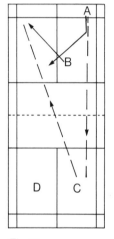

Fig. 98a

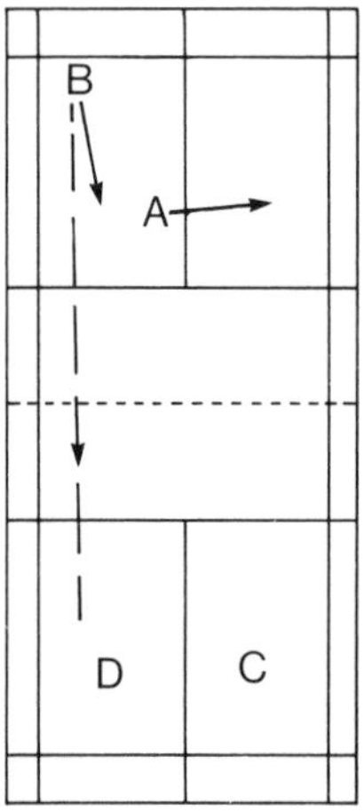

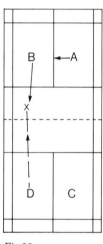

Fig. 98b

Fig.98c

Fig. 98d

From RC front and back attack to sides attack:

Fig. 98a
Player A in backhand RC and player B in MC; A smashes to C and approaches MC; C whips shuttle to forehand RC; B travels back to smash while A adjusts to front player position in MC.

Fig. 98b
B smashes and travels forwards to sides attack while A adjusts his position to sides attack, level with B.

From RC attack to FC front and back attack to sides attack:

Fig. 98b
After B's smash, he comes forwards to sides attack while A adjusts to the side to be level with B.

Fig. 98c
The defender blocks the shuttle to B's FC. B leaps forwards to attack and hits the shuttle between the opponents while A adjusts his sides position to cover B from the centre MC.

Fig. 98d
B quickly recovers and withdraws towards the MC into sides attack. A readjusts his position again to be level with B in sides attack.

Plate 24. Stefan Karlsson leaps in to make the kill.

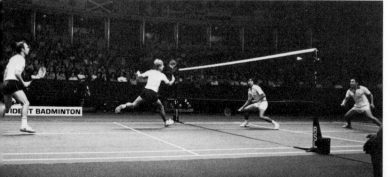

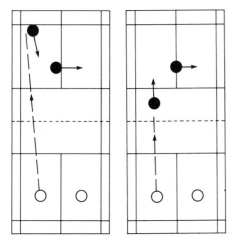

Fig. 99 (left)
The RC attacker smashes and travels quickly towards the MC. He leaves space in the RC. If the defender whips a lob over the incoming attacker's head back to the RC, the attacker will have to stop, change direction and return to the attack in the RC. As the all-court attacker is quick he will recover quickly to do so, but might be just late enough not to get behind the shuttle to maintain the force of the attack. The defenders may be able to counter-attack.

Fig. 100 (right)
The FC attacker withdraws towards the MC. If the defenders can control the speed and use some deception they can make the attackers commit themselves too early. Here, a defender with good racket head control can feint as if to whip the shuttle to the RC, causing the withdrawing attacker to prepare for the overhead attack. The defender then checks the racket head speed and drops the shuttle into the FC. He catches the attacker out.

The defence – midcourt situation

The defence must not be caught in a slugging rally unless they can match the speed of the all-court attackers. They must be able to control the pace of the shuttle, to change the pace by slowing the shuttle down, and to change the direction of its flight. Both features, pace and direction, are necessary to upset the rhythm and the timing of the all-court attack players.

As the attackers continually work towards the midcourt to maintain control, *they can be caught out by hitting the shuttle back to the court area they have just left,* rather than by hitting the shuttle to the space they are travelling towards. They are adventurous and committed to going forwards from the rearcourt to the midcourt, or backwards to the midcourt from the forecourt. They move into a space, hit and move out. They depart from spaces at speed. *They can be wrongfooted and caught slightly off balance by hitting the shuttle to those spaces.* See the examples below (figs. 99, 100).

In general, defenders must be able to match an all-court attacking pair in racket skills even if they cannot or choose not to play an all-court game themselves. The English world class pair, Mike Tredgett and Martin Dew, possess excellent racket control which they use to absorb such an attack; added to which they use intelligent deception to regain the attack. Their battles with Kihlstrom and Karlsson provide many interesting examples of how to contain and gain the attack against all-court attack players.

Front and back attack and defence – midcourt and forecourt situation

In this situation the shuttle is just below net height in the forecourt or midcourt. To some extent the situation is neutral with both sides evenly balanced. They spar for an opening, to gain a lift. Neither side has clearly gained the attack, nor is either side defending – although, to be accurate, we might consider that hitting from below the net constitutes defending against a possible attack.

Such a situation occurs when one player opens the rally with a low serve, or when the front players are engaged in a forecourt rally and the rear players are in the midcourt covering any replies that get past the front players. For example, figs. 101 and 102 illustrate the low serve and two types of reply to the serve.

This is a 'cat and mouse' situation. Neither side is able to dominate the attack and so neither side is actually in a defence situation. Accuracy, control and deception are required here to

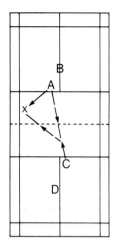

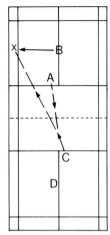

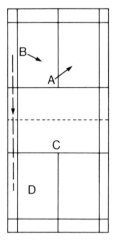

Fig. 101
1. A serves low to C who plays a net reply to A's forecourt. The two opposing front players play a net rally, each threatening the other's reply to force a lift in the FC or MC which can be hit down.

The rear players on each side are positioned in the MC, continually adjusting their positions relative to the shuttle position in the FC.

Fig. 102
2. A serves low to C who pushes the shuttle down to the MC away from B. C is now ready in the FC to intercept and attack any replies to the FC or MC. A is ready to cover any of C's interceptions to the FC. D is ready to cover and attack any replies that get past C.

avoid lifting the shuttle and, instead, to make a reply which gains a lift. The stroke-moves each side plays, whether to the forecourt or midcourt, will be determined partly by the relative strengths and weaknesses of the players. For example, if B is usually a front hit-player now positioned in the midcourt as the rear player, and C is a front hit-player in his usual position in the forecourt, then B might be wary about hitting the shuttle to the forecourt where C can attack it. The most appropriate move might be to drive the shuttle past C to the midcourt towards D, and for A to drop back level with B into sides attack (see fig. 103). This move would

Fig. 103

allow B to make his way to the forecourt as hit-player if a forecourt situation should follow. Alternatively B might decide to whip the shuttle to the right or left corner of the opponents' rearcourt and manoeuvre D into the rearcourt. This stroke-move would be appropriate if D was usually a front set-up player and not much of a threat in the rearcourt. Such a move would reverse the positions of the opponents and, perhaps, allow A and B more chance to gain the initiative in the attack.

There are a number of moves possible in this type of neutral situation. In the examples shown, I have drawn attention to the fact that some consideration must be given to the preferred functions of the players when making a stroke-move in the situation.

Chapter 6 Serving and Receiving Service

The serve is the opening move of each rally and because the server must hit the shuttle upwards and expose his side to a possible attack from a receiver balanced ready to attack, it is often considered to be one of the most significant moves in the game and essential, therefore, that players serve accurately and intelligently. A serve-move should be chosen and directed according to the probable replies of the opponent. It is possible, to some extent, to predict the type of reply the receiver may play; to do this, you should learn about the opponent's game and consider the implications with respect to your serve-move and his replies.

The basic serving positions are shown below (see fig. 104; see also plate 7 on p. 46). The players take up a forecourt/midcourt, front and back formation with the receiving side holding a slight advantage – ready to attack the rising shuttle. At this point there is a mini contest. The server can serve low or high, or flick or drive. The receiver does not know what to expect. How can the server 'attack' the receiver and obtain a reply to the serving side's advantage? How can the receiver counter the server's moves and maintain the attack? Let us see. We will start with the server.

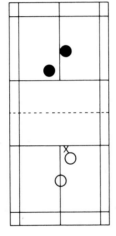

Fig. 104
The basic serving positions.

Note: serving side shown in the lower half of the diagram.

The server

1. The low serve The low serve is aimed to skim the net and land on the front service line between the centre and the side of the court. The server has a wide angle of placement in which to aim the shuttle. He can use a forehand or backhand serving action (see plates 25, 26). The server is at a disadvantage, for he must hit the shuttle upwards. A good receiver will attack a low serve and hit down any shuttle which does not skim the net and fall immediately after crossing the net (see fig. 105). The server's task is to ensure that

Plate 25. *Kihlstrom concentrates on the forehand serve.*

Plate 26. *Ivana all set to play a backhand serve.*

the receiver does not hit the shuttle until it falls below the level of the net. If he succeeds, the receiver must hit upwards. The onus then falls upon the receiver to prevent the serving side from attacking his reply.

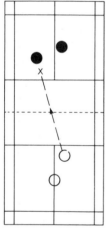

Fig. 105
The shuttle flight in the low serve.

Receivers differ in the extent to which they are a threat to the server and in the types of reply they make. These two factors influence the type of low serve used by the server, as the following examples show.

a. The receiver stands in the forecourt/midcourt
Usually the receiver takes up this position to cover the serve to the rearcourt. There is no pressure on the server, who can serve low with ease and force a lift (see fig. 106).

Fig. 106
Receiver stands in the MC. He is unable to reach the net to attack the shuttle before it begins to fall into the FC. Receiver reaches the shuttle late and must hit upwards.

b. The receiver is a front hit-player
This receiver will usually stand close to the service line, ready to attack the low serve. He will be skilful at hitting down shuttles which are close to the net, creating pressure on the server to hit the shuttle accurately over the net. To deal with this situation, the server can vary his serve in several ways.

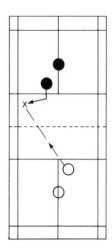

Fig. 107
Server serves wide of receiver. Receiver comes
forwards to find that the shuttle has been hit away
from his forward flow of movement. He has to
change direction or twist and stretch to reach the
shuttle—too late to hit down.

1. He might do a flick serve to catch out the receiver who anticipates the low serve and comes forward to attack too soon. If the receiver is caught out, he might be less adventurous and wait longer before attacking the low serve the next time; this takes some of the pressure off the server.
2. The server can direct the shuttle wide of the receiver and cause him to change direction, stretch to the side and, hopefully, hit the shuttle when it has fallen below net level (see fig. 107).
3. The server can serve directly at the receiver, but deliberately serve short. The idea is to cause the shuttle to drop quickly below net height. This is a risky move and should only be used against the receiver who travels forwards very early and very fast to attack the shuttle. There are several consequences of this serve-move. The receiver might be committed to hit down and thus hit the shuttle into the net; he might try to change his stroke and be forced to lift; or realise that the shuttle will fall short, but be unable to avoid colliding with it because he has travelled forward so quickly that he cannot get out of the way. Finally, he might be able to avoid the shuttle and allow it to fall short. The serve is then lost.

c. The receiver is a front hit-player who uses one grip only
A receiver can hit the shuttle in several directions from the forecourt: straight, or to the right or left of the court. There are receivers who have sufficient skill in racket control that they can hit the shuttle anywhere. There are others, particularly at the lower levels of play, who will attack the serve and hit their reply in one direction only. Very often this is because they use one single grip to receive (forehand or backhand) and do not change their grip during the stroke-move. It is perfectly natural for a forehand-grip player to move his arm across his body and direct the shuttle towards the right of the opponent's court. Similarly, it is natural to move the arm across the body when using a backhand grip and to direct the shuttle to the opponent's left court. It is for this reason that players must practise hitting the return of serve to the right and the left when using a forehand grip and likewise with a backhand grip. Meanwhile, the server can make use of this habit. If the receiver is a forehand grip player, the server should aim the shuttle at his chest or left shoulder; as he attacks the shuttle he will follow the natural movement of the arm across his body to hit the shuttle forwards and to the right side of the server's court. If the receiver is a

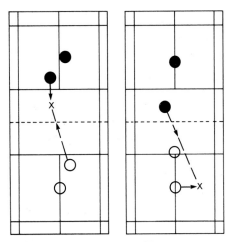

Fig. 108 a, b. Forehand receiver hits to opponents' right court.

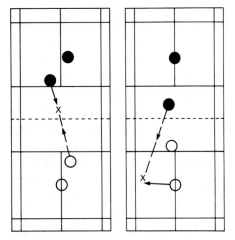

Fig. 109 a, b. Backhand receiver hits to opponents' left court.

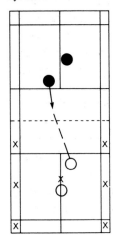

Fig. 110
Replies to the low serve.

x shuttle aimed to
these places by
receiver

2. The flick serve

backhand player, the server can serve to the chest or right shoulder and expect a reply to the left side of the court. The server is ready for any replies to the forecourt and his partner is ready for the push or attempted kill to a particular side of the midcourt (see fig. 108a, b and fig. 109a, b). From there he can return the shuttle before the receiver has fully recovered. In the example given below, the hit-player's speed of attack is used against him because the serving side are aware of his habit of hitting in one direction only.

d. The receiver is a front set-up player

This receiver will be quick and agile in the forecourt, ready to attack and hit down any poor serves. He will not be as adventurous as the hit-player and so will not take chances. There will be less pressure on the server, who will feel less threatened when serving. There might even be some margin for error in the serve.

The receiver is likely to be skilful with his racket, for as a set-up player he should possess a range of replies to the serve. It should not matter what grip he uses; he should control the racket face to direct the shuttle where he chooses. If he cannot do so, the server must find out what his limitations are by serving to different parts of the forecourt and to different targets on his body, e.g. chest, shoulders. It could be, for instance, that he can return the serve to both sides of the court with his forehand stroke, but only to one side of the court with his backhand stroke.

The usual replies to the low serve will be:

1. A push down to the sides of the forecourt or midcourt, or at the server or his rearman.
2. A net reply from below the net to the centre, or the sides away from the server.
3. A whip from just below the net, over the head of the rear player to the corners of the rearcourt (see fig. 110).

In this serve, the shuttle is hit to travel on a shallow arc to pass quickly over the outstretched reach of the receiver. It can be performed with a forehand or backhand action. It is used for several reasons.

1. When the receiver becomes too much of a threat to the low serve – he may be very explosive or anticipate early and hit winners.
2. To manoeuvre the receiver to the rearcourt. The receiver may be a front player you would prefer to see in the rearcourt, or a player with a weak smash, or one who is slow go-

ing backwards and can be caught out by speed. The action must be similar to the low serve action so that you 'look as if to serve low' to the opponent. Just prior to impact you must whip the racket head forwards at speed to hit the shuttle up over the reach of the receiver.

Note: a number of servers use a backhand serve action to help in this, for this usually makes it more difficult for the receiver to judge whether the serve is to be a low or flick serve. Additionally, some players find the backhand action easier to learn and more successful than the conventional forehand serve.

The placing of the flick serve can increase the receiver's difficulty in making an attacking reply, as the examples below illustrate.

1. Fig. 111 shows a flick serve to the centre of the right service court. This is difficult to return if the receiver has been surprised. He must now get back quickly and play a 'round the head' shot. The initial reaction, as the shuttle is hit, is to transfer the weight onto the rear foot – an action which may direct his flow of movement away from the shuttle. This will necessitate a quick change of direction and travel towards the centre line. From that position most players will direct the shuttle towards the server's side of the court. The server can then wait for the shuttle to be hit towards the midcourt or forecourt, and attack it (see fig. 112).

Often a receiver in this situation may clear to the rearcourt and give the attack to the serving side, or try to block the serve and drop the shuttle into the forecourt. The serving side should be ready for both replies.

2. Figs. 113 and 114 show a flick serve to the centre of the left service court. This serve is useful for the same reasons as those given in the previous example: the receiver's initial transfer of weight onto his rear foot causes his flow of movement to take him away from the centre of the court, forcing him to change direction and jump backwards towards the centre to attack the shuttle. The smash reply is usually hit towards the opponent's left court where the server is now ready to cover the smash and a possible weak reply to the forecourt.

The serve to the centre line of the court can be alternated with the flick to the corner of the receiver's court. The shuttle travels diagonally across the court and has further to travel, as does the receiver. It requires a fast athletic receiver to travel back quickly enough to smash a good flick serve over

initial flow of ---►--- movement

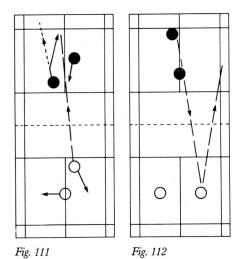

Fig. 111   *Fig. 112*

initial flow of ---►--- movement

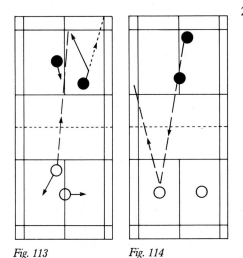

Fig. 113   *Fig. 114*

this distance, particularly to the left service court corner. The reply at the lower levels of play is usually a high clear, played to give the receiver time to recover.

3. The drive serve

The intention here is to drive the shuttle at the receiver. The shuttle skims the net and travels towards the receiver so quickly that he is forced to rush his reply. The serve is played as a surprise move designed to force a lift or an error. The shuttle has to travel upwards from below net height even on the drive serve, and for this reason it is best directed at the backhand side of the receiver; if directed at his forehand side, it is easy for him to raise his racket to block the shuttle into the forecourt or tap it down into the midcourt.

In performing this serve, there is a risk that the server may raise his racket head above the level of his hand and commit a fault serve. I have seen many an international player attempt a drive serve only to be faulted by the service judge. Their mistake is to drive serve from their usual serving position, from which they have to raise their racket head to the side, and so commit a fault. To ensure serving without committing a fault, the server should adjust his position and serve from a deeper base, e.g. one step further back. This will increase his distance from the net and allow him to hit the shuttle on a flatter trajectory across the net. If he catches the receiver by surprise he should be ready to step forwards and attack a weak reply to the forecourt (see figs. 115, 116).

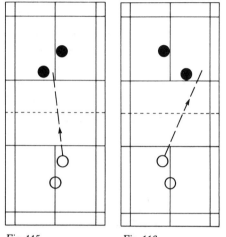

Fig. 115   Fig. 116

In both Figs. 115 and 116, server stands further back than usual to drive serve to receiver's backhand side.

4. The high serve

Here the shuttle is hit very high to fall vertically onto the long service line for doubles. A shuttle which falls vertically is more difficult to hit accurately than one which travels on a curved pathway. This serve-move is rarely used in top-level men's doubles because it creates a rearcourt/midcourt attack situation (see channel attack, page 61).

Its value as a move is determined by the sort of replies the opponents can make. If the receiver is a weak smasher, or tends to hit the shuttle on a flat trajectory, the serving side can benefit: they can attack the smash reply and gain the initiative. For this reason it is a useful move at the lower level of doubles, particularly in ladies' doubles. It is also a very obvious first move to use to manoeuvre a front player to the rearcourt. From his reply the shuttle can be returned deeper into the rearcourt, so keeping him pinned down as the rear player until the opportunity to attack occurs.

5. Serving from the side

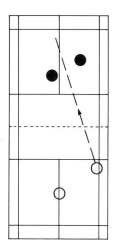

Fig. 117

It is usual for the server to stand in the midcourt/forecourt area by the centre service line, where he is ready to cover all replies to the forecourt. The receiver usually positions himself to divide the angle of return of all the serves possible to his right and left sides and above him (see figs. 118, 119 below). A variation on this serve position is for the server to serve from the side of the court. This occurs only when the server stands wide to serve to the receiver's backhand side. The intention is to unsettle the receiver and, possibly, restrict and reduce the effectiveness of his replies (see fig. 117). A well-executed drive or flick serve usually forces the receiver to make a backhand return, thus reducing his chances of attacking the serve. It is expected that the receiver and his partner will adjust their positions to reply to the serve, in order to make a move which will help them to maintain or gain the attack.

The receiver

The stance

Plate 27. Luan Jin takes up a backward attacking stance as he prepares to receive the serve.

There are different body movements required for receiving each type of serve. The one common factor is the stance (the starting position). Players usually adopt a backward attacking stance (see plate 27); from this stance the receiver must be ready to thrust away from a stationary position, forwards or backwards, to attack the shuttle. Good posture is very important; the trunk must be held in balance between the legs which are flexed ready to drive away from the spot. Many players could become more of a threat to the server if they stood correctly when receiving, and practised 'exploding' from the spot. The position is similar to that of a sprinter at the 'set' in the starting blocks: he concentrates his thought, tenses his muscles and 'explodes' forwards. Sprinters practise this crucial initial action because they realise its importance. Receivers should do the same.

The receiving position in the court

The position in the court varies according to the type of serve you expect to receive, and the replies you want to or are able to make. First, however, you should position yourself equidistant from the possible pathways of the shuttle to divide the angle of possible serves from any place in the server's court (see figs. 118, 119)– unless, for a tactical reason, you deliberately stand more to one side to leave space free for the server to serve into. This sometimes occurs when a player covers his backhand side to prevent the shuttle being hit there, and invites the serve to his stronger forehand side.

Distance from the short service line How far a receiver stands from the front service line depends on his skill and athleticism, and the type of serve he might expect to receive.

Replies to the low serve Now let us look at the various positions and replies the receiver can make to the different serves. I would like to stress here that we are not simply discussing the serve and the reply, but the actions of one human athlete trying to counter the actions of another.

There are several basic replies to the low serve. These are as follows:

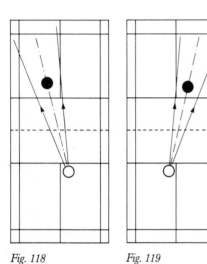

Fig. 118   *Fig. 119*

1. The kill

The intention here is to attack the serve. As the shuttle passes over the net the receiver springs forwards *and upwards* to reach out above the shuttle and hit it sharply to the ground. Many players make the mistake of just stepping forwards, and planting their front foot before hitting the shuttle. The result is that on many occasions they stop travelling forwards and hit the shuttle into the net or have to push it softly over the net, for the action of stepping forwards brings about a lowering of the body, with a stopping or slowing down of the forward movement, and makes it necessary to reach up to the shuttle as the body 'falls' below the shuttle. The emphasis on driving *forwards and upwards*, on the other hand, results in the receiver continuing to travel forwards to arrive earlier above the shuttle, making it an easier task to hit down for a winner. It is only after hitting the shuttle that the good receiver plants his foot, as he lands to recover. The sequence of movements when attacking the low serve are: drive forwards and upwards away from the stance to the net—hit the shuttle—land on the front foot and recover. It is *not* drive forwards, step and then hit, as many players do—and in so doing, allow too many servers to get away with poor low serves. If you get the opportunity, watch a good forecourt hit-player leap forwards and upwards to attack the shuttle at the top of the net. Plate 28 shows Mike Tredgett in action: one of the most attacking receivers in world class doubles. If you want to improve your net attack when receiving or acting as front player, then practise leaping upwards as you travel forwards.

Plate 28. *Mike Tredgett launches himself to make a kill.*

Plate 29. *Nora Perry stretches forwards to make a push reply.*

The hitting action for the 'kill' requires a quick strong action of the hand. This is performed as a 'tapping' action, so that the racket head *rebounds* after the hit as the player checks the racket head to prevent it hitting the net. It can also be performed as a 'brushing' action as the racket face hits across the shuttle to give it a fine glancing blow, again to prevent the racket head from hitting the net.

To be successful, the receiver must commit himself fully to the 'kill' and let his rear player worry about any replies that the opponent might make. The shuttle should be aimed at the server, or at his rear player, or to the sides of the midcourt.

2. The push

The initial intention is to attack the low serve and hit down to the forecourt or midcourt. The receiver springs up towards the net with his racket head held above his hand; on arrival he is too late to meet the shuttle as it passes over the net. The shuttle is some way past the net and has fallen below the level of the net. The push reply is used more in ladies' doubles, for the ladies stand further back to receive the serve and are not usually quick enough or early enough to kill the shuttle from above the net (see plate 29).

The serving side is confronted by a receiver who is leaping towards them with racket head up to attack the shuttle. Their usual reaction is to brace themselves for the downward hit. The front player (the server) would crouch and lean aside quickly to allow the rear player full view of the shuttle. The rear player would set himself in the midcourt in a front defence stance ready to make a reply (see plate 30). The response is to the receiver's advantage. He cannot hit down, but he can lower his body or racket hand and 'push' the shuttle flat across the net to the sides of the forecourt or midcourt, or at the body of the server or the rear player (see fig. 120). The shuttle does not travel as quickly or as steeply as in the kill, but achieves a positive effect in forcing a lift and maintaining the attack for the receiving side.

Plate 30. *Jane Webster as rear player intercepting the push to MC.*

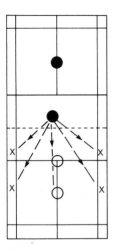

Fig. 120

Plate 31. Jane Webster plays an underarm net reply to the low serve.

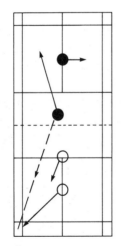

*Fig. 121
Receiver travels
forwards to attack the
low serve.*

*Fig. 122
Receiver lobs shuttle to
serving side's backhand
RC. Players adjust
their positions to attack
and defence formations.*

3. The underarm net reply

In this situation the shuttle is below the level of the net. The receiver must hit the shuttle from below with the racket head held below the level of his hand (see plate 31). The intention is to make a move which obtains a lift. The basic replies here are to 'push' or 'tap' the shuttle to the sides of the forecourt away from the server, or to play a 'tumbler' to obtain a mis-hit or weak reply.

If the server is a front hit-player, the receiver is under pressure. He must make a tight net reply (the shuttle passes very close to the net) or give the server the chance to 'kill' the shuttle.

4. The lob

If it is not possible to play a tight net reply or the receiver feels too much pressure from the server, an alternative reply is to whip the shuttle upwards to the corner of the rearcourt away from the rear player. This stroke-move relieves the immediate pressure. It does, however, create a rearcourt attacking situation, but for the moment this might be less threatening than the forecourt attack situation. The lob can be performed with a quick flick to catch the rear player by surprise and get the shuttle behind him. If successful, the receiving side may be able to regain the attack, depending on the rear player's reply. This sort of shallow lob is similar to the attack clear in its trajectory and its potential effect. If it is not possible to make this move, the shuttle being too far below the net, the receiver could hit a high lob deep into the rearcourt. The high lob allows the receiving side time to recover into a balanced sides defence formation (see figs. 121, 122).

Replies to the flick serve

The receiver who positions himself just behind the short service line exposes his rearcourt/midcourt area and invites the flick serve over his head. It requires a good athlete to travel backwards quickly enough to smash a good flick serve. Top class players, particularly front hit-players, are sometimes caught out by the flick. A front set-up player will be more cautious in attacking the net; and a rear hit- or set-up player will not be inclined to commit himself to attack the low serve unless it is a poor one. This player would be more inclined to invite the flick so that he could jump back and attack the shuttle.

At the top levels of play the players do tend to stand quite close to the front service line, particularly in men's doubles. The ladies are more cautious and tend to cover the possibility of the flick serve. In general, women are smaller and lack the strength and explosive speed of men. They usually stand further back from the short service line to receive the serve. The men threaten to attack and 'kill' the shuttle at the net and try to put pressure on the server. It is even more difficult for the server when the receiver is a tall athlete, for then any flick serve has to be hit on a high trajectory to get over the receiver, and height allows the receiver more time to travel backwards to smash the shuttle. The Danish doubles pair, Fleming Delfs and Steen Skovgaard, both over 6ft (1.85m) tall, were quite difficult to flick serve (see plate 32), and by crowding the net they would force the server to flick serve even higher.

Plate 32. Fleming Delfs intercepts the flick serve as Steen Skovgaard accelerates forwards to become the front player.

The basic replies to the flick serve are:

1. To hit down with a smash or fast drop shot. A slow drop shot reply is not an attacking move, and yet it can be seen often at the general club level of play when players have been caught out by the flick serve; it is the reply that the server hopes to obtain. You will see many instances of the server flicking the shuttle over the receiver's head and then moving into the

forecourt waiting to 'kill' the receiver's reply. If the receiver cannot hit a quick reply downwards he should hit the shuttle to the rearcourt.

2. The clear is a sensible move, to make time to recover and force the serving side as far away from the net as possible. The further the shuttle is behind the receiver after the flick serve, the higher he should hit it to ensure that it travels in a high arc to land deep in the rearcourt. After the clear-move, both receiving side players should adjust their positions and take up a sides defence formation relative to the shuttle position in the opponents' court.

At the general level of play it is sound policy to avoid creating a situation which exposes you to the flick serve – unless, of course, you enjoy leaping backwards and are not caught out by the serve. But if you, as the receiver, cannot stand just behind the front service line and spring backwards in time to smash the shuttle, then do not stand there. Stand further back!

I was once asked by an international player to help her with her return of serve. She told me that she was caught out too often by the flick serve. I asked her to take up her usual receiving position. She did so and stood with her front foot about 6ins (15cm) behind the front service line. She was not very tall nor particularly dynamic at springing backwards. Her position only increased any difficulty she might have found in receiving the flick serve. The obvious answer to the problem was for her to stand further back and reduce the force of the flick serve as an attacking move. No sensible server will hit a flick serve to a receiver already in position to see it coming and attack it. The only difficulty was that now she would be unable to attack the low serve and 'kill' the shuttle in the forecourt. I asked her how often she did spring forwards to 'kill' the low serve. 'Very rarely', was her answer. She usually played a push or net reply and occasionally flicked the shuttle to the rearcourt – all stroke-moves played from below the level of the net. It seemed that it really was unnecessary to stand so far forwards to receive the serve. In fact, though she was close enough to attack the low serve, she did not because she was too concerned about getting caught with the flick serve. She was positioned to go forwards and attack, but her thoughts were on going backwards, and so she did neither very well. We agreed that she would be better not even to consider the 'kill' as a reply to the low serve. She should stand further back, eliminate the flick serve as a possible threat and take the low serve late. She was a good net player with control and deception and quite happy to take on her opponent in a net rally. She had a good defence so did not worry about giving the opponents the attack in the rearcourt. After a discussion about the moves and their replies in the situation she adjusted her receiving position and stood further back. The benefit in competition was that she actually felt more relaxed, for the threat of being caught out had been removed. Being relaxed, she was much quicker to 'read' the low serve and in coming forwards to attack it. She became a better receiver.

It pays all receivers to reflect upon the situation. Do not let convention dictate how you receive. The ideal may be to attack the low serve, but how many players are capable of doing so? If you are a fit athlete, try to develop your speed in travelling forwards and backwards. If you are not, then position yourself to make those moves you are capable of. There are a number of appropriate replies to the low serve which do not require that you expose yourself to the flick serve. Practise these replies and you will enhance your chances of winning the rally by playing within your capabilities.

Replies to the drive serve

This serve is used as a move to surprise the receiver with speed and to force a weak reply. The usual reaction is to attempt a hurried smash action, which is what the server hopes for; but there is not enough time for this. If you are set in an alert attacking stance with the racket head held above the hand, the drive serve is not difficult to deal with; in fact it is extremely easy to make a reply, particularly if you position yourself in the midcourt away from the short service line.

To make a reply, raise the racket head higher and place the racket face in line with the oncoming shuttle; then tap the shuttle lightly down to the ground in the midcourt, to the sides of the forecourt or at the server, or up to the rearcourt. Very little movement of the racket head is needed to perform the action. It can be performed from in front, or to the right or left side of the body. If the shuttle is aimed at your backhand side, simply move the racket across your front to play a forehand tap from the backhand side. This is the sort of action you can practise in front of a mirror, so that you will react automatically when it occurs in a game.

Replies to the serve from the side

Fig. 123 illustrates the flick or drive serve aimed at your backhand side from a wide angle. Consider the receivers' positions. When the server takes up this position, the receiving side should adjust to a sides attack formation. The receiver adjusts his position in the midcourt to cover the drive or flick to the centre line on his backhand side. His partner stands in his section of the midcourt away from the receiver: this position does not obstruct the flight of the shuttle to the court, and allows the receiver full view of it and space to perform his stroke-move. In covering the serve to his backhand side, the receiver exposes the right side of his forecourt to the low serve. Servers sometimes make this move, but it is risky to do so because the receiver has time to see the serve and travel across to play a reply.

There are two stances which can be adopted to receive this serve. You can stand ready to use a backhand stroke or a 'round the head' smash. The latter is difficult if the opponent drives the shuttle on a low trajectory. Most receivers, therefore, prepare to reply with a backhand stroke-move.

Let us consider the replies to the serve to different parts of the court.

a. To the serve to the centre midcourt/rearcourt

The receiver is in a midcourt situation with the shuttle above net height on his backhand side. He can drive the shuttle back to the sides or centre, and even smash it if it is high enough; he can drop to the forecourt, or clear to the rearcourt. Look at the position of the server in fig. 123. It is obvious that he must return from the side to cover his midcourt and all replies on his side of the court. This is not easy to do, particularly if he hits a fast serve to a prepared receiver. A sensible reply is for the receiver to hit a backhand smash or drive to the centre midcourt between the two opponents as they travel to get into position. Alternatives are a quick drop to the left forecourt, or a whip clear to the corners of the rearcourt (see fig. 124). The drop to the forecourt will certainly obtain a lift in reply. The server's partner cannot travel to anticipate the move for he must also cover the whip over his head to his left rearcourt, and the smash or drive to the centre.

A receiver who is prepared for such a serve and has practised the replies should not be caught out; he should gain the attack quite easily. If you consider the merits of the wide serve from a positional point of view you might agree that it is a stupid serve-move to make: it is so difficult to cover the replies and so easy to lose the attack. Yet servers do use it and get away with it, mainly because receivers have not practised the replies and are surprised when they receive the serve.

b. The replies to the low serve to the right forecourt (see figs. 125a, b)

The server again puts himself into difficulties if the receiver is

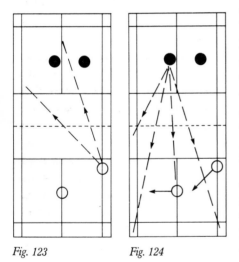

Fig. 123   *Fig. 124*

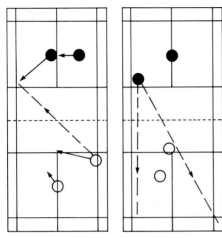

Fig. 125a
Low serve. Players
adjust positions.

Fig. 125b
Receiver plays one of a
choice of replies while
serving side get into
position.

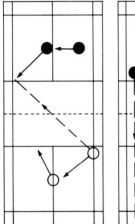

Fig. 126a
Low serve. Players
adjust positions.

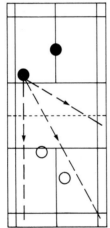

Fig. 126b
Receiver plays one of a
choice of replies while
serving side get into
position.

ready. The receiver can play a straight reply to the server's left forecourt. The server has a long way to travel to reach this reply and will be late arriving to hit the shuttle, if that is possible at all. The server's rear partner could travel into the forecourt to make a reply but this leaves the rearcourt exposed to the flick over his head – a flick either to the left rearcourt or to the right rearcourt. The latter move should be effective in wrong-footing the server, who is now making his way to the midcourt to cover his partner in the forecourt.

It is interesting to consider what might develop if the serving side anticipates these replies and adopts some policy to contend with them. For example, the server might decide to cover all replies to the midcourt and allow his rear partner to come forward and cover all replies to the forecourt. What can the receiver do (see fig. 126a, b)? He can still benefit from playing a lob to the rearcourt. A straight lob to the left rearcourt will, most probably, be too difficult for the server to reach in sufficient time to perform a strong forehand stroke-move. He will have to play a less threatening backhand stroke-move. Likewise a cross-court lob to the opponents' right rearcourt could effectively wrong-foot the server, whose flow of movement is taking him towards the centre midcourt. And finally, a cross court-reply to the opponents' right forecourt, the place from which the server has just departed, will have the rear player stretching and reaching the shuttle too late to attack.

It would seem that to serve from the side is a risky business. It can work as a move to upset inexperienced players who have not given much thought to the positions and replies in the situation. It is rarely used in good class doubles because of the weak position in which it places the serving side. I have discussed it in detail here because it is used quite successfully as a move in club doubles. Yet it is easy for the receiver to make a reply-move and to create a situation in which to attack, if he knows the replies. Now you do.

This discussion and the examples of the stroke-moves possible as replies in the situation created by the serve-move show that it is possible to work out what to do in any given situation in the game. The charts provide all the information you require. Add to this information a simple diagram of the court (see fig. 271 on p.223), and you will have all you need to resolve any problems concerning what you might do against various opponents.

Chapter 7 Mixed Doubles

Mixed doubles is a very subtle attacking game. Both sides try to maintain the 'front and back' attacking formation: a front player ready to hit down for a winner or obtain a lift, and a rear player ready to cover the replies to the midcourt and rearcourt. Both players must function as set-up and hit-players. They do not, however, play an all-court attacking game. Usually the lady looks after the forecourt and the man looks after the midcourt and rearcourt. The lady must try to create a situation which allows her man to hit down for a winner, and similarly, she should hit down whenever possible in the situation he creates for her. It is very much a team game. It is also very apparent when the players do not work for each other as a team.

We have in fact already looked at many of the situations which occur in mixed doubles.* If you have read this you will be familiar with those situations and have some idea of the positions you can take up and the stroke-moves you can make. It is important to understand the purpose of a mixed doubles pair for then you will appreciate their play. *They intend to maintain the attack throughout. They will do everything possible to create situations which enhance their chances of winning each rally. To do this they combine the strengths of the man and the lady in such a way that it becomes possible to make the moves necessary to fulfil this purpose.*

In general, *the most effective formation is for the lady to look after the forecourt, and the man, the midcourt and the rearcourt.* These positions are taken up on the assumption that the man is the stronger player in the midcourt and rearcourt, even though both players may be of equal ability in the forecourt. They may both function effectively as hit- or set-up players in the forecourt. They may also do the same in the situations in the midcourt and the rearcourt except for several important differences, related to their fitness.

*See the charts and Chapter 4; pages 63-64, for a discussion on the front and back attacking formation in the forecourt; page 73 for diagonal defence; pages 89-90 for front and back attack and defence in the mid-court/forecourt situations.

A man usually has greater muscular strength, speed and power. He can perform hitting actions much quicker and hit the shuttle harder, both important factors in putting pressure on the opponents and hitting winners. He also has greater explosive power which is necessary to change direction at speed or to accelerate from a stationary position to another place on the court. This may entail running or jumping to hit the shuttle, landing and stopping quickly to recover into position to cover any replies. These features apart, a woman can be just as creative in the rearcourt and midcourt as a set-up player, and as forceful as a hit-player; this is shown all the time in ladies' doubles. However, if she takes up the rear player role in mixed doubles, she will be exposed to the greater strength and speed of the opposing man.

There is no reason why a woman cannot train to develop the strength, speed and power to perform to a high standard in the rearcourt, and to equal the opposing man. Fitness training with weights will develop strength, speed and power. Court work on starting, stopping, travelling, changes of direction, jumping and landing in badminton situations can certainly improve speed and agility on the court. If women do attain the standard of fitness necessary to play at the speed of the opposing man then there is no reason why they should not play mixed doubles as ladies' and men's doubles are played. It would even be possible for a mixed doubles pair to play an all-court attacking game to good effect. There are some mixed pairs who do play as if in a level doubles game, but none who are successful at the top level against a conventional mixed formation, usually because the lady cannot cope with the force of the opposing man for any period of time in all the situations.

There is no good reason why boys and girls cannot be taught an all-court game before adolescence when there is more equality in fitness between boys and girls. It is when they grow apart in physical capabilities (strength, power and speed) that they can begin to develop more conventional mixed doubles positions.

Playing mixed doubles

We can now look at some of the situations which occur in mixed doubles. Let me remind you that pairs (a) adopt a 'front and back' attacking formation whenever possible; (b) try to create situations in which to hit winners or force an error; and (c) try to negate the strength of the other pair by reversing the positions of the opposing man and lady, i.e. manoeuvring the man to the forecourt and the lady to the rearcourt. All this makes for interesting patterns of play and development in the game. The serving positions, development from the serve, and the attack and defence situations differ from level doubles. These are quite easy to learn and understand if they are placed in some sort of logical order. The approach I follow here is to begin with an opening move – the low serve – and trace the development of play in attack and defence situations when the lady serves to the lady. After that we return to the serve and see how the play varies when the lady or the man serves to the opposing lady or man, using a variety of serves.

Development in play from the low serve

The lady serves to the lady
(see fig. 127)

The players stand in the conventional front and back attacking formation for a forecourt situation, similar to level doubles. The receiver stands further back from the service line – she is wary of the flick serve being used to catch her out or manoeuvre her to the rearcourt to weaken her side, i.e. reversing the positions of the man and the lady. She should stand back as far as she considers necessary to eliminate the flick serve as a threat, and yet in a position which will still allow her to travel into the forecourt to make a move which will help her to gain the attack. Obviously she will not reach the net in time to hit downwards unless she is very quick or stands close enough to the service line to allow her to do so but that would expose her to the flick serve. Much depends on her athleticism and skill.

The server can aim the shuttle to the right or left side of the receiver to obtain a predictable reply if she knows what sort of replies the receiver plays from various serves (see page 93). The server serves low and then steps forwards to threaten any replies to the forecourt. Her partner covers replies to the midcourt sides or centre just behind the server, and the lob to the rearcourt. The receiver steps forwards to hit down if possible. As this is unlikely unless the serve is a poor one, she approaches the net with her racket head held up, ready to push the shuttle over the net (see plate 33). The act of holding the racket head up presents a picture of a potential threat to the server: the receiver looks as if she will hit down. This 'picture' may persuade the server to hold still, to brace herself against the attack and defend against, rather than attack, the receiver's reply. The way a player holds the racket when preparing to hit the shuttle in the forecourt is sometimes suffi-

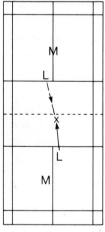

Fig. 127
M=Man, L=Lady.
  Note: Serving side shown in top half of court.

Plate 33. Karen Chapman threatens in the FC.

cient to make the opponents wary and cautious. In this situation, if the receiver can cause the server to wait, she will gain some *space* to push the shuttle across the net into the forecourt or mid-court, or *time* to drop her racket head below the shuttle and play a net reply to the sides of the forecourt. The situation is typical of the 'cat and mouse' play which is such a feature of mixed doubles.

Development

1. The receiver plays a net reply to the right forecourt

See fig. 128. The server immediately travels across to hit the shuttle from below net height. Her replies are: a push to the forecourt or midcourt; a net reply to the forecourt; a lob over the ladies' reach to the midcourt but too low for the rear man to hit down from the midcourt (this is risky and requires excellent control and timing); a whip cross-court to catch the rear man out; or a straight lift to the man's backhand corner. The lob to the rear-court is not a sensible move at the higher levels of play, but could be useful against a man who is slow to accelerate from the mid-court or has a relatively weak smash from deep in the rearcourt. You must assess your opponent's ability on these occasions.

The net reply creates the 'cat and mouse' situation with each side trying to force the other to lift the shuttle and give their own side the chance to make a winning hit. At this point both rear men are poised in the midcourt ready to cover any reply to the forecourt/midcourt area which gets past the front lady.

2. The receiver plays a push reply to the right midcourt

See fig. 129. The rear man goes across to hit the shuttle which is now below net height. (It is important that the rear man positions himself in the centre midcourt when his front lady is engaged in a forecourt rally; he should be ready to step *forwards* and *across* to hit the shuttle before it has time to fall too far below net height.

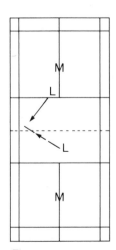

Fig. 128

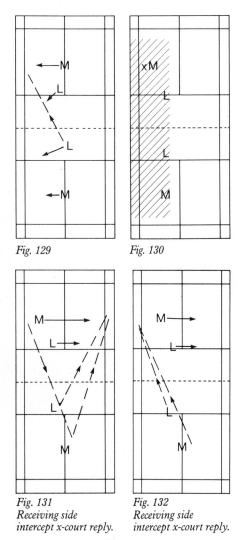

Fig. 129   Fig. 130

Fig. 131
Receiving side
intercept x-court reply.

Fig. 132
Receiving side
intercept x-court reply.

The higher it is when he hits it, the more chance he has of hitting the shuttle harder and flatter, and of putting pressure on the opponents. In the situation illustrated here the shuttle is too low in the court to do this. He must hit upwards.)

The opposing lady (the receiver) immediately recovers from the net and adjusts her position to cover any cross-court or straight replies to the forecourt or midcourt. The server (front lady) also adjusts her position to support her partners stroke-move by threatening the opponents' replies to the forecourt or midcourt. The receiver's partner (rear man) remains in the midcourt and adjusts his position slightly to the left of the centre line to cover any straight or cross-court replies which get past his front lady. He also covers the whip to the rearcourt. The new positions are shown in fig. 130. Both pairs are positioned on one side of the court which is where the play continues (see shaded area). The space here is now quite restricted by the players of both sides. The free space is on the other side of the court, but the approach there is blocked by the opponents who are covering any cross-court replies.

It is obvious what would happen if the rear man attempted a cross-court reply in this situation, particularly against alert, skilful opponents. The opponents, man or lady, would intercept the reply and hit the shuttle straight to the free space on the opponents' court before they could travel across to cover it (see fig. 131). Alternatively, they might hit the shuttle back to the place the opponents had just left in their rush across to cover the other side of their court (see fig. 132). *It is not very intelligent play to make a cross-court move when the opponents are positioned to cover the move.*

The cross-court move

When can you hit the shuttle cross-court? It seems a pity not to make use of all that free space on the other side of the court. The answer is that you can hit the shuttle cross-court to the open space when the opponents are not in position to cover such a move. The problem becomes one of creating a situation which allows you to make a cross-court move which will enhance your chances of winning the rally. To do this you must first manoeuvre your opponents out of position.

Manoeuvring the opponents out of position

As fig. 133 shows, much of the play takes places down one side of the court whilst the players spar for an opening and a chance to attack. The chance arises if the opposing man or lady can be

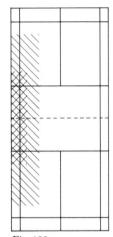

general area of play down the
side of the court

specific area of play to manoeuvre
opponents out of position

Fig. 133

drawn out of position to make a reply, particularly if he or she has
to make a late reply when the shuttle is near the ground.

As the players rally down one side of the court they will attempt to draw their opponents further to one side of the court
and even closer to the net. Fig. 133 shows the area into which
each side will try to hit the shuttle. The situation and the stroke-
moves used will vary slightly according to who is drawn out of
position. It is assumed in the discussion which follows that the
shuttle is well below net level and requires, at the least, a
moderately steep lift to get it over the net.

The lady drawn out of position

Reminder: the serving side are at the top half of the court
diagram.

Fig. 134 illustrates a situation in which the serving side lady
has drawn the opposing front lady towards the side of the
forecourt where the rally takes place. The receiving lady has
played a net reply. The serving side lady prepares to make her
stroke-move while the receiving side lady gets ready to cover the
forecourt replies. The serving side lady can play a net reply,
straight or cross-court, or a lob to the rearcourt. The lob will give
her opponents the attack. Whether or not she will lob depends
on how strong she considers the opposing rear man to be in his attack from the rearcourt, and also how skilful and confident she
feels against the opposing lady in the forecourt. In this situation
the opposing lady is ready to attack the straight reply but is too far
over to the right to intercept a tight cross-court net reply to the
open space on the other side of the forecourt. The chance of hitting a winner or forcing a weak reply are best if the shuttle is hit
cross-court to the forecourt. The serving lady hits it there.

At the higher levels of play, when playing against a skilful lady,
it is often necessary to use deception. In plate 34, Nora Perry

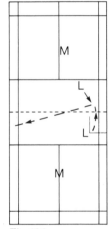

Fig. 134
*1. Receiving side lady plays a straight reply to
FC.*
*2. Serving side lady hits x-court net reply to other
side of FC.*

*Plate 34. Nora Perry deceives Imelda with a
x-court net reply.*

plays the cross-court net reply against the Indonesian player, Imelda. Imelda is poised to attack the straight reply from Nora Perry. Consequently, Nora Perry performs as if to play a straight net reply, so keeping Imelda's attention focused there and her body weight inclining slightly towards the right. Nora Perry 'holds' Imelda poised in that position until the last moment, when she suddenly switches the shuttle cross-court, leaving Imelda stranded and late in travelling across to make her reply.

It is obviously more difficult to hit the shuttle across the court to the side of the forecourt when the shuttle is below the level of the net. There are, however, many occasions in the game when a skilful lady will draw her opponent out of position and intercept her reply when it is above the net or sufficiently high to be hit down to the free space on the other side of the forecourt. The main prerequisite to achieve this is skilful use of the racket – to obtain the control and accuracy needed to place the shuttle over the net and into the side of opponent's forecourt. Once the opponent is drawn across the furthest extent she exposes the free space of her forecourt to the opposing front lady's replies.

The man drawn out of position

In fig. 135 the receiving side have played the shuttle to the space just behind the forecourt. The server's rear man travels forwards to make his reply.

The shuttle is low in the court. The receiving side position themselves to intercept any cross-court replies and threaten the straight reply. The serving side's front lady positions herself to cover the cross-court replies to her forecourt or midcourt, and to threaten any straight replies to her partner's stroke-move. The man is not in a good situation: he has to hit the shuttle from well below the net and has been drawn out of position to make his move, he has exposed his rearcourt and midcourt to the opponents' cross-court replies if they are quick to intercept the shuttle. He can play safe and lob the shuttle to the rearcourt but does not want to give the opponents an obvious attack; he decides to make a move which will enhance his chance of gaining the attack, and tries to hit the shuttle over the net, to skim the net, into the forecourt or midcourt.

This is what the opponents have anticipated. Their possible replies are:

1. The lady intercepts in the forecourt to hit the shuttle cross court to the open space. She could also hit the shuttle at the rear man as he tries to recover quickly into position. Or,

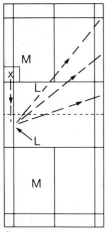

Fig. 135

2. The rear man meets the shuttle if it passes his front lady and hits it quickly cross-court. His options are to whip it to the opposite rearcourt corner, drive it to the midcourt, or tap it to the forecourt.

The serving side's front lady can do little against a fierce attack even if she does try to cover the cross-court reply. If she withdraws too far from her position in the forecourt she exposes her forecourt to the straight reply. Much depends on the height of the shuttle as the receiver's rear man hits the cross-court reply. The higher it is, the greater chance he has of hitting it hard and fast across the court. If the shuttle is low when he intercepts it he must play a softer reply, which gives the serving side more time to recover and cover the move.

Both players drawn out of position

The receiving side have hit the shuttle into the space just behind the serving side's front lady and ahead of her rear man. Both players are tempted to make a reply and both are drawn out of position. One will hit the shuttle and both will try to recover as quickly as possible to cover any cross-court reply to their move (see fig. 136).

The receiving side are ready to intercept a straight reply and, with both opponents drawn out of position, can easily hit the shuttle cross-court to the open side of the rearcourt, midcourt or forecourt. In this situation it might be more sensible for the players drawn out of position to lift the shuttle to the rearcourt, either cross-court away from the rear man or straight to his backhand side. Such a choice depends on the quality of the opponents and the skill of the player making the move.

Retrieving the situation

The cross-court move does not necessarily result in a winning hit. It is possible for the opponents to sprint across the court and make a reply in the situation. You should always be ready for this. *Never assume the rally is ended until you see the shuttle hit the ground.* Often, as is to be expected, the opponents may be late arriving to hit the shuttle, by which time it will be low in their court. Let us look at some possible replies in that situation.

1. Retrieving the cross-court move to the forecourt
This might be covered by the rear man if the front lady has been drawn out of position, e.g. in plate 34 where Imelda might be unable to reach the shuttle after Nora Perry's cross-court move.

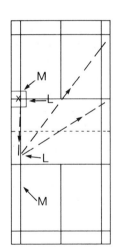

Fig. 136

Fig. 137
(Top) Man and lady adjust position to cover the reply to the x-court move.

(Bottom) Man and lady travel across to make a reply to the x-court move. The man travels forwards into FC. The lady takes up a position to cover him relative to the shuttle position.

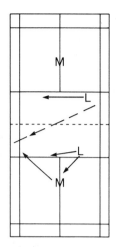

The replies to the cross-court move

Fig. 138
Serving side are caught out with a x-court move to their RC. The man sprints across to make a reply. The lady watches whilst she adjusts her position in the FC.

The receiving side adjust their positions to cover the replies, if any.

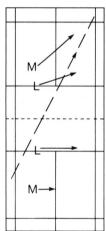

But as her rear man Christian is alert in the midcourt, he might find it easier than Imelda to travel to the forecourt and make a reply. He would travel forwards and across to hit the shuttle while Imelda would travel backwards and across to take up a position in the forecourt or midcourt to cover Christian while he made his move (see fig. 137).

2. Retrieving the cross-court move to the midcourt/rearcourt
In the midcourt and the rearcourt the man must recover in time to cover the cross-court reply. This would be easier to do in the midcourt than in the rearcourt, depending on how far he had been previously drawn out of position (see fig. 138).

The shuttle position is low in the forecourt, midcourt or rearcourt. The opponents are in position to attack any reply. In fact, relative to how low the shuttle is, the opponents will approach closer to the net to threaten the reply, particularly in the forecourt.

1. Replies from the forecourt (see fig. 139)
Two possible replies are (a) a move to the forecourt, straight or cross-court (the latter depends on whether the lady, in threatening the straight reply, over-commits herself and leaves herself open to the cross-court reply); (b) a lob to the rearcourt.

2. Replies from the midcourt (see fig. 140)
Here the shuttle can be hit on a flatter trajectory which increases the number of replies, e.g. a push or drive straight or cross-court, the whip to the rearcourt, and the low return to the forecourt. Much depends on the height of the shuttle in the court and the positions of the opponents as the shuttle is about to be hit.

3. Replies from the rearcourt (see fig. 141)
The shuttle in this situation is usually to the rear of the player (see the charts, rearcourt situation 7). His two attacking moves are the low return to the forecourt and the drive to the midcourt. The open space is in the direction of the straight return but, knowing this, the opponents will be ready to anticipate his reply. Once again, some deception is required. If the man can look as if he is going to play a straight reply to the forecourt or midcourt, he might tempt the front lady to anticipate early and move out of position towards the side of the court. He can then cross-court

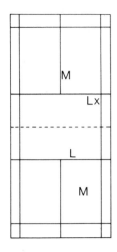

Fig. 139

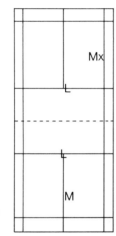

Fig. 140

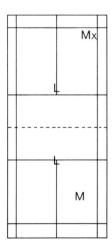

Fig. 141

the shuttle to the free space on the other side of the forecourt. It is a difficult situation for the rear man and how he extracts himself from it depends on his skill and accuracy, and the competence of his opposing lady. The rule is *to stay in balance and take the shuttle late to play a controlled reply, rather than try to take the shuttle early, whilst off balance and rush the reply.*

Comment The ability to draw the opponents out of position and create a situation in which you can hit a cross-court reply depends on the extent to which you can force them to make a straight reply. It hardly needs saying that players who attempt to hit cross-court when the opponents have the move covered expose themselves to a possible winning hit (see fig. 131, page 110).

Good positioning, with both the lady and the man ready to intercept and attack any cross-court reply, will force the opponents to play a straight reply. In general there is less risk attached to it. Nevertheless, to engage in a 'cat and mouse' game down the side of the court requires much accuracy and control in hitting the shuttle. Good racket skill is essential. At the lower levels of play, many players, particularly the men, do not try to force a lift by making a straight reply just over the net. They either lack the control and are not prepared to risk being intercepted and attacked, or do not consider it as a move in the game. What usually happens is that the men play a form of singles which completely ignores the fact they each have a lady operating at the front. They expect her to keep out of the way whilst they drive the shuttle fiercely at each other down the sides and cross-court. The lady is too far forward in the forecourt to intercept at the speed the shuttle travels. To intercept she needs to be positioned in the midcourt as she would be for sides attack in level doubles. But that will not do for her partner, who pushes her back into the forecourt where she is once again out of the way.

When the man cannot drive the shuttle he usually lobs it to the rearcourt and takes his chances on the smash. And if he cannot smash he clears and risks the smash from his opponent. On such occasions this can be less threatening with the chance of regaining the attack from the opponent(s). It is now that the man expects his partner to withdraw from the forecourt and help to defend. With her help there is a chance to intercept the shuttle and attack the opponent's smash. Such male 'partners' should not forget that mixed doubles is a team game.

Let us see what should happen when the shuttle is lobbed or cleared to the rearcourt at any level of play.

The lob to the rearcourt

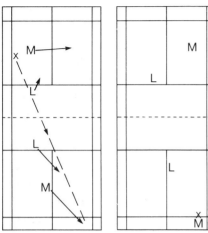

Fig. 142
Rear man lobs to RC.
Players adjust their
positions.

Fig. 143
Players in attack and
defence formations.

The rear man lobs the shuttle from the forecourt/midcourt area to the opponents' rearcourt (see fig. 142). The players travel to take up their respective attack and defence formations in the court (see fig. 143).

The attack

The attackers take up a rearcourt 'front and back' attack formation. The front lady positions herself behind the T relative to the shuttle position.

The defence

There are two defensive formations which might be taken up: the diagonal defence or the sides defence. In each one the lady positions herself to cover the cross-court smash, while the man positions himself to cover the straight smash. Let us examine each in turn.

1. Diagonal defence

The lady covers the cross-court smash and adjusts her base forwards relative to the position of the smasher and the sort of smash she can expect. She is committed to attack the smash. Her position is threatening to the attackers. If she intercepts the smash she can hit down for a winner or block the shuttle to the space in the midcourt behind the front lady and away from the smasher (see fig. 144).

The lady takes up a forward defence base because she also wants to ensure that she remains in the front of the court and is not manoeuvred to the rearcourt by a clear. If that should happen, the opponents will have managed to reverse the positions of the lady and the man – the very thing the defenders do not want to happen. Consequently, the lady must endeavour to take up a forward defence position whenever possible. She commits herself to covering the cross-court smash and any drop shot to the forecourt. She will leave any clear-move for her partner to cover. It is because of this that she has to position herself to cover the cross-court smash and not the straight smash. If she is positioned cross-court to the attacker his clear will travel diagonally across the court, and the longer flight will give her partner time to cover the clear to her rearcourt. Whereas if she is positioned to cover the straight smash, her partner will have less time to cover the straight clear over her head to the rearcourt. She would have to travel to the rearcourt to make the reply and their positions would be reversed.

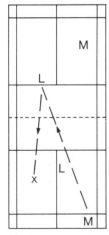

Fig. 144

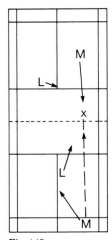

Fig. 145

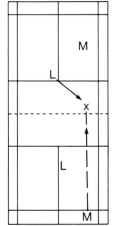

Fig. 146
Attack from right RC.
Front lady stands near
the T and is able to
reach the straight drop
in her partner's FC.

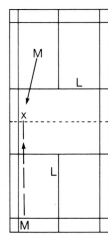

Fig. 147
Attack from left RC.
Front lady is further
away from the T –
may find difficulty in
reaching the straight
drop to her partner's
FC. Her rear man
must be prepared to
travel forwards to
make the reply from
FC.

Consequently, her partner must cover the straight smash, the clear to his own side of the rearcourt and the clear to his partner's side of the rearcourt. This positioning of the pair leaves a free space in the forecourt in front of the man. The opponents could hit the shuttle there in an attempt to draw the man forwards and once again reverse the positions of the man and lady (see fig. 145). The man does not want to be drawn forwards out of position, for if he is he exposes the midcourt and rearcourt to the cross-court reply to his move. We have seen this in the earlier examples. Hence it is the lady as front player who must be ready to anticipate the straight drop shot to her partner's forecourt.

There are some occasions when the man must be prepared to travel into the forecourt for the straight drop shot. This happens when the attacker is able to smash the shuttle from the left court, cross-court to the opponents' left court, to a right-handed lady. If she adopts a high defence stance (see plate 19, page 74) in forward defence, she is vulnerable to those smashes aimed at her backhand side, for they may get below her upheld racket. If she intends to maintain the high defence stance she will need to adjust her position. To protect the weak spot, she positions herself further over to her left to protect her backhand side and to ensure that she can play a forehand stroke. Consequently, she does not position herself to divide the angle of return equally. She moves to one side, leaving a larger gap on her forehand side (see figs. 146, 147).

2. Sides defence

When the opposing man has a powerful smash the lady will adopt a sides defence formation with her partner. She will still position herself to cover the cross-court smash for the reasons given. Her basic defensive stance may be 'front' or 'side-on defence' (see page 66); the choice will be determined partly by the power and the accuracy of the smasher and what stance she feels is most comfortable in the situation. Ideally, the front defence is best for then she would be able to revert to high defence, squat down below the shuttle and attack it if the smash is not too steep. It is unwise to prepare initially in high defence when positioned in the midcourt; a steep smash will get below the racket, catch the lady unprepared and may force a weak reply as she rushes to lower her racket head below the shuttle, too late to hit it hard. The usual stance (plate 11, page 67) in which the defender adopts a 'fighting' attitude, should enable her to switch to high defence in sufficient time to attack the shuttle. From the low position the situation is similar to any doubles situation. She can block to the forecourt, push to the midcourt or lob to the rear-court. Obviously, the replies to the forecourt and midcourt will create a situation more to her advantage, if successful.

This discussion of cross-court smashing does not imply that the man does not smash straight towards the opposing man, or to the centre between the two defenders. In general, the most weak-ly defended area in diagonal defence is the space between the two defenders. The straight smash obtains the usual replies with par-ticular emphasis on the push or drive to the midcourt and the block to the forecourt. Because of this, the smasher must be careful to hit the shuttle on a steep trajectory. If he hits a flat smash to either defender, he exposes his front lady to a flat drive reply which could travel too quickly for her to intercept and hit down. The rear man must play for his lady. He does not want her to withdraw too far from the forecourt to cover any cross-court drive replies to his smash. It should not be necessary for her to do so, for if that is necessary and she has been manoeuvred into a sides position level with her man, it is a simple step to keep her pinned down there, or clear to the rearcourt and maneouvre her to the rearcourt, thus reversing the positions of the man and the lady (see figs. 148, 149). The general rule is that the man should not hit flat smashes or drives, straight or cross-court, unless (a) his front lady is in a position to cover the reply and after hitting the shuttle is able to come forwards to attack in the forecourt; and (b) he can cover any replies which get past her. If he cannot guarantee these things, he should try to play a softer shot so that the shuttle falls after crossing the net and forces the opponent to hit upwards.

Having looked at the serve and traced the development when the lady serves to the lady, let us now return to the serve and discuss other variations in positional play when serving and receiving.

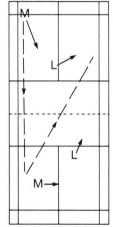

Fig. 148
Attacker hits a flat smash. Defender drives it x-court to lady who prepares to cover it. Players begin to readjust their positions.

Fig. 149
Sides lady blocks or pushes shuttle straight. Opposing front lady hits shallow lob over her head forcing her towards RC to make the reply.

The low serve: the man serves to the lady

See figs. 150, 151. To ensure that the man keeps control at the rear and the lady at the front, the man serves from the midcourt. His partner positions herself close to the T on his non-racket side. When he serves from the right court, she leans aside to allow him to serve wide, if necessary; and to allow the receiver an unrestricted view of the serve and the shuttle (see plate 35). When he serves from his left court she adopts the same position but stands normally in a forward attack stance (see plate 36). The trajectory of the serve is flatter than usual because it has further

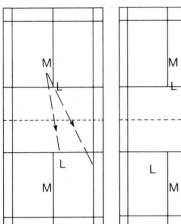

Fig. 150
Man serves from right
court.

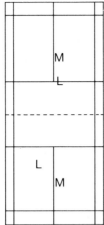

Fig. 151
Man serves from left
court.

Plate 35. Nora Perry leans aside as Thomas Kihlstrom prepares to serve
from the right court.

Plate 36. Ann Skovgaard ready to attack as
husband Steen serves from the left court.

Plate 37. Nora Perry drops below the shuttle in
order to return the shuttle with her racket head held
high.

to travel. The shuttle is hit to skim the net and fall quickly below
net height. The arc of the serve being flatter, it is difficult for the
receiver to play a net reply or a push with the racket head below
the hand, particularly on the forehand side. The receiver gains
more control from hitting the shuttle with her racket head high,
above her hand; but to do that she must lower her body to perform the action (see plate 37). From that position it is usually only possible to push the shuttle to the midcourt or forecourt sides;
hitting down is not possible with the shuttle below net level. Let
me remind you that the lady should be standing further back to
receive the serve to avoid the risk of being flicked. It is most
unlikely, therefore, that she will ever be quick enough to attack a
good low serve from above the net. In addition, as the man stands
in the midcourt to serve he has space to hit the shuttle to skim the
net at speed. An alert lady receiver will be ready to make the appropriate replies to this serve.

The lady's replies are (a) to push the shuttle to the sides of the
midcourt or forecourt and then adjust her position to cover the
opponents' replies to her move, in doing which she creates a

situation similar to her replies when the lady is serving to her; or (b) she could whip the shuttle to the rearcourt and try to surprise the rear man if he is slow to recover from his serve. The risk here is that he will smash if he is ready for such a stroke-move.

The low serve: the lady serves to the man

There are two formations in the receiving positions in this situation.

1. The receiver's partner positions herself close to the T in the forecourt (see fig. 152). She wants to ensure that she remains in the front to cover replies to her partner's (the man receiver) reply to the low serve-move. Consequently, the man receiving cannot commit himself to attack the low serve. He cannot risk going for the kill unless the serve is very weak and he can guarantee he will hit a winner. Should he go for the kill and the opposing man or woman whip the shuttle to his rearcourt there will be no player there to return it. His task, therefore, is to play a reply to the forecourt or midcourt which allows him to recover to his position behind the front lady and to cover all the serving side's replies to the midcourt or rearcourt. His partner will cover all the replies to the forecourt.

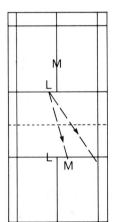

Fig. 152

To receive the serve he takes up a position behind the front service line, slightly further back than usual. This eliminates the possibility of being flicked, unless he moves too early, and yet still allows him time to travel forwards to play a net reply from just below net level to the sides of the forecourt or midcourt. If the man is very athletic and quick at travelling backwards he can stand further forwards to threaten the low serve. It is a matter for the individual man. What he must not forget is that he remains responsible for the rearcourt and midcourt after his reply to the serve.

2. The receiver's partner positions herself behind him in the midcourt (see fig. 153). The receivers reverse their positions to allow the man to attack and try to 'kill' the shuttle as it crosses the net. It is assumed here that the lady is skilful and confident in the rearcourt, and that the chance of a kill makes it worth 'weakening' the partnership in this situation.

The server now has a problem, for she knows that there can be no margin for error on the low serve. The opposing man shows he is prepared to commit himself fully to the attack, as indicated by the position of his woman to his rear. The server can prevent the attack if she serves a very accurate

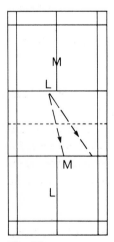

Fig. 153

low serve which the man cannot hit down. She could also use the flick serve to catch him out and make him less eager to explode into the attack next time. Finally, if she knows which way he tends to hit the shuttle from the net, she could serve to his forehand or backhand side, depending on what grip he uses, and allow him to hit down to the midcourt. Her rear man would be ready and could counter-hit the attempted kill, whipping the shuttle to the sides of the midcourt or rearcourt before the opponents had fully recovered.

The low serve:
the man serves to the man

See fig. 154. The same situation and possible moves occur as when the lady serves to the man, except that now he must also contend with the drive serve. Since the server is positioned further back he can drive the shuttle horizontally at speed. It is not a difficult move to reply to if the receiving man is ready, and then he also gains the chance to attack the serve.

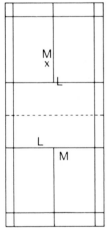

Fig. 154

Development in play from high serves

Within this category are drive, flick and high serves. The *drive* serve is used to hit a fast rising shuttle which skims the net, reaches the receiver between shoulder and just above head height. The server's intention is to force a mis-hit, a hasty or a weak reply. The *flick* serve is used for several reasons:

1. To try to get the shuttle over and behind the receiver to gain a winner or a weak reply.
2. To catch out an eager attacking receiver who is anticipating the low serve.
3. To make the receiver more cautious in attacking the low serve.
4. To manoeuvre the lady to the rearcourt.

The *high* serve is generally used when serving to the lady. Its purpose is to manoeuvre her to the rearcourt and reverse the positions of the man and the lady. The receiver has plenty of time to travel into position to smash the shuttle, and so it is not a very intelligent move to use against the man unless, of course, the man is relatively weak in the rearcourt and hits a reply which can be counter-attacked.

Serving to the lady

It makes little difference who serves high to the lady. The effect is the same: the receiving lady is manoeuvred to the rearcourt

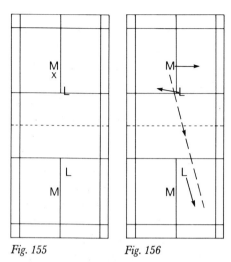

Fig. 155   Fig. 156

Fig. 156. Server adjusts his position to cover the straight smash. His front partner adjusts her position to cover the x-court smash.

Lady receiver travels back to attack the high serve (flick serve).

The replies of the lady in the rearcourt

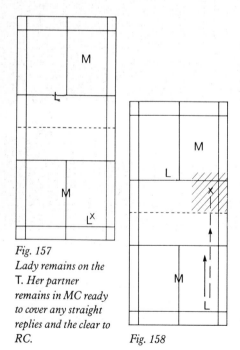

Fig. 157
Lady remains on the T. Her partner remains in MC ready to cover any straight replies and the clear to RC.

Fig. 158

behind her partner who remains in the midcourt. The differences, though insignificant, are as follows:

1. When the man serves from the midcourt, the receiving lady has more time to perceive the flick serve and can prepare sooner, especially as she will stand further back to receive the serve in anticipation of the flick serve used as a move against her (see fig. 155).

2. The serving man's partner must adjust her position to cover the cross-court smash to the right court when he serves from the right court—even though it is highly unlikely that the receiving lady will smash cross-court (see fig. 156).

When the receiving lady is *caught out* by a flick serve and *cannot* get sufficiently behind the shuttle to hit down, *she should clear high to the rearcourt.* This would be a sensible move to give her time to recover into position, rather than for her to attempt to hit a drop shot or a weak smash which would provide her opponents with an easy chance to win the rally. Should such a situation occur, the serving side lady would not cover the cross-court smash but remain on the T, ready to attack any weak reply to the forecourt (see fig. 157).

We will assume here that the lady is in a position to smash effectively. However, the receiving side still have a problem. Though the lady can smash, their positions have been reversed. The 'weaker' player has been manoeuvred into the rearcourt. How do they now revert to their stronger positions and retrieve the situation? This problem arises at any time during a rally when the lady is manoeuvred into the rearcourt. The solution is for her to play a *transition move.* The only safe place in the court is in front of the man positioned to defend against the straight smash (see fig. 158).

The lady can make two basic replies which are reasonably safe. *She can play the straight drop shot to the forecourt or the straight smash to the midcourt. Furthermore she must ensure that she hits the shuttle steeply downwards by whatever means she is able.* The opponents will be unable to attack a shuttle which is falling quickly below net level. Immediately she has made the stroke-move she must travel quickly forwards to take up her front player position. The opposing man replies to the straight smash whilst his partner travels across to reply to the straight drop shot. If the opposing man's partner is unable to reach the shuttle in the forecourt the man must be ready to do so for her. The receiving lady travels forwards to the forecourt whilst the opponents make their reply

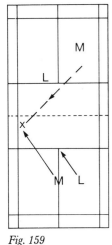

Fig. 159

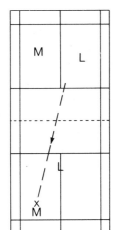

Fig. 160
Opponents anticipate the straight drop or smash reply from the lady. She clears to RC or drops x-court to FC.

to her stroke-move. If she has smashed, the opposing man may whip the shuttle back over her head, drive it straight at her or drop to her forecourt. Her job is to cover all the replies which are hit straight towards her and are within her reach, and still get to the forecourt as quickly as possible. She will leave the lob over her head to her partner, for that is his responsibility. Her partner remains watching and alert in the centre midcourt. He is ready to cover the cross-court whip or drive, the lob over his partner's head as she rushes forwards, and the cross-court reply to the forecourt, if the lady looks as if she cannot reach it (see fig. 159 and plate 38). It is always a sensible policy to play a safe stroke-move when making a transition move; but whenever the opponents begin to assume that one will be played and position themselves to cover it, alternative moves should be used. In the previous example, the serving side lady and man might position themselves closer to the forecourt and midcourt to cover a straight reply. They restrict the space. It is not difficult to exploit their expectations by hitting the shuttle to the spaces they leave unguarded (see fig. 160).

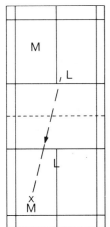

Fig. 161
Lady takes up forward defence position expecting a weak smash.

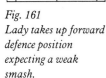

Fig. 162
Lady takes up a sides defence position expecting a strong smash.

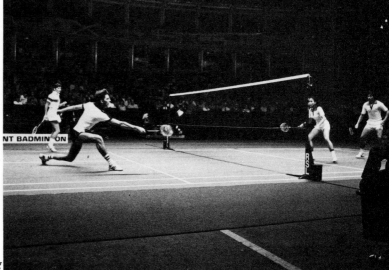

Plate 38. *Billy Gilliland covers the FC as Karen Chapman looks on.*

The flick serve to the man

This serve-move results in the usual front and back attacking formation and the diagonal or sides defence, depending on the probable force of the attack (see figs. 161, 162). The lady covers the cross-court smash.

Receiving the flick serve   The most attacking reply is to smash. The shuttle travels quickly and may result in a winner or a weak reply. It is most important that speed is not sacrificed for control and accuracy. It is all too easy to hit hard and flat; such speed can be counter-productive and can allow the opponents to drive the shuttle back past the front lady. The most important feature of the rearcourt smash in mixed doubles is the trajectory of the shuttle. It must be hit steeply to force the opponents to hit upwards and to give the front lady a chance to intercept a shuttle which flies *upwards* towards her rather than *horizontally* at her. If the man cannot get behind the shuttle sufficiently to hit it steeply with power, he should hit it less strongly, slice it, and bring his racket head further over the top of the shuttle to hit it downwards at a slower pace.

Conclusion

You should now know what sort of situations obtain in mixed doubles and how the lady and man combine as a team. It should be obvious that intelligent co-operation between the man and the lady is essential if they are to unify as a pair.

In mixed doubles, to a greater extent than in level doubles, each pair tries to adopt a 'front and back' formation even to the point of doing so when defending; for example, the lady takes a forward position in 'diagonal defence' ready to attack the smash. Mixed doubles is the most advanced form of attacking doubles play. The players are required to be adventurous opportunists as well as to show imagination, patience and control in their use of stroke-moves. How far the players are able to show these qualities will depend on their individual strengths and how these are utilised together in the partnership.

If you have read the book carefully you should be able to identify accurately what technical and/or tactical aspects of your play you must work on to strengthen your partnership and improve your chances of success in competition. Parts Three and Four will help you to do this.

Part Three

Performance

Chapter 8 Your Performance in the Game

There are two separate though related aspects to think about here: your performance as individual players and your combined performance as a pair.

Performance as a pair

Doubles is a team game. Two players must combine to form one unit—to play as if one. We know from experience that it is possible to put together two highly skilled individual players who somehow fail to combine those skills to form a successful doubles pair. Often this is due to a lack of knowledge about how to combine their strengths and adopt positions on the court which allow them to blend and harmonise as a unit. Sometimes it is a matter of luck that two players merge to form a good pair; then with continual play and experience together they learn to co-operate, help each other and combine to play intuitively as one unit.

I believe that it is quite possible for any two players to form a partnership and achieve considerable success as a pair. To do this they need to analyse each individual's game in different situations and to discover what situations each one prefers and how each one likes to operate in them. Does one prefer the rearcourt or the forecourt? Does one like to function as a hit-player, or a set-up player, or both—i.e. the all-court player? As front player, does one stand in the midcourt or on the T in the forecourt when the pair are in a front and back attacking formation? If one positions himself in the midcourt, can he jump sideways to intercept and attack the drive or push reply to the sides? And from that position can he travel forwards quickly enough to attack the shuttle above the net in the forecourt?

All the information players need to know in order to play as a pair can be read in the charts in Chapter 2, and in the section on playing doubles. To learn to play as a unit can be achieved by working together in specific practices and with continual experience in competition, the true test of performance as a pair. Chapter 10 describes and explains how and what to practise.

Individual performance

Your skill in hitting the shuttle and your ability to do the work and withstand the physical and psychological pressures of play will effect your joint strength as a doubles unit. A study of the charts indicates that there is much you must learn in order to perform competently in doubles. These things can be listed as follows:

1. You must learn the various techniques of hitting the shuttle, i.e. the strokes and the variations on the strokes. You should then be able to hit the shuttle from anywhere in your court to anywhere in your opponents' court to make the necessary moves in a given situation.

2. You must learn how to travel from one situation to another, position yourself to hit the shuttle, and recover from that stroke-move to travel into a new position in time to cover the possible replies. To do this requires good balance and footwork.

3. You must be able to meet the physical demands of the game. Any fitness training must be designed to improve your ability to travel easily between situations and to perform stroke-moves in those situations. The fitness training must link up with travelling and hitting techniques. This is achieved by continuous work over a period of time.

4. You must learn to make the appropriate stroke-moves. Hence you must learn all the stroke-moves possible in a situation, then you can find out what is appropriate in practice by discovering what is actually possible for you and your opponent. To do this you require more knowledge of your own game and that of your opponents. If, for example, one opponent is in a rearcourt attack situation in which there are six stroke-moves, then you can plan accordingly and create situations which may be to your advantage; for example, when you serve low to a front hit-player who tends to hit the shuttle in one direction only from the top of the net, you can anticipate this reply.

    The charts provide you with a checklist of possible moves, their replies and how to recover after making a move with respect to the sort of situation you have created. You can use that checklist to assess what your side—and your opponents —can do. If you find that you have any weaknesses, you can devise practices to correct those weaknesses. It could be, for example, that you never try to intercept the push or drive down the line when you are the front man in an attacking situation. More often than not your rear man has to travel forwards after his smash to cover that reply, and by the time he reaches the shuttle it has fallen below net height and he must hit it upwards. Consequently the situation is slightly to your disadvantage, for you have lost the attack. You might not realise that it could be your job to leap sideways to intercept the shuttle and hit down, while your partner adjusts his position to sides attack.

If you are not aware of this the charts will indicate it, for they provide a list of stroke-moves which affect your actions in any specific situation. One good reason for attacking the reply in the midcourt is to meet the shuttle as early as possible and maintain a downward attack. If you are not sure why you attempt a particular stroke-move—what the purpose is—then read through the charts and find out. The answer is there.

In the example in question, you should work out why you do not intercept the shuttle early in the midcourt. There could be several reasons. It could be that you stand too far forward, near the T in the forecourt instead of in the midcourt, and so have less time to perceive the shuttle and the opponent is successful in hitting the shuttle past you. It could be that your footwork and agility are inadequate: you see the shuttle and are in the correct position but not sufficiently athletic to leap across, hit the shuttle, land and recover quickly into position to cover the replies. The problem is to identify the cause and then devise some practice(s) to improve your performance in making the necessary stroke-move in this situation. There is much you can learn and practise if you want to improve your performance and become a better doubles player. It will certainly help if you are clear about what features of your performance can be improved and just how you can work to improve them. So, first, let us look at performance in some depth and later I will suggest some ways in which you might improve it, both for yourself as an individual and for your partnership in a doubles team.

Performance and standards

The word 'performance' is used here in two ways, both of which are important in your development as a doubles player. First, we can talk about successful or unsuccessful performance when we refer simply to whether you won or lost the game. We simply state a fact about the result of the game, e.g. 'They gave a successful performance', meaning that they won the game. This does not tell us very much and is not really interesting. Second, we can say that they gave a good or poor performance, regardless of whether they won or lost the game. It is quite usual for a player or the partnership to come off court and be told that they have played well even though they lost. There is no contradiction in saying that they lost but gave a good performance, or won but played badly.

It is important to understand in what sense a performance is good or bad, quite apart from the result of the game, otherwise you will learn nothing and make little progress, if any; for progress is dependent on learning and you should try to evaluate your performance and learn something about it each time you engage in a contest. But this is only possible if you know how to evaluate your play. You must realise that comments of the 'good' and 'bad' type are judgements about the quality of your performance with respect to standards of excellence in some aspect of the game. Either your performance comes up to standard or falls below standard in some way.

Nevertheless, although it is important that you attain good standards in performance, it is even more important that you are successful in the game. *Trying to win is the point of the game. Hence the successful performance of your partnership is the main target.* The ideal and most satisfying state is to give a performance which is both good and successful. *You should try to win and also attain the desired standards of excellence in the game.* In fact, your chances of success are increased if both partners attain a good standard of performance.

At this point the framework, as illustrated in the charts, becomes useful in identifying the inter-related features of performance and demonstrating the standards of excellence you should try to attain. It contains the sum total of all those aspects of the game you must learn in order to become a good player in a good doubles side. The framework is the game. It serves as a measure by which you can assess your knowledge and understanding, simply by comparing what you can do with what you ought to do to reach the highest standard of performance possible, i.e. perfection. This is personified in the notion of the complete player within the complete team, as seen in the pair of all-court players who reach the highest standards in all the aspects of the game and thus win unless equalled by another pair. To be realistic, perfection for many is an unattainable ideal and, for the few, it is a state touched for odd moments rather than sustained. It possesses an elusive quality. Nevertheless, it is the distant destination all players must seek if they want to become better players; for to try to become a better player, even to improve one's footwork in the forecourt, or the accuracy of the smash, is to seek standards of excellence (i.e., what counts as good) on the road to perfection. The beginner takes his first steps along that road as soon as he steps onto the court and hits his first shuttle.

In addition there are a further set of related standards. These are the practical standards of performance set by different opponents at different levels of play within the game. These are easy to recognise, for they range between those of the beginners and of the current world champions. Between these two levels are a number of steps which must be climbed, each one more difficult and demanding. It is possible to compare progress in the different levels of play with climbing a pyramid (see fig. 163). At the bottom of the pyramid there are numerous players, some quite content to remain there, others keen to improve and reach the next level; and so on until only a few remain striving for the top and capable of reaching it. When they do, they remain there until displaced by a pair below.

world champions
contenders
international players
players in countries, states, regions
players in clubs, leagues
beginners

Fig. 163
The different levels of play indicate practical standards of performance relative to the players on the pyramid.

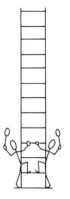

Fig. 164
Standards of excellence in performance in the game.

There are many routes up the pyramid, with the choice of route and method of travel depending on the way the game is organised in different countries throughout the world. Access to each level is gained by success in competition. It is obvious that, at some stage, a pair needs access to international competition to become a valid contender for the title of world champion. It should also be obvious that success in competition at any level of play in general, and at the top level in particular, is most unlikely unless the players have also attained high standards of excellence in all the various aspects of the game.

These levels of play are important. They give you the chance to test your progress on the journey to becoming better individual players and a better doubles pair. However good your practical knowledge of how to perform the stroke-moves, and your tactical knowledge of when to perform them in a given situation, there comes the time when you must test that knowledge and your skill on the court. The test is to compete against other pairs. If you can progress from club player to the club team and win the club doubles championships you have become a better player. From there you can continue to progress, becoming the best at each level in terms of doubles success, as you also become better as a player. Remember that 'better' here is not only relative to other players and the levels set by those players. The opponents at each level of play are a test of your progress, not only towards the top of the players' doubles pyramid, but also towards the ideal of perfection. This ideal, with its objective standards of excellence within the different parts of the game, runs parallel to the pyramid though separate from it (fig. 164). The objective standards of excellence are quite different from the practical standards set by the players.* Even the world champions, who are on top of the

---

*For example, the purpose of the attack clear as a stroke-move is to get the shuttle over the opponent's head and make him travel to the rearcourt. There are several sets of standards involved here. With respect to the way you hit the shuttle, a good standard of skilled performance would be described as smooth, fluent, neat, rhythmical and efficient stroke production. The shuttle would be hit with control and accuracy just above the reach of the opponents to the desired place in the rearcourt. As a stroke-move it would be of a good standard only if it caught the opponent out, i.e. the shuttle got behind the opponent, caused him to be late in getting to the shuttle, reduced his chances of making a scoring hit, and created a situation to your advantage.

These are objective standards of good performance determined by the nature of the game and what good players at the highest level are capable of achieving consistently in the game. At a lower level of play a beginner may attempt an attack clear as a move but perform it with excessive movement in a crude fashion. Consequently it does not send the opponent all the way to the rearcourt. Nevertheless, it could still be effective as a move at that level of play because the opponent, as a

pyramid, can still work towards the ideal of perfection as set out in the framework, and become better players in the sense of becoming more complete players within the context of the doubles game.

The 1983 All England and World Champion mixed doubles player, Nora Perry, emphasised this point to me when discussing her partnership with Thomas Kihlstrom of Sweden. Nora, recognised as one of the leading doubles players in the world, if not the best, and a previous winner of all the major doubles titles in ladies' and mixed doubles, commenced her partnership with Thomas Kihlstrom in the 1982-83 season. Though a world class player, she began to train and practise even harder with Kihlstrom. They would play twenty sets of doubles in practice, trying out new moves and positions to improve their play as a doubles team. They believed that there was room for improvement, that they could become better players. As a result they won thirty-nine consecutive matches and every major title in the world that year.

They were sensible to work so hard, for the champions who rest on their laurels risk losing the title of 'best pair'. In defeating opponents, they unavoidably 'teach' their opponents about their (the champions') game and also about the opponents' own game. Hence an ambitious and intelligent pair of contenders will begin to do whatever is necessary to eliminate weaknesses and devise ways to improve their standards of performance in the various aspects of the game, so that the next time they meet the champions they are better equipped to challenge for the title. No champions can afford to stand still. Like all players they must aim at the twin targets necessary in any progress towards becoming better players, that is, the ideal of perfection inherent in the framework which is personified in the complete player; and the intervening targets of the different levels of players (though in the world champions' case their only threat is from the contenders in the pyramid).

To sum up briefly: you test yourself against other pairs to measure your progress on the road to perfection, the elusive ideal;

---

beginner, may find that even such a crude clear is to his disadvantage. Although we recognise that beginners are well below the objective standard of what counts as 'good' when compared with the standards set within the framework and the ultimate ideal of 'perfection', they are capable of playing below this standard and still attaining the practical standards relative to their level of play. At their level this would be sufficient to win the game.

and to help you there is the framework, which makes it possible to test and measure yourself accurately and also provides the means of improving your performance by giving you a frame of reference within which you can assess any aspect of your performance in the game. The task now is to take a close look at the different aspects of performance and to try and work out the desired standards of excellence inherent in each part.

The components of performance

Performance comprises three inter-related components. These are skill, fitness and attitude, each of which can affect the others. The onset of fatigue can cause a breakdown in skill level, whereas a high level of skill and fitness can increase confidence and influence determination and adventurousness in play. Alternatively, lack of confidence or fear in play often has a disastrous effect on skill and fitness. When all three are in tune and functioning at the highest level the player will experience feelings of being at one within himself—complete harmony as a unified being, as though he can do nothing wrong. He becomes lost in the moment as if space and time had ceased to exist. The racket feels a part of him, an extension of self, and seems to become large and magnetic in quality, attracting the shuttle which hovers in front like some huge parachute. His side of the court seems the size of a postage stamp and the opponents' court looks as big as a football pitch. How can one not succeed?

Such moments, though rare, are authentic experiences. When they do occur they are the result of much hard work and conscious effort to improve the standard of performance in each of the major components. Let us look now at each briefly in turn.

Skill Skill consists of the technical and tactical aspects of performance.

Technical skill

The technical aspects are the strokes and footwork, i.e. the various techniques of hitting the shuttle and travelling from one situation to another to do so. The emphasis here is on the art of moving in the game. This is most apparent if you reflect upon the ways in which we describe skilful players. We talk about the strokes in terms of a 'powerful' smash, a 'gentle' drop shot; the player 'caresses' the shuttle over the net, and possesses a 'flashing' backhand. The same can be said of the general movement around the court when we refer to the player as graceful, flowing, gliding, skimming the ground, and performing 'explosive' leaps and 'featherlight' landings.

In using such descriptions, we not only 'paint' a picture of the player in action but also evaluate the way he performs and suggest that he comes up to some standard of excellence that we admire and enjoy. We become concerned here with the beauty of the movement and use aesthetic words to describe it as we see it. Usually we are even more specific than this and refer to stroke production as neat, tidy, economical in time and effort (all necessary to hit the shuttle with control and accuracy). The footwork we refer to as quick, light, nimble, balanced and controlled; here we are more concerned with the mechanical efficiency of the technical performance than with its beauty. In general, the descriptions we use are a combination of physical and aesthetic descriptions which sometimes overlap, as when we use the word 'powerful' which tells us something both about the force used to hit the shuttle and about the quality of the movement of the player in his execution of the stroke. Both kinds of description imply that there are standards of performance which we believe are the mark of a good player. To reach these, a player must become very proficient in using his racket, and in his footwork and general movement about the court. It is worth commenting further on the techniques of hitting and travelling in the game.

Hitting and travelling techniques
Badminton doubles is a hitting game which involves the delivery of 'blows' to the opponents. There is, of course, no physical contact with the opponents. Nevertheless, the game involves the aggressive element of attack. The racket is the weapon that delivers the 'blow'. The game is played at speed, making a quick recovery after each hit essential. *The rule to follow is 'hit and move.'* Balance and control are important factors in recovery. Players who travel to a situation to make a stroke-move and lose balance will be slow to recover. Poor hitting and travelling techniques can upset balance and slow the recovery.

Hitting techniques
The racket is very light and can be used easily to apply much force with the minimum of strength and movement. There are a number of different grips which allow you to hold the racket in different ways to hit the shuttle in various situations. The grip serves two functions. First, it enables you to control the racket face and so direct the shuttle to any place in the opponents' court.

Second, it enables you to control the racket head to apply more or less force to the shuttle in the chosen direction.*

The racket should be held in front of the body with the racket head higher than the hand ready to hit the shuttle from anywhere in the space around the body. This is the attack position (see plate 39). For rearcourt moves, the racket is simply lifted back ready to hit the shuttle from a high position (see plate 40). The force of the blow will be determined by the weight and the speed of the

Plate 39. Karen Chapman poised with her racket held ready to attack any replies to Gilliland's smash.

racket head. With the lighter racket head you can generate more speed, and help towards this by holding the racket near the bottom of the handle (so increasing the length of the racket), and by keeping your trunk relatively still during the hitting phase. Just allow your arm and shoulders to perform most of the hitting action. This will also assist balance and recovery.

In the midcourt and forecourt less movement of the arm is required since the shuttle is often hit at your side or in front and the movement is usually performed with a quicker action. The trunk should still be held in a state of balance to allow you to deliver quick 'blows' from the midcourt and forecourt. It helps here to shorten the racket by holding it near the top of the handle. You will find it easier to hit and recover at speed. Many top players change the position of their hand on the handle to lengthen or shorten the racket. They shorten it particularly in defence, to attack the smash and engage in a sides attack 'slugging' contest; or to attack in the forecourt and 'kill' the shuttle or play spinners and tumblers.

Plate 40. Steen Skovgard with racket positioned ready to smash as Chandra and Christian set themselves to defend.

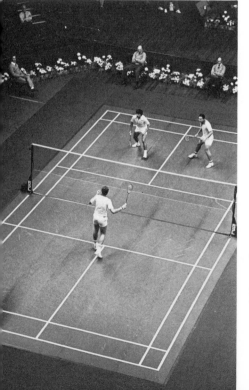

*You can read about the grips and strokes in my earlier books *Badminton for Schools* and *Better Badminton for All*, both published by Pelham Books.

Speed of hitting, the ability to generate force and to recover quickly, all depend on your ability to tense and relax your muscles quickly. To reach the necessary quality of movement in your hitting technique you require a conscious awareness and control over your bodily state. All the strength, speed and agility that comes from fitness training will not improve the quality of movement unless you are aware of the sensation of tension and relaxation in your muscles and can control that state throughout your performance. The same quality of movement is required in your technique of travelling over the court to make the stroke-moves. You must be able to travel easily from one situation to another, and in this respect good posture and carriage in conjunction with good footwork is most important. If the trunk rests lightly and balances easily on the hips, without strain, it becomes easier to travel around the court. The legs seem to have less work to do, for the trunk 'rides' on them without being a burden to them. In play it is important to carry the trunk round lightly on the legs so as to travel around the court without strain. The tactical benefits of good technique with quality of movement are seen as you take less time to travel to the shuttle and to recover from your stroke-move to cover the reply, and produce even greater control and accuracy in the execution of the stroke-move. Thus you can maintain an effective attack.

Travelling techniques

The means of travel between situations can vary. Between the midcourt and the rearcourt it usually takes the form of sprints, sidesteps and jumps. These are performed lightly with a softness of foot which improves the speed of travel and indicates a concern for quality of movement in the body. The action of accelerating from a particular stance, e.g. defensive, is achieved by flexing the knees, lowering the upright body and then using the strong thigh muscles and the muscles of the lower leg and foot to push rapidly into the floor to thrust you away from the spot. Similarly, the same muscle groups in the leg act as brakes and allow you to slow down or stop to make the stroke-move, before thrusting you away to recover and travel to a new situation. The speed of travel, and starting and stopping, is partly dependent on the relationship between the trunk and the legs and the overall quality of muscular tension in the body.

Travel between the midcourt and the forecourt is performed either by taking steps to travel up to the shuttle to arrive in balance, or by stretching to extend the reach. The most common action is the lunge, similar to that used by the fencer, which is an action that maintains the body in balance and aids speedier recovery. With training and an awareness of posture and balance you should learn to stretch into a deep lunge at speed with maximum control and possess the strength and technique to recover smoothly from the lunge with control.

Any training in travelling around the court should include:

1. Pushing off quickly from the spot with short sprints in backward, forward and diagonal directions to stop quickly in balance before you push off to recover.

2. Sidesteps towards the corners with a jump to smash and then a controlled landing before pushing away to recover.

3. Exercises designed to increase flexibility in the legs, hip joint and lower back to ensure the ability to perform full deep lunges in forward and sideways directions whilst the trunk remains centred and in balance.

Tactical skill

This term refers to the use of stroke-moves and the positions your side adopts to defeat the opponents. The emphasis is solely on how the opponents are played. When we describe and evaluate the tactical aspects of performance we tend to apply words concerned with mental attributes: a good player in this respect reaches a high standard if he uses common sense, plays intelligently, is shrewd, imaginative and creative. These are the standards we want a good player to attain. Hence to become a good player you must make stroke-moves which are appropriate in the situations that occur during the rally. Then, and only then, can you be said to have reached the desired tactical standards and to deserve such descriptions as 'intelligent' or 'imaginative'. To reach these standards in the technical and tactical aspects of skilled performance requires much work in practice and competition.

The technical and tactical skill required are clearly shown in the charts. Skill in playing requires a combination of both in the form of stroke-moves played in situations in accordance with the principle of attack. To ensure a good performance there are various standards expressed in physical, mental and aesthetic judgements of performance that the execution of a stroke and the choice of a stroke-move must attain. If you want to become a better player with respect to skilled performance then you must look critically at your performance in these terms.

Fitness   Fitness refers to the player's physical and mental states. For instance, a person may feel fit but might be proved to be quite unfit by a few minutes' hard exercise, while a highly trained player who is superbly fit could go on court and not feel fit. The purpose of being fit is to improve our capacity for hard physical work and to delay the onset of and quicken the recovery from fatigue. Here we are concerned mainly with fitness for badminton with respect to physical performance in the game and, to some extent, with 'feeling' fit to play the game.

If you are unable to do the work required, i.e. the amount of work at the rate the game is being played, then your technical and tactical skills will suffer. You will fall below your standards in stroke production and become inefficient, make errors and lose accuracy and control. You might also begin to make errors in judgement and 'read' the game badly. No matter how intelligent you are as a player, if your moves do not create the situations you intend because the shuttle does not go where you aim it, you will reduce your chances of winning. In addition, if you are too tired to get into position to cover the replies in the situations you create, then you will obviously lose any advantage you have played for and may perhaps lose the rally. It is easy to see that your skill and fitness are separate but interdependent aspects of your performance. So also are attitude and fitness. It is most important that, if you have trained hard and achieved a high standard of fitness, you should actually feel fit when you step onto the court. It would be most disappointing to feel listless, lethargic, tired and drained of energy, and this can happen if you are not in the right state of mind before and during a game. In general, however, this problem of attitude arises more in the singles game than in doubles, for in doubles a good level of fitness is usually more conducive to helping the player feel confident and eager to compete.

Fitness components

There are a number of fitness components that need developing. These are: agility, flexibility, local muscular endurance, cardiovascular and respiratory endurance, strength, power, speed and the correct maintenance of body weight.

Agility is the ability to change direction quickly with control whilst travelling at speed. This is something you must be able to do in the game while travelling from one situation to another.

Strength is to do with the amount of force you can exert with your muscles. It is closely related to power, which is the capacity to exert the maximum force in the shortest possible time. A powerful player is not only strong but can exert force quickly.

Speed is the ability to move quickly, e.g. to perform a smash or to travel from the midcourt to the forecourt. The speed at which a player moves is dependent on (a) reaction time and (b) movement time. Reaction time is the time taken between the initial perception of the stimulus (the shuttle being hit or flying through the air) and the player's first muscular movement in response; it relates to the speed at which information travels through the nervous system to the muscles which make the response. Movement time is the time taken from the start to the end of the movements the player makes in his response. It is largely dependent on how fast the muscles will contract. This feature can be improved with the right sort of training. Training for strength and power, key components of speed, are necessary as are exercises designed to improve fast racket work and fast footwork.

Though reaction time cannot be improved with respect to the speed at which information is transmitted through the nervous system, it can be improved if the player learns to select information about his opponent's probable move at an early stage in the situation. He can learn to 'read' the behaviour of the opponents and anticipate the move. It is helpful here to ignore the rule of 'watch the shuttle' and follow the rule of 'watch the opponent' as he prepares for his stroke-move. By doing so it is possible to obtain clues about his intention and thus to be able to anticipate and make an earlier response to his move.

Local muscular endurance is the capacity for the continuous work of particular muscle groups before the onset of fatigue. The fit player can work more intensely for longer periods before he becomes tired.

Cardiovascular and respiratory endurance is the capacity to keep up demanding activity for long periods of time, particularly when it involves large muscle groups. The popular name for this component is 'heart and lungs' endurance, because it is involved with the transportation of energy to the working muscles. As badminton demands much running and jumping, starting and stopping, a constant supply of oxygen (energy) will be needed by the heavily worked muscles. This can only be achieved if the heart and lungs are capable of working efficiently for long stretches of time.

Flexibility is the ability to move your limbs through the full range of movements required to meet all the twisting and turning and stretching that the game demands. It reduces the risk of joint and muscle injury caused by placing excessive stress on the body during competition. All players should develop the habit of warming up by doing slow stretching exercises and maintain this habit as part of their daily training (see pages 155-162).

Maintenance of correct body weight is important to ensure that you do not do more work than is necessary, but are capable of doing all that is necessary without undue fatigue. If you are overweight, you carry an extra load and must do more work to transport yourself around, which results in an increase in your energy output. Alternatively, if you are below your correct weight it is most likely that you will either be too weak to do the work or have insufficient energy stored in the body. Correct body weight is maintained by a combination of exercise and diet.

On getting fit

There are three essential factors in the development of badminton fitness. These are training, rest and diet.

1. Training

The purpose of training is to make your body function more efficiently. To do this you must improve the level of efficiency of the components of fitness. Different types of exercise(s) are used for this purpose, e.g. running, skipping, stretching, weight training. Exercise is work. When you exercise you move. All movement is dependent on muscular contraction of varying degrees of intensity and rate over a specific period of time. To perform a power smash, for example, requires muscular contractions of a higher intensity and rate than is needed for the low serve. There are two main factors to be considered in improving the efficiency of the working muscles: (a) the quality of the contraction of the muscles, which is considered to represent the strength of the muscles; and (b) the supply of energy to the muscles.

(a) Muscular contraction. The muscle comprises two types of muscle fibre. These are slow contracting and fast contracting fibres—commonly known as 'fast twitch' and 'slow twitch' muscle fibres. They function as their labels suggest. The 'slow twitch' fibres are used to a greater extent in endurance-type activities, whereas 'fast twitch' are used to a greater extent in speed activities. Badminton is a game which entails both, though in

doubles there is a greater emphasis on speed than endurance. The doubles player has to accelerate quickly, like a sprinter from the blocks, or launch himself upwards into the air to smash, with the explosive quality of a shot putter. For these reasons any training programme must include exercises which develop both types of muscle fibre. Badminton players must work on endurance, strength, speed and power exercises.

(b) Energy supply. If muscles are required to perform work they require energy. All muscular activity – those muscles involved in running and jumping, and the muscles of the heart and respiratory system – requires a constant supply. The energy comes from two main sources: the oxygen from the atmosphere, and the chemical energy which comes from food. Both undergo a complex series of changes before being converted into the energy used in muscular activity.

There are two types of energy system. These are the aerobic energy system, which is dependent on oxygen; and the anaerobic energy system, which is dependent on chemicals obtained from food and is stored in the muscles in the form of adenosine triphosphate and phosphocreatine (ATP-PC), and lactic acid (LA).

The aerobic energy system, essential for badminton play, relies on the transport of adequate supplies of oxygen from the atmosphere to the working muscles. Oxygen is required at the working muscles as part of their reaction to provide energy. The lungs, the blood stream and the heart are all involved in this transfer and must be highly efficient to ensure that oxygen reaches the muscles with the minimum of delay. When the intensity of exercise is such that a supply of oxygen is adequate for the demands of the working muscles, the oxygen system is used. Activities of a long-term nature such as middle distance running operate mainly on the oxygen system. The training for these events is aimed to develop a highly efficient oxygen system. Such events are characterised by lengthy periods of exercise with some, but little, variation in intensity. This is called *steady state work,* the oxygen energy system being used almost exclusively throughout.

The anaerobic energy system comprises the ATP-PC and lactic acid systems, and is used substantially in badminton doubles where the intensity of the play fluctuates from slow movement to rapid play during a rally. In such a game the oxygen system is not always sufficient. Shortly after you have started to move quickly the aerobic method of supplying energy to the muscles becomes inadequate. The muscles work so rapidly that the energy they require cannot be met by the transfer of oxygen from the atmosphere. Energy has to be obtained quickly from the supply in the working muscles. The two components of the anaerobic energy system make the energy available in different ways. The first one to be activated is the ATP-PC system in which the primary fuel is a chemical, phosphocreatine, stored in the muscle cells. The breakdown of this chemical makes the energy available very rapidly. Very short, intense activities which take only a few seconds will get their energy from this source. It provides energy for about four to five seconds before it needs replenishing. Thus, an explosive movement such as a backward jump smash will use the ATP-PC system. The second component of the anaerobic energy system is the lactic acid or LA system. It is called lactic acid because the chemical fuel glycogen, stored in the muscle, is converted into energy, forming lactic acid as a waste product. Energy can be produced rapidly by this system, but the muscles cannot tolerate a high quantity of this waste product; they cease to function effectively and can become quite painful – one such result is cramp. If the activity is of such high intensity that the anaerobic system is used exclusively, then the available energy will last for only 40-50 seconds. After that the lactic acid builds up and the player is forced to reduce the intensity of the activity and switch to the oxygen energy system until the anaerobic energy systems are 'refuelled'.

Any training programme has to develop these energy systems, each of which operates for a specific period of time working at a certain intensity. The ATP-PC system is best developed by working at the appropriate maximum effort for periods of 5-10 seconds and allowing three times that period to recover, i.e. 15-30 seconds. The work/rest ratio is 1/3. This applies also to the lactic acid system which is best developed by working for periods of 40-60 seconds at the appropriate maximum effort with a rest period twice the length of the work period. The oxygen system requires work at an appropriate intensity for periods in excess of three minutes. The rest period is the same as the work period, a ratio of 1/1.*

---

*For more information about fitness training specific to badminton, reference can be made to *Get Fit for Badminton* by J. Downey and D. Brodie (Pelham Books, 1980) and *Badminton – A Physiological*

This discussion is intended to emphasise the importance of fitness training for any player who wants to meet the demands of the game. However, in planning the programme it is important that players and coaches understand what different forms of training do to the body. There is, unfortunately, more ignorance than is necessary amongst players and coaches about the physiology of exercise. Consequently, athletes could be at risk if they push too hard in training without taking adequate precautions. For example, they should ensure that the relationship between work load and work rate is correct. They should get the balance right between work and rest. If not they may suffer injury or unnecessary strain and be unable to complete their training programme simply because, for instance, their rest periods are not of sufficient duration in relation to the amount and intensity of the work they are undertaking. Alternatively, players might train but not increase their level of fitness simply because they failed to do work of sufficient intensity.

There is no reason for ignorance in this area. There are plenty of books written by sports scientists about the physiology of exercise and how to train for fitness in different sports. Furthermore, in England, the Sports Council has set up a National Coaching Foundation whose task is to educate coaches in the different theoretical aspects of their sports—one such aspect being the physiology of exercise. Coaches and players would all benefit from enrolling on such a course.

In the meantime, players and coaches are advised to be sensible when working on the practices listed later in this book. In these it is possible to intensify the work to achieve a specific training effect, i.e. to develop agility, strength, power and the energy systems. Where appropriate, instructions on how to do this are provided. The main emphasis, however, is on the development of technical and tactical skill—the ability to make the appropriate stroke-moves in the situations which occur in the game.

2. Rest

A certain amount of rest is important to allow the body to recover

---

Evaluation by Finn Mikkelsen and Birger Rasmussen of the August Krogh Institute, Copenhagen. The latter was a study presented to the badminton coaches' international coaching conference at the first world championships, Malmo 1977. Copies of this should be obtainable from the International Badminton Federation (24 Winchcombe House, Winchcombe Street, Cheltenham, Gloucestershire) or the coaching committees of the national governing bodies.

from the work. This includes the rest taken during training and the rest gained between training sessions doing other things or in natural sleep.

3. Diet

A correct diet ensures that the body is supplied with the essential fuel to provide the energy to meet the demands of play; and that correct body weight is maintained.

It is most important in any training programme that the correct balance is attained between these three factors.

Fitness standards

The standards of fitness are to some extent built into the fitness components. The fit player should be strong, fast, powerful, agile, flexible, tireless, lean, athletic and muscular. We might also add that he should be dynamic and explosive.

A higher level of fitness is often reflected in a better quality of movement on the court. This might be expected, for if fitness is specific to badminton and a player becomes badminton-fit by training on those movements that occur in the game, then necessarily that player is going to become a better mover in the game. The quality of fitness is related to the quality of skilled movement in the game. The significance of these fitness standards is that they are targets for any player who wants to become better, in terms of becoming a more complete player as well as of wanting to climb to the higher levels of play on the pyramid. They are necessary standards, for they arise from the demands of the game as reflected in the framework.

Training for fitness

Although it is not the intention in this book to discuss specific training methods, it is possible to provide additional guidelines to getting fit. There are a number of principles that should be considered in training for fitness. These are:

1. Build up a *general* level of fitness, i.e. an efficient cardio-vascular and respiratory system. When you have reached a general level, then

2. Train *specifically* for badminton and develop badminton fitness.

3. *Overload* the training. Increase the amount of work that you do in training until it exceeds what the game demands.

4. Make the training *progressive*. Getting fit is a gradual business and you must overload the training gradually.

5.   Make sure that the amount of work, i.e. the amount of overload and the rate of progression, is *specifically* selected and arranged to suit your individual needs. General training may be all right to some extent for a group of players but eventually the work you do must suit you. Every individual player is different and requires a different training programme.

6.   *Measure* your progress. Test yourself and then keep a record to see how you are improving. Remember that the fitter you become the slower is the rate of improvement.

7.   Make the work *interesting*. Some *variety* is important.

Finally, even though fitness training appears to be hard work (due to the principle of overload and progression), it can still be enjoyable. For most players it can become a regular part of their daily lives. Eventually, the beneficial effect of regular training and a concern for the quality of movement in play will improve your badminton fitness. The rewards come from the experience of training with a feeling of well-being, and the end result, a better performance in your game.

Attitude   Attitude is by far the most complex aspect of performance and is inextricably bound up with skill and fitness in contributing to good performance. It is relatively easy for a player to attain a high standard of fitness and technical skill with hard work and practice over a period if time, and then, with lots of experience in competition, to develop a good level of tactical skill in the game. There are players who do this and yet do not achieve the sort of success they are capable of solely because their attitude lets them down in some respect. Problems concerning attitude affect players at all levels. In this chapter I simply want to discuss what might count as an appropriate attitude to the game and how such an attitude can enhance your performance as a player.*

The appropriate attitude to the game

Attitude refers to a player's behaviour. If it comes up to the recognised standard then there should be a good performance. If we want to know what counts as an appropriate attitude we must examine the game to find out.

It is safe to assume that a player takes up the game *voluntarily*.

---

*For a detailed discussion on attitude read my book *Winning Badminton Singles* (A & C Black).

If so, it would seem that he considers it a *worthwhile* game to play and that he continues to do so for the *enjoyment* he gets out of it. The enjoyment can come from the exercise, the hitting of shuttles, general movement about the court (twists and turns, jumps and leaps, sprints and changes of direction), the challenge of the contest and that it is an *absorbing,* dynamic and *interesting* game to play. The more he plays the more he will *care about how he performs* and will begin to take some *pride in his performance* and the success he achieves; in which case he will be more ready to *commit himself* to the standards of excellence within the different aspects of performance in the game. At this stage it could be said that he has a *love of the game* solely for the interest and enjoyment it provides.

No doubt, as he continues to play and improves his skill and fitness he will give little thought to his attitude. In fact in playing the game for its own sake he will already be forming an appropriate attitude to it. *For the game is a contest in which the player and his partner compete with the opponents to win. Trying to win is the point of the game.* It is because both sides try to win that the game becomes interesting, for each side becomes a test of the performance of the other side. This takes time, for badminton is a game that goes on for a period of time and calls for a certain degree of skill to defeat the opponents. The game becomes more absorbing as the struggle to win becomes more difficult. The players must be interested in and committed to the task of winning. To do this requires a certain degree of *persistence* in their efforts until the game is over. At the same time, being committed, there will be a serious effort to win and *determination* shown in doing so. Such a commitment will require complete *concentration* since all attention is focused on defeating the opponents. We might conclude at this point that certain attitudes are necessary if the players really can claim to play the game as a contest.

There is a further source of attitudes which arises from the fact that the game is played with other competitors. As it is a social game, in the sense that it is played by human beings, *the manner in which it is played* is important. It is expected that the players should adopt certain moral attitudes because badminton is a game within the world of sport. Man has devised various sports throughout his history and has done so, with few exceptions, for the purpose of his enjoyment and to enhance the quality of his life in some way. In sport we enjoy many things: the competition, the challenge, test of skill and courage, the physical movement and so on. All the different activities have some point to them.

The point of mountain climbing may be to 'get to the top' or to test skill and character on a new, difficult route; of archery to hit the gold; and of a game, to win. For all athletes there is the challenge of succeeding in the particular point of their chosen sport.

Fundamentally, the main point of sport is *enjoyment* and consequently it would seem to negate the whole purpose of sport to try to win at the expense of enjoyment. Any behaviour that lessens the enjoyment of sport in any way might, therefore, be considered to be undesirable and to be avoided if possible. If athletes adopted certain moral attitudes undesirable behaviour would certainly be avoided. And it is only right and proper that they should adopt certain moral attitudes, for sport entails social relationships and the principles which govern behaviour in any social relationship apply also to those in sport. Morality is essentially concerned with how people behave towards each other in all aspects of life. It determines what sort of attitude is appropriate in a game. Hence it would be expected that players should show some *respect for their opponents and partner, fairness, honesty and consideration for their interests* in the game. When people make requests for 'sportsmanship' and the game to be played in the right spirit they are making an appeal that morality should prevail; and rightly so, for in such a context moral attitudes are as much a part of behaviour in the game as determination, concentration, adventurousness, courage and so on. Badminton is a part of the world of sport and has something to do with enhancing the quality of life for those who participate in it. If not, the game would hardly seem worth playing.

We can summarise this part of the discussion by concluding that certain attitudes are logically intrinsic to the game and operate as the appropriate standards which players should try to attain in the 'attitude' aspect of their performance in the game. They include care, pride of performance, love of the game, enjoyment, commitment to the standards, concentration, perseverance, determination, respect and consideration for the other players, fairness and honesty. Such attitudes are central to the game and the basis of all other positive attitudes which may be expressed in the game.

Part Four

Training and Practice

Chapter 9 Preparation and Training for Play

It is not the intention here to provide a complete training programme for players. In fact, the emphasis throughout this part of the book is placed firmly on the development of skill. Yet skill, whether technical or tactical, is partly dependent on fitness. Without a fit body it is unlikely that a player would be able to perform to a high level in some of the situations which arise during play. For example, it is unlikely that any player could leap backwards to twist in the air, smash the shuttle, land lightly in balance and power himself forwards unless he possessed a high degree of flexibility, agility, strength and speed of movement. Furthermore, it is unlikely that he could continue to do this unless he also possessed a highly efficient energy system.

In this chapter I have selected exercises designed to improve certain aspects of fitness related to moving in the game. These are flexibility, strength, speed, power and agility. The exercises will improve skill in moving for they include work on balance and footwork, particularly in the jumping and landing, running, sidestepping, stopping and starting that goes on in the game. The benefits of training the body in these aspects of fitness by completing various exercises will be apparent when carrying out the practices on court. It is important to remember the advice given on pages 144-5 about the relationship of work and rest when performing strenuous exercises. Any form of exercise will require energy from either the aerobic and/or anaerobic energy system and in this respect any training must take the form of 'steady state' work or interval training.

Those readers who want to know how to plan a fitness training programme which includes all the relative aspects of fitness should refer to the books mentioned earlier (pages 144-5).

Exercises for flexibility

Flexibility is the name given to describe the range of movement at the joints in the body. At each joint the bones are connected up in such a way as to allow a certain type and range of movements. The movement occurs when one set of muscles contract and another set extend. Bend your arm at the elbow and you will see your biceps contract while your triceps (the muscles to the rear of your upper arm) extend. This dual relationship of opposite sets of muscles applies to all those muscles which control movement at the joints in the body.

The stretch range of a muscle can be increased by exercise just as the contractile strength can. When the muscle does not stretch to its maximum extent you will find that you have a limited range of movement. Try to touch your toes and you will most probably find that the muscles of your back and the back of your legs feel tight. They need stretching if you want to be able to touch your toes.

There are many ways of developing flexibility. In sports activities it is usually developed in conjunction with strength, for movement only takes place when the muscles contract. Owing to the nature of the movement in many sports, muscles have to contract at speed and against resistance of different sorts. In athletics shot putting is an excellent example of this, whereas in badminton jumping to smash demands rapid contraction of the leg muscles to push off from the floor. In most of the exercises that follow, the contractile strength of the muscles is developed in conjunction with muscle stretching. Muscle strength is used to stretch their opposite muscle groups and enable the player to increase his range of movements at the joints. The method used is called 'slow stretching'. It is recommended by physiotherapists and exercise physiologists as a safe and effective way of extending the stretch range of muscles at the joints.

You will most probably find them boring to do. I do, for I would much rather swing my limbs around in rhythmic fashion to music. But I have found from experience that that is nowhere near such an effective means of achieving greater flexibility. What you must do is get down to the work and discipline yourself to exercise regularly. If you do you might just find yourself less prone to injury and able to perform to a higher level of play, in the sense that you will be able to move and reach for shots with an ease that you never thought was possible.

In addition to increasing the range of movements at the joints, 'slow stretching' is valuable as a method of warming up before any strenuous exercise, in fitness training or on-court practice and play. It is absolutely vital that all players do this. I asked a physiotherapist of thirty years' practical experience with top class athletes from all sports about the importance of 'slow stretching exercises.' We discussed their value: how they increase the range of movements at the joints, reduce the risk of muscle injury (torn muscle tissue, torn tendons and damaged ligaments) and how they prevent the occurrence of later injuries which appear gradually because of the nature of some sports. For example, games such as badminton and other racket sports are one-sided body games. The players are usually either right-handed or left-handed. There is a tendency in play to stretch the muscles more on one side of the body than the other. One side of the body usually gets worked and stretched more than the other side which can be neglected. The body is used asymmetrically. Over a long period of time the player finds that he cannot get away with this unequal use of muscles and injuries begin to occur as a direct result. Then the player experiences pain, discomfort and restricted movement. He ends up visiting physiotherapists to sort himself out. I know this because I am myself being 'sorted out' with a right-side neck and related shoulder injury which is the direct result of thirty years of right-sided tennis, badminton and swimming front crawl. I might have avoided much of this if I had performed slow stretching exercises daily, using both sides of the body on each exercise to ensure symmetry in the stretching and strengthening of the muscles. I left it rather late to realise that these exercises *should be performed daily if possible and always as part of the training, practice and competition warm-up, and rehabilitation after injury to the muscles.*

My friend the physiotherapist insisted that if I intended to write about 'slow stretching' exercises I must make that point most firmly. He also emphasised that I should make it very clear how to perform the exercises properly to obtain maximum effect. He believes that many athletes do stretching exercises without really stretching as far as they could and so never achieve their full range of movement. When I think of many badminton players I know I am inclined to agree with him. Let us take the first one below and explain how to perform a stretching exercise properly.

1. The neck joint (a) *Head turning* (see fig. 165). Stand or sit upright with your

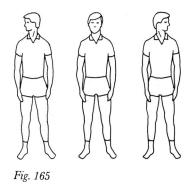

Fig. 165

head properly balanced on your shoulders in a neutral position. Turn your head slowly to the right until you feel the muscles on the left side of the neck begin to tighten (a pulling feeling). You have now arrived at the point where you cannot turn your head any further – or think you cannot. Now you must try to turn it further and stretch the muscles on the left side of your neck even more to do so. That is what you are aiming to do each time. *Extra stretch equals extra distance.* To do this you *press* your head round further using your right neck muscles to do so. *Press hard that extra distance for about 3-5 seconds* and then *release* the strain and effort for several seconds. Begin again and continue until you have completed 5-10 repetitions. Then *repeat the exercise on your left side to ensure symmetry.* Turn your head slowly to the left and begin pressing.

Note: If you feel too much tension in your neck muscles after you release then shake your head lightly to 'loosen' the muscles. It is a good policy to 'shake out' in this way to 'loosen' muscles after any of the following strenuous stretching exercises.

Now if you turn your head from side to side after the stretching exercise you should find that you can move it further with greater ease than before. You should experience a similar feeling in the movement at any joint after doing the exercise.

You might find some books and articles recommend 'slow stretching' for a period of between 10-20 seconds. I think that this is both too long and quite unnecessary. It is unlikely that a young player or an unfit person could maintain the muscle strength to stretch muscles for this period of time. It is also quite probable that the muscles could go into spasm which is something you do not want to experience. It is quite sufficient to stretch for about three seconds only and do more repetitions if you want to.

There are numerous exercises for all parts of the body. If you want to obtain some idea of the full range then arrange to visit a ballet, modern dance or olympic gymnastics class performing their stretching exercises. For now, learn the exercises included here which have been arranged in order to allow you to work systematically through the different joints of the body. Once you have learned these and grasped the general idea you can quite easily make up your own.

(b) *Head side-leans* (see fig. 166). Position as before. Sit or stand upright. Lean the head to the right until you feel the muscles tightening on the left of the neck .That is the limit of your range of movement. Now press your head further over to the right, using muscle strength to do so. Maintain the pressing for 3-5

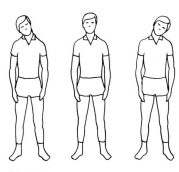

Fig. 166

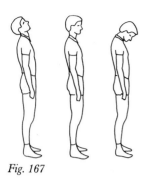

Fig. 167

seconds and then release. Complete about 10 repetitions. Now repeat on the left side.

(c) *Head forwards and backwards leans* (see fig. 167). Position as before. Tilt the head forwards, chin towards your chest, until your feel the muscles tightening at the back of your neck. Now press further for about 3-5 seconds. Do 10 repetitions or more. Repeat the exercise but tilt the head backwards until you feel the muscles at the front of your neck begin to tighten. Now press further for about 3-5 seconds. Release. Complete 10 repetitions or more.

2. The trunk

Fig. 168

(a) *Trunk twisting* (see fig. 168). Stand upright or sit on a stool. Fold your arms. Twist to the right as far as you can move. Now press further for about 3-5 seconds. Release. Complete 10 repetitions. Repeat with twisting to the left.

(b) *Trunk leaning* (see fig. 169). Stand upright with arms by your side and palms facing inwards towards your legs. Lean over to your left, reaching down with your left hand and allowing your right hand to slide up the body and your right elbow to bend. Now press further down for 3-5 seconds. Release. Complete 10 repetitions. Repeat on the right side.

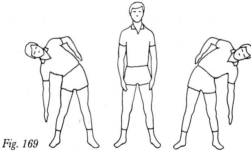

Fig. 169

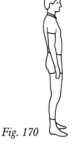

Fig. 170

(c) *Trunk bending* (see fig. 170). Stand upright, legs straight and knees pressed back. Bend forwards, allowing your hands to hang down in front of you. Now press further and try to reach further down with your hands. Hold for about 3-5 seconds and release. Complete 10 repetitions.

(d) *Trunk arching* (see fig. 171). Stand upright with legs apart, hands resting on your hips. Arch backwards, allowing your knees to bend forwards and your head to tilt backwards. Press further for 3-5 seconds. Release. Complete 10 repetitions.

(e) *Trunk arching* (see fig. 172). Lie face down on the floor. Place your palms on the floor by your chest. Arch backwards while looking upwards and using your arms to push your chest further

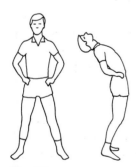

Fig. 171

Fig. 172

away from the floor. Press further for 3-5 seconds. Release. Complete 10 repetitions.

3. The shoulder joint

(a) *Arms upwards backwards press* (see fig. 173). Stand or sit upright. Lift your arms straight and vertical above your head with palms facing forwards. Press backwards and maintain the pressing for 3-5 seconds. Release. Complete 10 repetitions.

Fig. 173

Fig. 174

Fig. 175

(b) *Arms sideways backwards press* (see fig. 174). Stand or sit upright. Extend your arms out sideways with palms facing down. Press arms backwards and increase the pressing further for 3-5 seconds. Release. Complete 10 repetitions.

(c) *Bent arm backwards press* (see fig. 175). Sit or stand upright. Bend and lift the arms back in the preparation-for-the-smash position. Press backwards further for 3-5 seconds. Release. Complete 10 repetitions.

Fig. 176

4. The hip joint

(a) *Forward stretching* (see fig. 176). Sit upright on the floor with your legs together, straight ahead. Press your knees down to the floor. Slide your palms down your legs and try to reach your feet and beyond while you press your head down to your knees. Press further for 3-5 seconds and release. Complete 10 repetitions. This exercise also stretches the lower muscles of the back as well as the back muscles of the upper leg.

(b) *Side stretching* (see fig. 177). Sit upright with straight legs positioned apart, knees pressing down to keep the legs straight. Place your palms on the ground just behind your hips. Press your legs further apart and keep pressing for 3-5 seconds. Release. Complete 10 repetitions.

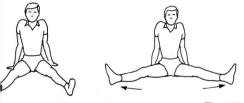

sitting position

Fig. 177

sitting position

Fig. 178

(c) *Side stretching with forward stretching* (see fig. 178). Sit upright with legs apart and knees pressing down. Lean forwards with your palms sliding forwards along the ground. Try to press your trunk to the ground as you press your legs outwards. Press for 3-5 seconds and release. 10 repetitions.

(d) *Hurdle stretch* (see fig. 179). Sit on the ground with one straight leg in front of you and the other leg bent, placed to the side and behind you. Press your legs down to the ground. Lean forwards and slide both hands down the front leg to reach your foot. Press further for 3-5 seconds and release. Complete 10 repetitions. Repeat with the positions of the legs reversed.

Fig. 179

Fig. 180

(e) *Side splits* (see fig. 180). Stand upright with your legs apart, as wide as they will go. Press the knees back to make the legs straight. Hold on to a support if necessary. Press the legs down and outwards as you try to push them further apart. Hold for 3-5 seconds and release. Complete 10 repetitions.

Fig. 181

(f) *Forward splits* (see fig. 181). Use a support if necessary; two chairs or the floor will do. Stand with your feet apart in a forward and backward position. Make sure that the front toes are pointing forwards and the rear toes are pointing to the side (at right-angles to the front foot). Place your hands on the chairs positioned on either side of you, making sure your arms are vertical. Push your legs further apart while lowering yourself and taking some of your body weight on your arms. Once your legs are as far apart as they will go press further and allow some of your bodyweight to

Fig. 182

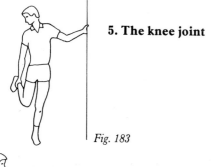

5. The knee joint

Fig. 183

Fig. 184

assist you in pressing down. Hold for 3-5 seconds and release. Complete 5 repetitions and change the positions of the legs. Repeat.

(g) *The lunge* (see fig. 182). Stand upright as for forward splits. Lower your upright trunk by bending the front knee. Keep the rear leg straight and the front foot flat on the floor. Lower yourself into a deep lunge and press downwards, making sure that you keep your trunk and head upright. Hold for 3-5 seconds and release. Complete 5 repetitions and then change over the legs. This exercise also increases the range of movements at the ankle joint if you keep your front foot flat on the floor and make sure that your knee bends over the foot.

(a) *Standing knee bend* (see fig. 183). Stand upright. Bend your right knee behind you. Grasp the ankle with your right hand to assist you to bend the knee further. Bend and pull with the hand for 3-5 seconds and release. 10 repetitions. Change over and repeat with the left leg.

(b) *Deep squat* (see fig. 184). Stand upright. Bend your knees and lower yourself into a deep squat position. Allow your heels to come off the ground. Rest your fingers on a chair or wall to aid balance if necessary. Press down for 3-5 seconds and release. 10 repetitions.

(c) *Knee extend* (see fig. 185). Sit on the floor with your legs stretched out in front of you. Tense your thigh muscles and press your knees down to the floor. If you extend the whole leg and press hard your heels should leave the floor. Hold for 3-5 seconds and release. Complete 10 repetitions.

Fig. 185

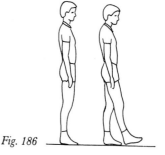

Fig. 186

(d) *Knee extend* (see fig. 186). Stand upright. Lift your right leg forwards until the foot leaves the ground. Tense your leg muscles and press the knee back locking the leg quite straight. Hold for 3-5 seconds and release. 10 repetitions. Change legs.

6. The ankle joint

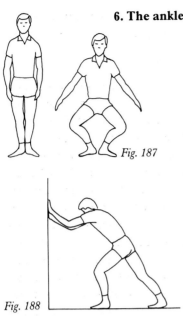

Fig. 187

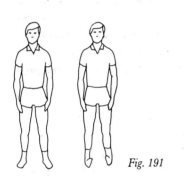

Fig. 188

Fig. 191

(a) *Plié* (see fig. 187). Stand upright with feet together though turned outwards about 45°. Keep the trunk and head upright and bend the knees to lower you. This one has the effect of seeming to make the bottom stick out. Keep your feet flat on the floor. When you feel the muscles are tight at the back of the lower legs, press down further. Hold for 3-5 seconds and release. 10 repetitions.

(b) *Wall press* (see fig. 188). Stand upright with one foot in front of the other. Place your hand against a wall at arm's distance away from your front foot. Lean forwards and press your rear heel away from you until you feel the muscles tightening at the back of your rear leg. Press further for 3-5 seconds and release. 10 repetitions. Change legs.

(c) *Sit upright on the floor with legs stretched out in front of you* (see fig. 189). Press the knees down to the floor and pull the feet and toes towards you. Maintain a strong pull for 3-5 seconds and release. 10 repetitions.

Fig. 189

Fig. 190

(d) *Sit as in the previous exercise* (see fig. 190). Extend the feet and toes away from you. Press away firmly for 3-5 seconds and release. 10 repetitions.

(e) *Outward press* (see fig. 191). Stand upright. Roll your feet over so that the soles face each other and the weight is supported on the outer surface of each foot. Use a chair or wall to support some of the body weight if necessary. Press for 3-5 seconds and release. 10 repetitions. This exercise can be performed with each foot in turn. It can be done in the sitting position.

Exercises for speed

Speed of movement is closely related to muscle strength. If you want to move quickly your muscles must be able to contract quickly. How quickly they contract depends on how well you have developed the 'fast twitch' muscle fibres and what amount of resistance you must overcome. For example, if you intend to jump sideways to intercept a shuttle in the midcourt you need strength in the leg muscles to propel your body upwards against the downward pull of gravity. The contractile strength of the 'fast twitch' muscle fibres must be developed for this sort of explosive jump.

Speed of movement is also clearly related to flexibility. If you strive to reach a shuttle in the forecourt and perform a deep lunge to do so, you might find that in your effort to reach the shuttle you lunge deeper than your muscles will permit. The stretch range of the muscles has not been increased sufficiently. You might have missed exercising for a few days. This happens and the result is excessive stretching of the muscles for which they are not prepared. Something tears and you end up with an injury. The exercises below will develop strength as you perform them. They will not develop flexibility. For that you must work on flexibility exercises and if you do not you will not obtain the full benefit from these speed exercises. You will have to work well within your muscle stretch range in order to avoid injury. Be advised. Complete your flexibility exercises and do a proper warm-up before you commence the following speed work exercises and the later exercises on power, strength and agility.

One final comment. The·exercises entail much jumping and travelling on the floor of the court or some other space. In a game you would perform these actions while your attention is focused on the shuttle or your opponent. Do not look at the floor when you do these exercises. Keep your attention focused forwards and learn to sense where you are in relation to the floor or any other obstacle through the muscles and by peripheral vision (see page 171).

1. Fast feet and legs Most of these exercises will develop foot and leg speed, for all travelling entails the use of the feet. The exercises here do not involve travelling but simply speed work in one place.

(a) *Patter steps.* Stand upright with the weight resting on the balls of your feet. Prepare yourself and then commence running on the spot with very fast small light steps, the feet hardly leaving the ground. Do this for 5 seconds and rest for 10-15 seconds. Complete 5 repetitions or more.

(b) *Astride jumps.* Stand upright as in the previous exercise. Prepare yourself and then commence astride jumping very fast. Your knees remain flexed throughout and the feet just skim the ground. Work for 5 seconds and rest for 10-15 seconds. 5 repetitions or more.

(c) *Scissor jumps.* Stand upright with one foot in front of the other, balanced evenly between your feet. Knees are flexed and weight on the balls of your feet. Prepare yourself and then change the feet position very rapidly continuously for 5 seconds. The knees remain flexed and the feet skim the ground. Rest for 10-15 seconds. 5 repetitions or more.

(d) *Knee raising.* Stand upright with weight resting on the balls of your feet. Prepare yourself and then begin sprinting on the spot snapping your knees up as fast as possible. Quick light steps. Work for 5 seconds and rest for 10-15 seconds. 5 repetitions or more.

2. Explosive start

One of the most important requisites in badminton is the speed of acceleration from a stationary position to travel to some other part of the court. Many players are of equal ability in travelling at speed once they have reached maximum speed. The great players, however, like good sprinters, are quick off the mark. This ability can be improved with practice. Key features are good balance and posture, concentration and good technique. The speed of the first step and the push-off (the simultaneous drive into the ground away from the spot by the supporting foot) are crucial. The first group of exercises helps to improve the speed of the first step; the second group, the step and the push-off.

Note: in badminton it is usual for players to make the initial step with the same side foot as their racket hand: thus right-handed players step out on their right foot and left-handed players with their left foot. All these exercises are for right-handed players and therefore relate to the right foot unless stated otherwise; left-handed players should reverse the exercise to suit their movements.

One-step exercises

(a) *Stand in the front defence stance* (see plate 12). Trunk and head upright, knees flexed and weight resting lightly on the balls of your feet. Prepare yourself. Step towards the right forecourt, place your foot down and then push back into the front defence stance. The knees remain flexed throughout and the foot skims the ground. Perform this 5 times without stopping, as fast as possible.

Perform the same exercise in the following directions: right midcourt, right rearcourt, left forecourt, left midcourt, left rearcourt. It is easier and clearer if the directions are illustrated with a sign, as I will do with the remaining exercises.

• represents the centre of the court and your starting position.

represents the direction and corner of the court from the centre if you are facing the net.

shows the court and the direction of travel.

The exercise you have just performed is shown below in this notation.

It will be obvious once you perform them that to take one step towards the left rearcourt, midcourt or forecourt causes you to pivot or twist round to your rear or in front. It might help to carry a racket to practise the movement with the preparation for a stroke at the same time.

(b) *Combination steps.* In the game you often have to step in one direction, return to a stationary position and step out in a new direction. Complete the facing exercises. Each is a two-step exercise. Perform 3 repetitions as fast as possible, i.e. step, return — step, return, three times.

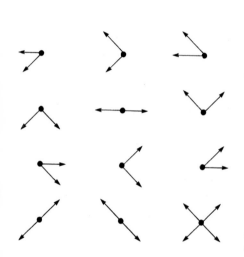

One-step and push-off exercises

The previous exercises concentrated on the *step*, prior to sprinting or jumping to a new position in the court. There are also occasions when the player must thrust away from the spot as he takes an extended stride to reach the shuttle. This action can be performed from a stationary position, as happens when you are defending and make a sudden lunge to reach a smash or fast drop shot, and also while you are travelling, when you push off and leap forwards in a giant stride to hit the shuttle from the top of the net. All these actions are dependent on the explosive movement of the push-off and the outward speed of the stepping leg.

I will describe the first exercise and then illustrate the additional ones in the notation given above.

(a) *Stand in the front defence stance.* Prepare yourself with knees flexed, ready to stretch away from the spot. Push down into the floor as you extend the rear leg rapidly and stride out onto the right foot. (Your left foot — the big toe — remains in contact with the ground in this exercise: see plate 41.) Land and push back to recover into the defence stance. Repeat 5 times as fast as possible.

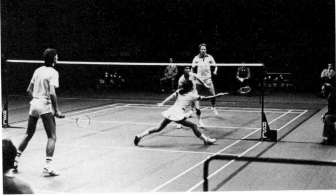

Plate 41. Karen Chapman pushes off her rear foot as she stretches out to make a reply.

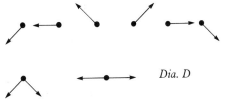

Dia. D

It assists the quality of the movement to prepare as if to hit the shuttle each time you step out.

Select from the facing exercises. Complete 5 repetitions of each exercise.

3. Trunk and shoulder twists

Much of the force used to hit a shuttle is related to the speed and extent of rotation in the trunk and shoulders. Certainly the readiness to hit a shuttle is related to the speed of preparation of the racket, which for high shuttles does require rotation of the trunk and shoulders, to the right for forehand and 'round the head' strokes, and to the left for backhand strokes. The speed of preparation can be improved with practice.

(a) *Stand upright with racket held in the attack position in front of the body.* Tense the muscles of your bottom and legs, so immobilising the lower half of your body. Prepare yourself. Twist to the right to prepare to hit a shuttle. Return to the starting position. Do this 10 times as fast as possible. Rest and repeat for backhand strokes. Remember to keep the muscles tensed in the bottom and legs throughout the exercise.

4. Hip swings

During a game you will always try to be in balance, that is with your hips centred between your feet, even though your shoulders might be well forward of your feet, or your bottom might 'stick out' behind them. At times you have to be prepared to move out of balance, as when you launch yourself backwards to smash a shuttle which has got behind you. Then you must hit the shuttle and somehow adjust your balance very quickly to land with your feet in position to allow you to push forwards immediately. There is much movement of the feet from one side of the hips to the other, i.e. either in front or behind or to the right or the left. The following practice is designed to improve the speed at which you make the adjustment into balance.

(a) *Stand in the defence stance,* knees flexed and trunk and head upright. Lean forwards more so that your shoulders are well ahead of your feet (see fig. 192). This is the starting position. Prepare yourself. Jump forwards with both feet skimming the

Fig. 192   Fig. 193

Fig. 194

ground to place them in front of you (see fig. 193). Perform this action, swinging both feet forwards and backwards behind and in front of your hips, for 10 repetitions.

(b) *Stand in the defence stance as above* (see fig. 194). This time the exercise is to swing your feet from one side to the other, from the right to the left continuously for 10 repetitions. Prepare yourself. Jump off both feet to place them to your right side and then jump to swing them across to your left side. Do this continuously as fast as you can.

5. Fast hands

Speed of hitting is partly dependent on how fast you can move your hands. This is particularly so for work in the midcourt and forecourt when engaged in a speed rally. The hand operates mainly from the wrist joint which is constructed to allow a range of movements. Hold your hands in front of you with the palms facing one another. You will find that you can move the palms forwards and backwards, the little finger side of the hand up and down, and you can rotate the hands. Badminton hitting usually comprises a mixture of all three types of movement with the main movement being the sideways movements of the hand (between the little finger and the thumb) and a partial rotation of the hand.

The extent of movement possible at the joint depends on how much the muscles will stretch, and the speed of movement is dependent on the contractile strength of the 'fast twitch' muscle fibres. An excellent exercise for hand speed is 'chopping'.

(a) *Chopping*. Hold your hands out in front of you with arms flexed and palms facing. 'Chop' with your hands, up and down as fast as you can. Do this for a count of 5 seconds and then rest. Complete 10 repetitions. You can practise this movement at any time. The more you work on the hands the more you will stretch the muscles at the wrist joint and develop speed.

Exercises for power and strength

The exercises below are mainly for work on the legs and entail much jumping and landing. Such activity requires good balance and so it is important that good posture is maintained when performing them. An upright trunk and head balanced on the spine (not tilting forwards or backwards) is essential. For good posture, strong abdominal muscles and back muscles are required to keep the trunk in balance. Sit-ups and back strengthening exercises should be an expected part of general fitness work in a training programme. The landings should be light to reduce the chance of injury and to aid recovery speed. When you do these exercises think about how you do them and make every effort to land lightly. It helps to land on the balls of the feet and to use the strong leg muscles to soften the landing. In these exercises your legs function as springs to thrust you away from the gound, and as shock absorbers to cushion the landing. So concentrate, work hard and you will become a better mover on the court.

Note: Do not do these exercises without a thorough warm-up.

1. Two-feet take-off

(a) *Rebound jumps* (see fig. 195). Stand upright with knees slightly flexed and weight evenly balanced on the balls of your feet. Prepare yourself. Jump upwards, land, do a small rebound jump as a preparation for another higher jump. The flight pattern of the jumps is shown below. Complete 10 rebound jumps trying to get higher on each jump.

Fig. 195

(b) *Rebound tuck jumps* (see fig. 196). These are sometimes named 'double knee jumps'. The exercise is similar to the previous one but now the knees are 'snapped' up to the chest on each high jump before landing and doing the transition rebound jump. Complete 10 tuck jumps.

(c) *Tuck jumps.* The jumps are now performed without the rebound action. Prepare youself. Perform consecutive tuck jumps, i.e. 'jump, land lightly, jump, land, jump, land . . .' Snap the knees up to your chest on each jump. 5-10 repetitions.

(d) *Pike jumps* (see fig. 197). This jump is similar to a tuck jump in that it is continuous without a rebound on landing. Prepare yourself. Jump up raise your legs straight and apart in front of you as you reach forwards to touch your toes. Land and repeat continuously. 5-10 repetitions.

Note: Do not do this exercise unless you are very flexible in the legs and lower back and have also completed a thorough warm-up.

Fig. 196

_ Fig. 197

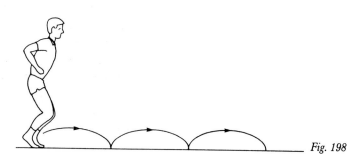

Fig. 198

(e) *Two-footed long jumps* (see fig. 198). The intention here is to jump with feet together as far as you can travel on each jump. Prepare yourself and begin jumping for distance. Complete 5 consecutive jumps without stopping.

(f) *Two-footed high jumps* (see fig. 199). The intention here is to jump for height and distance. These can be performed with or without a rebound jump. The directions: forwards and sideways. Prepare yourself. Complete 5 forward high jumps. Rest. Complete 5 high jumps to the right. Rest. Complete 5 high jumps to the left. Rest. It might make it more interesting if you set up obstacles to jump over, e.g. skittles, chairs, lines on the floor. Take care if jumping over a solid obstacle.

Fig. 199

(g) *Vertical smash jumps.* The intention here is to jump for height and mime the smash action. These can be performed with or without a rebound jump. Complete 5 consecutive jumps on the spot and then 5 in the following directions:

Dia. E

Perform a rebound jump to return to the starting position each time you jump away from the spot.

2. Single-foot take off (a) *Lunge jumps.* The intention here is to spring from the push-off foot to the stepping foot and spring back again from the stepping foot to the push-off foot. This is performed as a continuous sequence of jumps from one foot to the other. Perform in the direction shown. Try to increase your distance on each jump. Jump to the left side of the court to land on the left foot. Complete 10 repetitions.

Dia. F

(b) *Hopping.* Hop for distance and height. Continuous hops. Right foot−5 hops; left foot−5 hops. Complete 2 repetitions.

Exercises for agility

Agility is one of the most important fitness components in badminton. It entails speed, power, strength and flexibility. A player may possess each of these components to a high degree but unless he can co-ordinate them all within the *agility* factor he will always be lacking in his ability to move well on the court. A high level of agility is a key factor in badminton for the game demands so much of it from the players: the quick sudden changes of direction, the scrambles to retrieve a situation, the twists and turns, the stopping and starting, the quick footwork and adjustments in the step pattern to get into the correct hitting position, and central to all this−a fine feel for balance. These features of the game are all a consequence of agility. So how can we develop it? Like everything else in the game we can develop it by playing, if the pace is fast enough and the player is up to the standard of play. It can be developed in general in other games. Netball, basketball, football and rugby require a high degree of agility, as do tennis and squash. Childrens' playground games of dodge ball, tag and variations on chasing each other are early ways of learning to be agile (these are all reasons why children should be encouraged to play a variety of games in their schools' physical education or sports programme). But if a player does not possess agility to a high degree then the following exercises may contribute towards that development. It will be further improved in play as he becomes more equipped to contend with more difficult situations in the game.

1. Fast feet (see fig. 200) The intention here is to sprint between chairs placed close together. The closeness of the chairs forces an abrupt change of direction, i.e. to run, check the momentum and push off in a new direction. The pathway zigzags rather than curves as would happen with the chairs some distance from each other.

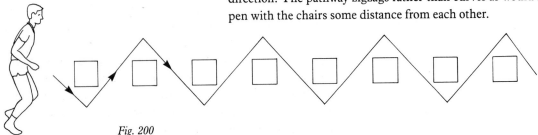

Fig. 200

(a) *Get ready in the starting position at the end of the column of chairs.* Run between the chairs as fast as possible by dodging through them until you reach the end. Rest as you walk back to begin again. Complete 5 repetitions.

(b) *Repeat the exercise but this time travel backwards.* You will be able to see the chairs out of the 'corner of your eye' as you travel. Take care and your speed will increase as you practise.

(c) *Sideways travelling.* This time, travel betwen the chairs sideways. Face one way only and lead first with your left side until you reach the end. Return with your right side leading. The pathway will zigzag but your movements will involve you in travelling forwards and backwards to work your way between the chairs (see fig. 201).

Fig. 201

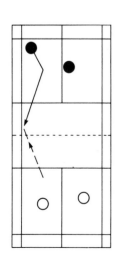

Note: As you improve in these exercises try not to look down at the chairs or obstacle. Look straight ahead and develop your peripheral vision and the ability to feel your way with your feet. To feel your way with your feet is to develop your kinaesthetic sense, to know where you are in the muscles. Peripheral vision is the ability to see things on the periphery of your vision, 'out of the corner of your eye'. Both features are prerequisites of the good player.

2. Diagonal push-offs

It is usual to be sprinting in one direction and have to change direction abruptly in the single action of checking the flow of movement on one foot and pushing off the same foot in a new direction. This occurs when you are returning to the centre midcourt from the right rearcourt and have to change direction to reach the shuttle in the right forecourt (see fig. 202).

This next set of exercises is designed to develop the strength and power to do this effectively.

(a) *Diagonal stepping* (see fig. 203). Stand upright and look straight ahead. The exercise entails running with feet apart while you step from your right side to your left side. Take ten steps at high speed, pushing from side to side on each step. Complete 5 repetitions. Now repeat this backwards. Complete 5 repetitions.

(b) *Diagonal leaps* (see fig. 204). This is a similar exercise to the previous one. The exercise begins with four fast steps, continues with four medium leaps, to four fast steps, to four large leaps to four fast steps and rest. Complete 5 repetitions.

Fig. 202

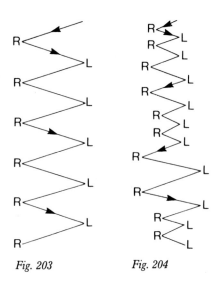

Fig. 203   Fig. 204

Exercises for quality of movement

Any footwork exercise can be performed with the emphasis on the quality of movement. In this context it implies a lightness, a softness of foot, when a player moves around the court with such a quietness of foot that he is barely heard. To do this requires good posture with the trunk held lightly as it 'takes a ride' on the legs. To practise this quality is quite easy if you remember to travel lightly all the time. It may be difficult at first until you become stronger, but as you do and also develop a fine sense for balance and control of your movements about the court, you will begin to move lightly. You will run across the court softly and quickly, change direction by using your strong leg muscles to cushion the shock as you stop abruptly to push off in a new direction. Jumps will be performed with the trunk held lightly in balance as the leg muscles propel you into the air. Landings will be performed again with the trunk held lightly under control and not allowed to slump as your legs bend to absorb the force of the impact with the ground, then having done so extend rapidly to push you away from the spot into some new direction. To achieve the feeling of lightness you must be conscious of it. If you have experienced what I am describing in badminton or any activity, and I am sure you have felt it or seen it in others, then work towards it and try to retain it. Practise running and stopping abruptly, yet lightly. Practise jumping up and landing without a sound and without your trunk falling towards the ground as you land. Practise jumping and landing with your arms held apart and still, so allowing your legs to do all the work.

Skipping is a fine exercise for developing quick light footwork as well as developing the aerobic energy system. First, make sure that you use a good skipping rope. A leather skipping rope is best as it has sufficient weight to rotate through the air quickly, so allowing you to turn the rope faster with the minimum of arm movement. A good 'skipper' uses only his hands to turn the rope. If you do not use a leather rope then make sure you use conventional rope which is flexible and yet heavy enough to turn quickly through the air. Second, ensure that the weight is carried on the balls of the feet which perform a variety of step patterns to a steady rhythm. Rhythm is very important – one reason why boxers skip to jazz or pop music; it is also less boring to skip to music when skipping for long periods of time. Third, do not look down at your feet or the floor as you skip. Look straight ahead and doing so will help you to keep your trunk upright and develop good posture. Fourth, set a period of time for the exercise, or a set number of turns of the rope. I find this latter method quite dull and uninteresting as it distracts attention from the rhythm, especially if you have to count up to a thousand. These days it is easy to use music since cassette tape recorders can be attached to the body. If you cannot skip easily in a rhythm then get a rope and practise hopping to four beats on one foot and then changing to the other foot. It will soon come with practice. Then alter it to light hops to two beats before you change feet. After that vary it with running on the spot, doing double-footed tuck jumps as you try to turn the rope several times before you land again. I believe that Tjun Tjun, the great Indonesian doubles player, used to turn the rope over four times before his feet touched the ground to continue performing numerous repetitions of this exercise.

Work at this and you will find that you will become more alert and lighter on your feet in the game.

Chapter 10 Practices

The practices in this chapter are designed to improve your technical and tactical skill in doubles. Some are included in order to help your individual performance and some to aid your team performance. The routines used can be adapted either to develop some aspect of your fitness, e.g. the anaerobic energy sytem, agility, speed, or to improve your attitude in play. For example, 'going for the kill' can be a risky business as you might make an error, especially in the forecourt when trying to 'kill' the shuttle when a faint chance arises. But if you practise hard at hitting winners from faint chances, your confidence will increase as you become more successful on each attempt. What was once a faint chance becomes a strong possibility. Then in a game when the shuttle is close to the net you can leap forwards to attack it, knowing that you have done so successfully hundreds of times in practice.

It is most important that you understand what aspect of your performance is the main point of each practice. If you are doing ten fast continuous repetitions of a 'backward jump smash and recovery' routine then the emphasis is clearly more on fitness than technique; if the emphasis were on technique there would be a pause between each repetition while you analysed your movements and tried to perfect them each time. There are numerous routines listed in articles and books which do not always make clear what the routine is designed to do, which often results in confusion about the real point of the routine. Make sure that you fully understand the reasons for each routine.

Finally, remember the saying, 'practice makes perfect *what you practise*.' Practise with quality. Decide clearly what aspect of your performance you want to improve; make sure the practice is the right one for you and that you know how to complete the practice properly – then work hard.

The practices given in this chapter take place in the situations which occur in the game, i.e. the rearcourt, midcourt and forecourt. In each situation there are a number of stroke-moves which can be practised—many players already do these in their singles practices. Consequently there are numerous routines available and many more which can be devised. It is possible to work out a practice routine for any stroke-move(s) and the reply(ies) in any situation in the game. (Look at the charts for the complete range of situations and stroke-moves in the game.) These practices are either technical or tactical. *In a technical practice the emphasis is on how you perform with respect to your strokes and footwork. In a tactical practice the emphasis is on what you do to your opponent.* In tactical practices you will work alone or with your partner, practising certain stroke-moves and your response to the replies in certain situations.

The basis of all practice is the *principle of attack,* 'at all times try to create a situation in which it is possible to make a scoring hit'. Each tactical practice ends with an attempt to hit a winner—an attempt which either succeeds or fails. It is to be expected that mistakes will be a normal feature of such practices until you learn to contend with the situation; the greater the risk of failure in your attempt to hit 'a winner in a situation, the more likely you are to make an error. This is particularly so in many of the practices included here, for I have selected or devised those which require speed and adventurous play, expressive of the spirit of attack. But if you practise, undeterred by your mistakes, you will make less mistakes and become a good doubles player. Quality practice can be exciting and stimulating. Enjoy yours!

Technical practices

Most of these practices are designed to improve the ability of one player, either as the attacker or the defender. The main player in the practice is identified as P and the player that assists him as F (the feeder). In some practices there may be two feeders, e.g. a 1 v. 2 practice *(one player* versus *two players).* The practice may be an 'attack and defence' situation or an 'attack and counter-attack' situation, when both sides hit out at each other. A typical example of this is a midcourt sides attack situation. In such practices, although the emphasis may be on one player, it is inevitable that his feeder(s) also improve from the practice they complete in acting as feeders; they will be expected to hit the shuttle at speed and/or to place it with control and accuracy to some place in the court for the *player* to perform his practice.

Technical practices include work on: (a) hitting technique, (b) hitting and travelling technique, and (c) travelling technique.

The best way to improve travelling technique is to practise shadow badminton sequences; that is to perform all the movements required, without the shuttle. Thus if a player finds it difficult to hit at speed whilst travelling and jumping in a particular situation, he should work on his footwork, jumping, landing and recovery until these movements are adequate for the job he has to perform in that situation. If they are, he should not find it difficult to leap up and hit the shuttle. Shadow badminton routines are excellent for improving all aspects of badminton fitness and the quality of movement.*

When the emphasis is on speed in a practice then make sure you achieve speed. Go for it without concern for mistakes. If the practice emphasises leaping forwards, backwards or sideways to attack the shuttle and go for the kill, then do that. Don't hold back and play safe. Throw yourself around the court; commit yourself fully to an honest attempt. If you want to become fast at moving or hitting the shuttle then practise being fast. Do it! If you want to be adventurous then practise being adventurous. The point I want to emphasise here it that to become a fast, powerful, adventurous player you cannot begin slowly and work towards speed. You must hit out and go for speed and learn to control your energy and movements while maintaining this all-out commitment to speed and adventurous play. There are times, of course, when great doubles players play safe, in that they play a percentage move—one that gives nothing away and yet contributes towards creating a situation in which they can eventually hit a winner. It is a mistake to think that the principle of attack means that you must blast away at the opponents regardless of the consequences. To be adventurous does not imply that one is reckless. Good players are patient and will play simple neutral moves until the chance arises for full commitment to hit the winner; then they are prepared to have a go. But they can only do so if they have practised hard and know from their practices that they are capable of hitting winners off faint chances. It is usually the opponents who feel the full force of this attitude to the game, for they feel under constant pressure. They know that the other team will keep coming at them and should they make an error and hit a weak reply they know that the other side will go for the winner, indeed that they will snap up the faintest opportunity to do so. That is pressure. At the top levels of play the ability to apply and

* See my book *Better Badminton for All* (Pelham Books, 1982) for these routines.

maintain pressure is the only factor that separates the winners from the losers. Mind you, a great deal of work goes into developing that ability. The practices which follow will help you to do the same.

Practices for attack – 1   The first group of practices for attack (practices 1-27) emphasise the work of the rear player in a doubles attacking formation.

Rearcourt situations – jump smashes

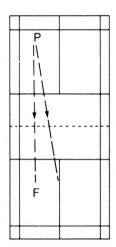

Fig. 205

Practice 1

Aim: To improve the vertical jump power smash.
Players: One player (P) and one feeder (F).
Instructions: Players position themselves as shown (see fig. 205).
F holds 5-10 shuttles ready for single feeding.
F hits a high doubles serve to P.
P performs a vertical jump and hits a power smash.
F allows the shuttle to hit the ground (to let P see the effect of his smash and experience hitting a 'winner').
Work schedule: 10 smashes, 5 to centre, 5 straight. Pause between each smash. Hit the shuttle as hard as you can.

Practice 2

Aim: To improve the vertical jump sliced smash.
Instructions: Complete as for practice 1.

Practice 3

Aim: To improve the vertical jump fast drop shot.
Instructions: Complete as for practice 1.

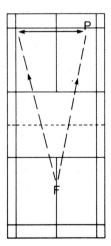

Fig. 206

Practice 4

Aim: To improve the running jump power smash.
Players: One player (P) and one feeder (F).
Instructions: Players position themselves as shown (see fig. 206).
F holds 5-10 shuttles ready for single feeding.
F hits a high doubles serve to the right RC.
P runs across, jumps high and hits a power smash straight or to the centre. He lands and recovers towards the centre.
F hits a high doubles serve to the left RC as P lands and recovers.
P sprints across to jump up and hit a power smash straight or to the centre.

Work schedule: 10 smashes then rest. Complete 1-5 repetitions of the practice.

Note: this practice entails a high degree of fitness. Allow adequate rest—three times the work period. Alternatively, reduce the number of smashes: begin with 4 and work up to 10.

Practice 5

Aim: To improve the running jump sliced smash.
Instructions: Complete as for practice 4.

Practice 6

Aim: To improve the running jump fast drop shot.
Instructions: Complete as for practice 4.

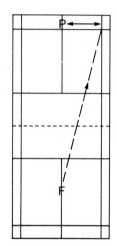

Fig. 207

Practice 7

Aim: To improve the running jump smash; to improve agility.
Instructions: Players position themselves as shown (see fig. 207). F holds 5-10 shuttles for single feeding.
F serves high to the left RC.
P runs across, jumps, smashes, lands and returns to the centre.
F serves high to the same corner as P is travelling towards the centre.
P checks his flow of movement and changes direction to return to the left RC to jump and smash.
Work schedule: 5 power smashes, 5 sliced smashes, 5 fast drop shots.

Practice 8

Aim: To improve the running jump smash; to improve agility.
Instructions: Complete as for practice 7. (F serves to the right RC; the players adjust their positions accordingly.)

Practice 9

Aim: To improve the running jump attack; to improve agility.
Players: One player (P) and one feeder (F).
Instructions: P stands in the centre RC. F positions himself in centre, right or left MC (see fig. 208)
P has a free choice of smash (power or sliced) and the fast drop shot, straight or to the centre.
F has free choice of corner to serve to.
F holds 5-10 shuttles. Single feeding.
Work schedule: 10 smashes. Complete 1-3 repetitions.

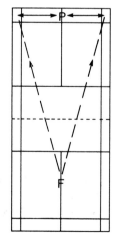

Fig. 208

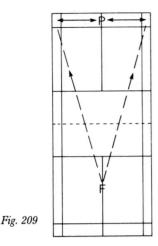

Fig. 209

Practice 10

Aim: To improve the running jump smash; to improve agility and speed.

Players: One player (P) and one feeder (F).

Instructions: Players position themselves as shown (see fig. 209). The players play a continuous rally.

F serves high to the right RC.

P runs, jumps and smashes and returns to the centre RC.

F replies with a lob to the left RC.

P runs, jumps and smashes.

F lobs alternately to each corner.

P smashes to the centre.

Work schedule: 10 smashes. Complete 1-5 repetitions.

Fig. 210

Practice 11

Aim: To improve the running jump power smash; to improve agility and speed.

Players: One player (P) and two feeders (F). 1 v. 2 practice.

Instructions: Players position themselves as shown (see fig. 210). The players play a continuous rally.

Either feeder serves high to RC corner.

P runs, jumps and smashes to either sides or centre of MC.

Power smash only.

F lobs to any RC corner.

Work schedule: 10 smashes. Complete 1-3 repetitions.

Practice 12

Aim: To improve the running jump sliced smash; to improve agility and speed.

Instructions: Complete as for practice 11.

Practice 13

Aim: To improve the running jump fast drop shot; to improve agility and speed.

Instructions: Complete as for practice 11.

Practice 14

Aim: To improve the running jump power, sliced smash and fast drop shot; to improve agility and speed.

Instructions: Complete as for practice 11. (P has a free choice of smash or fast drop shot.)

Midcourt/rearcourt situations – jump smashes

In these practices the player travels diagonally from the mid-court, where he may have been operating as the front or rear player, or 'sides' attacker, to jump towards the corner of the rear-court. He smashes the shuttle, lands and recovers quickly towards the midcourt.

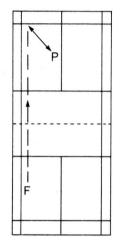

Fig. 211

Practice 15

Aim: To improve the side-on jump smash.

Players: One player (P) and one feeder (F).

Instructions: Players position themselves as shown (see fig. 211). F serves a shallow lob straight to the RC corner.

P steps towards the corner and jumps off his right foot so that he travels through the air with his right side leading. He stays sideways on throughout the action. He smashes the shuttle which is slightly to his rear.* He lands on both feet, rebounds or performs a deeper (knees bend) landing and thrusts away from the spot towards the MC.

F serves again as P arrives in the MC.

*Note: P may have to close the racket face slightly if the shuttle is to his rear. For this he uses a multi-purpose grip or backhand grip, and hits with slice.

Work schedule: 10 smashes, 5 to centre, 5 straight.

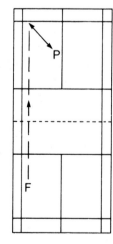

Fig. 212

Practice 16

Aim: To improve the side-on jump smash.

Players: One player (P) and one feeder (F).

Instructions: Players position themselves as shown (see fig. 212). The players play a continuous rally.

F serves to the RC corner.

P steps, jumps and smashes to land and recover quickly towards the MC.

F replies with a lob back to the RC.

Note: In a continuous rally P needs time to recover after each smash. It is advised that P hits the smash with less power and F feeds from a deeper base.

Work schedule: 10 smashes, 5 straight, 5 centre.

Practice 17

Aim: To improve the spin-jump smash.

Players: One player (P) and one feeder (F).

Instructions: Players position themselves as shown (see fig. 211).

F serves a medium high lob to the RC corner.

P steps towards the corner and jumps off his left or right foot into the air to get behind the shuttle. He rotates (spins) as he prepares to hit the shuttle so that he is facing into the court as he smashes. He smashes, lands with his right foot now in front, and runs forwards to the MC. The smash can be a power smash or a sliced smash.

F allows the shuttle to hit the floor and serves another shuttle when P is balanced and ready in the MC.

Work schedule: 10 smashes, 5 straight, 5 centre.

Practice 18

Aim: To improve the spin-jump smash; to improve agility and speed.

Players: One player (P) and one feeder (F).

Instructions: The players position themselves as in fig. 212.

F is in the centre of his side of the midcourt.

P smashes straight or to the centre.

The players play a continuous rally.

Work schedule: 10 smashes. Alternate the direction to the centre and straight.

Practice 19

Aim: To improve the scissor-jump smash; to improve flexibility, strength and agility.

Players: One player (P) and one feeder (F).

Instructions: Players position themselves as shown (see fig. 213). F serves a shallow serve to the left RC corner.

P travels backwards, jumps and twists his shoulders as he arches his back to perform a 'round the head' smash. He lands and recovers to the MC.

F serves again when P is balanced and ready.

Work schedule: 10 smashes, 5 straight, 5 centre. The smashes can be power or sliced.

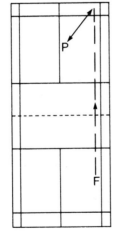

Fig. 213

Practice 20

Aim: To improve the scissor-jump smash; to improve flexibility, speed, strength and agility.

Players: One player (P) and one feeder (F).

Instructions: Complete as for practice 19 except that the players play a continuous rally. P needs more recovery time; P hits with less power; F takes a deeper base.

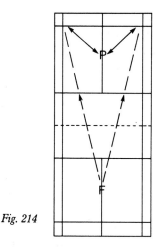

Fig. 214

Practice 21

Aim: To develop a variety of jump smashes.

Players: One player (P) and one feeder (F).

Instructions: Players position themselves as shown (see fig. 214).
F serves alternately to the left and right RC.

P uses a side-on or spin-jump smash from his right RC and a
scissor-jump smash from his left RC. He lands and recovers
quickly to the MC.

F serves as P arrives in the MC.

Work schedule: 10 smashes, all straight.

Practice 22

Aim: To develop a variety of jump smashes; to develop
flexibility, speed, strength and agility.

Players: One player (P) and one feeder (F).

Instructions: The players play a continuous rally.

P smashes to the centre.

P hits with less power and F takes a deeper base.

Complete as for practice 21.

Practice 23

As for practice 22.

F now has a free choice of direction to return P's smash.

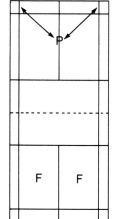

Fig. 215

Practice 24

Aim: To develop a variety of jump smashes; to develop
flexibility, speed, strength and agility.

Players: One player (P) and two feeders (F). A 1 v. 2 practice.

Instructions: Players position themselves as shown (see fig. 215).
The feeders (F) can return the shuttle to either corner of the
RC.

P can smash straight or to the centre and recover to the MC each
time.

P can smash with less power and Fs take a deeper base if
necessary.

Work schedule: 10 smashes. 3 repetitions.

Midcourt situation – jump smashes

The player is operating in the midcourt as the front player or as a
'sides' attacker. He jumps to the side of the court to smash a shuttle which has been lobbed down the line within his jump stretch
reach. He might take off from one foot or two feet and lands on

two feet to rebound back into position. The practice takes the form of a continuous rally to emphasise the jump and rebound-landing action. The player should land lightly and be quick to recover. The 'smash' is more of a quick downward tap, for it is an interception to maintain the attack rather than an attempt to hit a winner. It is either the 'dink' smash (arm outstretched) or a bent-arm smash.

Practice 25
Aim: To improve the quickness and lightness of the jump and recovery; to develop skill in intercepting high shuttles and hitting down quickly and steeply.
Players: One player (P) and one feeder (F).
Instructions: Players position themselves as shown (see fig. 216). F serves a quick lob down the line.
P jumps high to the side with racket prepared, reaches up and taps the shuttle down to F, lands and rebounds towards the MC. F lobs the shuttle back down the line for P to repeat the action. The players play a continuous rally.
Work schedule: 10 smashes to F.

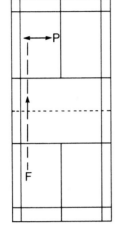

Fig. 216

Practice 26
Aim: To improve the jumping and landing technique; to develop skill in intercepting high shuttles on the right and left sides of the body.
Players: One player (P) and one feeder (F).
Instructions: Players position themselves as shown (see fig. 217). The players play a continuous rally.
F lobs the shuttle alternately to the right and left side of P. P jumps up and taps the shuttle down from his right side and with a 'round-the-head' action from his left side. Lands and rebounds quickly and lightly into position.
Work schedule: 10 smashes.

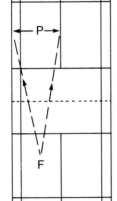

Fig. 217

Midcourt and rearcourt situations – jump smashes

Practice 27
Aim: To improve skill in jumping to perform a variety of smashes from RC and MC situations.
Players: One player (P) and two feeders (F). A 1 v. 2 practice.

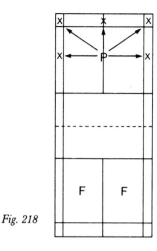

Fig. 218

Instructions: Players position themselves as shown (see fig. 218).
Each feeder holds 3-5 shuttles.

The feeder in the right court serves his shuttles first.

The players play a continuous rally.

F serves a high lob to the MC or RC positions as shown.

P travels and jumps to smash with power or slice anywhere in
the opposite MC (he can try to hit a winner); lands and recovers
into position.

F lobs the shuttle back to P's MC or RC.

P jumps up to smash.

Work schedule: Each rally is continuous play until the rally
breaks down. When it does the appropriate feeder serves another
lob. *The feeders must rally with control* to ensure that P is able to
practise his various jump smashes in the MC and RC. When
each rally breaks down, pause and allow P to get ready before
starting again. Although P must be fit to perform this practice,
the Fs must remember that the emphases is on technique and
not fitness. *Rests are necessary.* With this sort of practice P
should improve his ability as the rear player in doubles.

Practices for attack – 2 The following group of practices (practices 28-46) emphasise the
work of the front player in an attacking formation.

Midcourt situations
Practice 28

Aim: To improve skill in leaping or diving sideways to intercept
a drive or a push; to develop fast racket work; to develop power,
agility and good balance; to develop an adventurous attitude.

Players: One player (P) and one feeder (F).

Instructions: Players position themselves as shown (see fig. 219).
F holds 5-10 shuttles.

F hits the shuttle at medium to fast speed so that it skims the net
and rises towards the MC.

P dives across and attempts to hit it back at speed; he lands,
adjusts his balance and recovers quickly into position.

F serves another fast shuttle when P is ready.

Work schedule: 10 shuttles.

Note: This practice can be repeated with P intercepting and
blocking the shuttle to the FC, though as it is easier to block the
shuttle than to hit it back at speed, the practice is described for a
speed reply. The player operates as a hit-player.

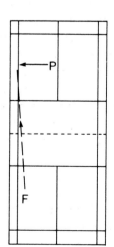

Fig. 219

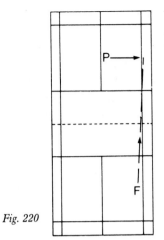

Fig. 220

Practice 29

Aim: As for practice 28.

Instructions: Complete as for practice 28.

The players position themselves as shown (see fig. 220).

P intercepts and hits from the backhand side.

Practice 30

Aim: As for practice 28.

Players: One player (P) and two feeders (F). A 1 v. 2 practice.

Instructions: Players position themselves as shown (see fig. 221).

Each feeder (F) holds 5 shuttles.

One feeder begins and drives a rising shuttle down the line.

P leaps or dives across, hits the shuttle, lands and adjusts his balance to recover in the MC.

The second feeder then hits his shuttle down the line on his side of the court.

P leaps across and hits it, then recovers into position in the MC ready for the next shuttle.

Work schedule: 10 shuttles.

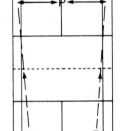

Fig. 221

Practice 31

Aim: To improve skill in fast hitting in the MC; to develop alertness and quick reflexes; to develop concentration.

Players: Two players. 1 v. 1 practice.

Instructions: Players position themselves as shown (see fig. 222).

The players face each other alert and ready to attack.

One player drives the shuttle at the other. It is important to skim the net.

The players rally at speed, hitting the shuttle from in front of the body. The hitting action is a fast tapping action. There is little time for any follow-through of the racket head; the technique is to check the head, so causing a slight rebound of the racket head on impact with the shuttle.

The shuttle is aimed at the opposing player to try to catch him out, e.g. not ready with his racket to counter-attack.

The rally takes the form of a 'slugging' contest.

When the rally breaks down one player serves another shuttle at speed.

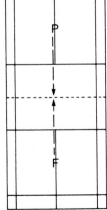

Fig. 222

Work schedule: 10 rallies.

Note: If the shuttle falls below net height a player should make a *push* reply to the midcourt. This will prevent the shuttle rising as it crosses the net.

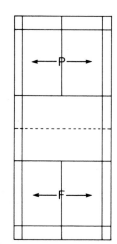

Fig. 223

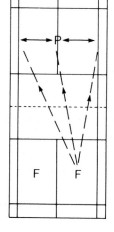

Fig. 224

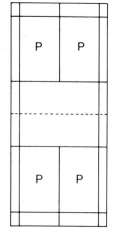

Fig. 225

Practice 32

Aim: To improve skill in fast hitting in the MC; to develop skill in moving and recovering.

Players: Two players. 1 v. 1 practice.

Instructions: Players position themselves as shown (see fig. 223). Complete as for practice 31 except that now the players move each other from side to side. Each aims the shuttle at the other or to the right or left side of the other, a sufficient distance that the other player has to jump or stretch to the side to hit the shuttle. As soon as the shuttle is hit the player moves back into position to cover the reply. The emphasis is on 'hit and move'.

Work schedule: 10 rallies.

Practice 33

Aim: To improve skill in fast hitting in the MC; to develop fast reflexes and speed of recovery.

Players: One player (P) and two feeders (F). A 1 v. 2 practice.

Instructions: Players position themselves as shown (see fig. 224). Feeders hold 5 shuttles each.

The feeder in the right court serves his shuttles first. He drive-serves to skim the net.

The feeders' task is to hit at speed or push the shuttle to the sides or centre of P's MC. They try to get the shuttle past P or hit it at him and force an error.

P 'hits and moves' to cover his court and counter-attacks to force the feeders to miss or make an error.

Work schedule: 10 rallies.

Note: If P is hopelessly out of position and slow to recover, the Fs should hit a slower shuttle to give P time to recover before they speed up the rally again.

Practice 34

Aim: To improve skill in counter-attacking in the MC.

Players: Four players. A 2 v. 2 practice.

Instructions: Players position themselves as shown (see fig. 225). One side act as the servers. Each server holds 5 shuttles.

One server hits a fast drive across the net.

The four players rally at speed until one player hits a winner or forces an error.

The players return into position and the server hits another shuttle.

Work schedule: 10 rallies.

Note: If the shuttle falls short of the MC or drops below net level, the players should push the shuttle to the MC before they speed up the rally again. If one side lifts the shuttle high in the MC the other side can smash for a winner.

Practice 35
Aim: To improve the ability to 'go for the winner'.
Players: One player (P) and one feeder (F).
Instructions: Players position themselves as shown (see fig. 226). F holds 5 shuttles.
F drive-serves to aim the shuttle above P's racket shoulder, about bent-arm smash height (hold a racket and mime the impact of a bent-arm smash to get an idea of how high this is).
P smashes the shuttle at a fast pace towards F's stomach.
F flicks the shuttle up above P in the MC or up in the FC.
P jumps up from the spot to wherever the shuttle may be, smashes a 'winner' and recovers.
F *allows the shuttle to hit the ground.*
P gets ready and F serves another shuttle.
Work schedule: 10 rallies.

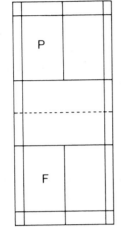

Fig. 226

Practice 36
Aim: To improve skill in counter-attacking in the MC; to improve the ability to 'go for a winner'.
Players: One player (P) and one feeder (F).
Instructions: Players position themselves as in fig. 226).
F holds 5 shuttles.
F drive-serves to aim the shuttle above P at bent arm smash height.
P smashes at a fast pace towards F's stomach.
F counter-hits to skim the shuttle across the net at P.
The players engage in a counter-attacking rally from the MC until one player lifts for the other to smash for a winner, or one player makes an error.
When the rally ends the players get into position and F serves a second shuttle.
Work schedule: 10 rallies. F serves 5 shuttles, P serves 5 shuttles.

Forecourt situations
The practices which follow will develop and improve the skill of the front player as either a hit-man or set-up man. In these practices I have emphasised the role of the player as a hit-man only.

My view is that if a player is quick enough and adventurous enough to attack the shuttle at speed, he should find it relatively easy to perform a softer shot, e.g. the block. I leave it to players and coaches to adapt the practices to develop the skills of the set-up player. The set-up player needs to practise set-up moves as much as the hit-player needs to practise the hit-moves. The practices are continuous rallying unless stated otherwise.

Practice 37
Aim: To develop racket speed in the FC; to develop control and accuracy; to develop quick reflexes.
Players: One player (P) and one feeder (F).
Instructions: Players position themselves as shown (see fig. 227). F hold 5 shuttles.
P stands in the forecourt in the forward attacking stance (see plate 6, page 42).
P must tap the shuttle *as it crosses the net* and is *not allowed* to step back outside the forecourt.
F drive-serves the shuttle to skim the net.
P taps it back at speed and recovers with his racket hand ready for the reply.
F hits the shuttle back at speed and the players rally at speed (as fast as possible) until the rally breaks down.
Work schedule: 10 rallies. 1-3 repetitions.
P performs 5 rallies with a forehand grip and 5 rallies with a backhand grip.
F has a free choice as long as he feeds accurately. This he will do if he watches only the shuttle and not where he is hitting it to. So F senses where the net is and hits the shuttle hard towards it—to skim it.

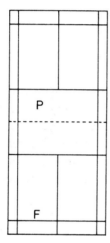

Fig. 227

Practice 38
Aim: To develop racket speed in the FC; to improve skill in travelling in and out of the FC; to improve the ability to 'go for the winner'.
Players: One player (P) and one feeder (F).
Instructions: Players position themselves as shown (see fig. 228). F holds 5 shuttles.
P is behind the service line in a forward attacking stance.
F serves the shuttle and aims it about 12ins (30cm) above the net.
P jump-lunges forwards and upwards to tap the shuttle back to F, lands and rebounds back behind the service line.

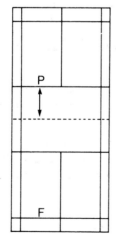

Fig. 228

F hits the shuttle back to the same spot.

P jumps forwards and taps it to F, lands and recovers.

F hits the shuttle back for the third time.

P jumps forwards and hits the shuttle down for a winner from the top of the net, lands and recovers behind the service line. *It is most important that P recovers. He must develop the habit of assuming that the shuttle will always be returned.*

F takes another shuttle and the players repeat the practice.

Work schedule:

(a) 5 rallies – P, forehand grip.

(b) 5 rallies – P, backhand grip.

(c) 5 rallies – P, alternates as F feeds to one side and then the other.

(d) 5 rallies – F has a free choice of which side of P to hit the shuttle.

Practice 39

Aim: To develop fast racket speed in the FC; to develop agility and quick reflexes; to improve the ability to 'kill' the shuttle.

Players: One player (P) and two feeders (F). A 1 v. 2 practice.

Instructions: Players position themselves as shown (see fig. 229).

P stands behind the T in the forward attacking stance.

The feeder in the left court holds 5 shuttles.

F serves the shuttle about 3-6ins (7-15cm) above net height.

P jumps forwards and taps the shuttle to waist height, at or to the sides of the feeders, lands and recovers quickly.

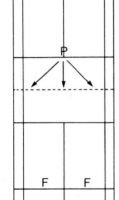

Fig. 229

F returns the shuttle at the same height to the right or left FC.

After the fourth hit of the rally P can attempt to 'kill' the shuttle whenever he decides.

Work schedule: 5-10 rallies.

Midcourt/forecourt situations

Practice 40

Aim: To improve the ability to change from MC to FC attack; to develop speed and agility; to improve the ability to 'go for the kill' in the FC.

Players: One player (P) and one feeder (F).

Instructions: Players position themselves as shown (see fig. 230)

P stands in a forward attacking stance in the MC operating as front player.

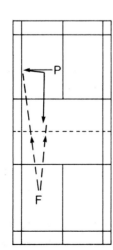

Fig. 230

F holds 5 shuttles.

F drive-serves down the line.

P leaps across and hits the shuttle hard at F and recovers quickly towards the MC.

F blocks the shuttle to the FC.

P changes direction and leaps forwards and upwards to 'kill' the shuttle. He commits himself fully to the 'kill' and then recovers behind the service line to threaten any reply.

F allows the shuttle to hit the floor.

Work schedule: 5 repetitions.

Practice 41

Aim: To improve the ability to change from FC attack to MC attack; to develop speed and agility.

Players: One player (P) and one feeder (F).

Instructions: Players position themselves as shown (see fig. 231). P stands in the forward attacking stance behind the T.

F holds 5 shuttles.

F serves the shuttle about 12ins (30cm) above the net into the FC.

P leaps forwards and upwards and taps the shuttle back to F, and then rebounds back towards the MC.

F drives the shuttle down the line to try to get it past P.

P leaps across and slashes or taps the shuttle back across the net at F or to the centre, then recovers quickly in the MC to cover any replies. *F lets the shuttle fall.*

Work schedule: 5 repetitions.

Note: F must regulate the speed of the shuttle to allow P time to recover and leap across in the MC. F and P can play a continuous rally or F can feed single shuttles depending on his control.

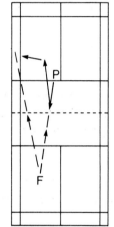

Fig. 231

Practice 42

Complete as for practice 40 but perform the practice with P in the left court hitting backhand stroke-moves.

Practice 43

Complete as for practice 41 but perform the practice with P in the left court hitting backhand stroke-moves.

Practice 44

Aim: To improve the speed of the attack in the FC and MC; to develop agility and flexibility; to develop adventurous play.

Players: One player (P) and one feeder (F).

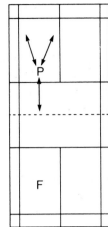

Fig. 232

Instructions: Players position themselves as shown (see fig. 232). The players play a continuous rally or F hits single shuttles. F holds 5 shuttles.

F serves the shuttle above net height in the FC.

P leaps forwards, taps the shuttle to F and recovers quickly behind the service line.

F lobs the shuttle above P whilst he is recovering.

P pivots to place his right foot behind him as the take-off foot to jump backwards and smash the shuttle at F, then lands and recovers.

F blocks the shuttle to the FC.

P leaps forwards and taps it at F and recovers.

F lobs the shuttle above P whilst he is recovering.

P pivots and leaps backwards to smash at F, and recovers.

F blocks the shuttle to the FC.

P leaps forwards, *hits a winner and recovers.*

F *allows the shuttle to hit the floor.*

Work schedule: 5 repetitions.

Practice 45

Complete as for practice 44. This time the practice begins with the feeder serving a lob to the MC for P to smash. The sequence is MC-FC-MC-FC-MC (smash a winner).

Practice 46

Complete as for practice 44. This time the feeder can feed in any order. On the fifth feed the player hits a winner.

Midcourt situations: 'defence and attack' practices

In this group of practices the emphasis is on the defender. Let me remind you that there are a number of variations in defence. First, the player may take up a 'side-on' or 'front' defensive stance. Second, he may adopt a deep, centre, or forward base in which to position himself. Third, he may defend with his racket in low or high defence. Refer again to pages 65-73 if you have forgotten these. There will be opportunities in the practices to try out and develop these variations.

Throughout the practices the defender is the player (P) and the attacker is the feeder (F).

Before we begin the practices let me also remind you that to defend is not a casual business. *In defence you must attack the opponent.* You should adopt a *fighting attitude.* It is hard work. When you hit a high lob, make sure that the attacker remains right at the rear of his court so that his smash is less effective. When you whip the shuttle down the line or cross-court, hit the shuttle too fast and high for the front player to intercept, and too quickly for the rear man to recover and hit a good smash. When you block the shuttle it must be accurate and quick so as to get the shuttle below net level before the opposing front man can attack it. Finally, you should always be alert and ready with your racket to drive back the smash or, at the least, to push it low over the net past the front man in order to gain the attack. There is too much sloppy play in defence in general and not enough work and fight. Players don't want to be defending in the game; they want to be attacking. So, attack and get out of the defensive situation and into an attacking one. Work hard and you will be quite surprised at the effect it will have on your game. Be positive!

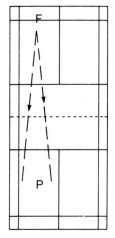

Fig. 233

Practice 47

Aim: To improve the ability to lob to the RC; to improve skill in defending on the forehand and backhand side.

Players: Player (P) and feeder (F).

Instructions: Players position themselves as shown (see fig. 233). The players play a continuous rally.

P serves high to F.

F (a) hits 5 smashes to P's forehand and 5 to P's backhand.

(b) hits 10 smashes alternately to P's forehand and backhand.

(c) hits 10 smashes to either side.

P lobs high and deep to the RC.

Practice 48

Aim: To improve the ability to lob to the RC; to develop a 'fighting attitude'.

Players: One player (P) and one feeder (F).

Instructions: Players position themselves as shown in fig. 233. Players play a continuous rally.

P serves high to F.

F tries to smash a winner or force an error.

P lobs all smashes high and deep to the RC to try to keep F pinned in his RC and away from the net.

Work schedule: 5 rallies.

Practice 49

Aim: To improve the ability to lob to the RC; to develop a 'fighting attitude'.

Players: One player (P) and two feeders (F). A 1 v. 2 practice.

Instructions: Players position themselves as shown (see fig. 234).

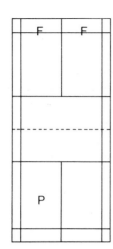

Fig. 234

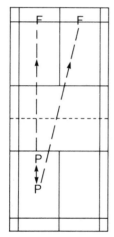

Fig. 235

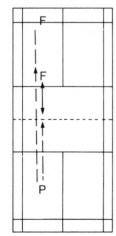

Fig. 236

(a) P stands in the left court.

P serves high to any part of the RC.

F tries to smash a winner in P's left court.

P lobs the shuttle to either RC for Fs to smash.

Work schedule: 5 rallies.

(b) P stands in the right court. Complete as in (a).

Practice 50

Aim: To improve skill in using 'high defence' to lob; to develop speed in moving between centre and forward defence.

Players: One player (P) and two feeders (F). A 1 v. 2 practice.

Instructions: Players position themselves as shown (see fig. 235).

(a) P stands in his left court.

P serves high to the feeder in the court directly opposite him.

F smashes at P who is in centre defence.

P squats and uses 'high defence' to hit the shuttle to the RC diagonally opposite him, then moves forward into forward defence.

F smashes X-court at P.

P hits the shuttle high to the RC directly opposite him and moves back to centre defence ready to receive the straight smash.

Work schedule: 10 smashes.

(b) P stands in his right court. Complete as in (a).

Practice 51

Aim: To improve skill in performing the block; to improve the speed in recovery.

Players: One player (P) and two feeders (F). A 1 v. 2 practice.

Instructions: Players position themselves as shown (see fig. 236).

P serves high to F in the RC.

F smashes at P.

P blocks the shuttle to skim the net and recovers quickly ready to attack.

F (the front man) steps forwards and taps the shuttle at P and then recovers.

P lobs the shuttle up to the RC and prepares to defend.

F smashes; P blocks etc.

Work schedule:

(a) 5 forehand blocks, 5 backhand blocks.

(b) 10 alternate blocks (forehand–backhand).

(c) 10 blocks–free choice of stroke.

Note: P can block the shuttle with the racket head low or high.

Practice 52

Aim: To improve skill in performing the block and the lob; to develop a fighting attitude.

Players: One player (P) and two feeders (F).

Instructions: Players position themselves as shown (see fig. 236). P serves high to the RC and prepares to defend.

F smashes.

P can block or lob.

F (the front man) and F (the rear man) try to hit a winner. They must hit smashes and net taps or kills only (no drop shots).

Work schedule: 5-10 rallies.

Practice 53

Aim: To improve skill in performing 'the drive' return to the smash.

Players: One player (P) and one feeder (F).

Instructions: Players position themselves as shown (see fig. 237). P serves high to F and prepares to defend.

F smashes towards P.

P *steps forward* and meeting the shuttle early drives it horizontally across the net back at F.

F drives the shuttle at P.

P lobs it to the RC for F to smash again.

Work schedule:

(a)   5 smashes to P's forehand side.

(b)   5 smashes to P's backhand side.

(c)   10 smashes alternating forehand and backhand.

(d)   10 smashes – free choice of side.

Note: I have said that P should step forwards to drive the smash. This is not always possible. However, it is important that P meets the shuttle when it is high, to allow him to drive it horizontally across the net at speed.

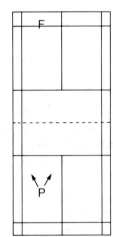
Fig. 237

Practice 54

Aim: To improve the drive and the whip.

Players: One player (P) and two feeders (F). A 1 v. 2 practice.

Instructions: Players position themselves as shown (see fig. 238).

(a)   P stands in the left court.

P serves high to F and prepares to defend.

F smashes at P in the MC.

P drives the shuttle straight or X-court.

F drives it back.

P whips the shuttle straight or X-court.

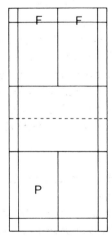
Fig. 238

F smashes. P drives it back . . .

(b)   P stands in the right court. Complete as for (a).
      Work schedule: 10 smashes. Continuous rally.

Practice 55

Aim: To improve the drive, whip and lob.

Players: One player (P) and two feeders (F). A 1 v. 2 practice.

Instructions: Players position themselves as shown in fig. 238.
The players play a continuous rally.
P defends using a drive, whip or lob.
F and F attempt to hit a winner.

Work schedule:

(a)   P in left court. 5 rallies.

(b)   P in right court. 5 rallies.

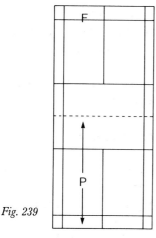

Fig. 239

Practice 56

Aim: To improve speed off the mark in defence; to develop a
fighting attitude.

Players: One player (P) and one feeder (F).

Instructions: Players position themselves as shown (see fig. 239).
P serves high to the RC and prepares to defend.
F can smash, attack clear, or check-smash. He wants to catch P
out and make him late getting to the shuttle in the RC or the
FC.

P must reply as follows:

(a)   lob the smash for F to smash again.

(b)   smash the attack clear. If he cannot do that and must clear
      then he has been too slow and/or weak to 'power' away from
      his defensive stance to the RC. A good defender should be
      able to smash the attack clear.

(c)   meet the check-smash in the FC before the shuttle falls
      below the netting. The closer he meets the shuttle to the
      top of the net the more effective can his reply be.

Work schedule: 10 rallies. Each rally ends after P's reply to the
attack clear or the check-smash. The players get ready and P
serves high to the RC to commence a new rally.

Practice 57

Aim: To improve the ability to defend; to improve speed off the
mark and speed of recovery.

Players: Two players (P) and two feeders (F). A 2 v. 2 practice.

Instructions: Players position themselves as shown (see fig. 240).

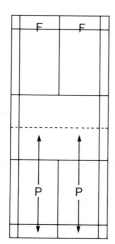

Fig. 240

The players play a continuous rally.

Ps defend and Fs attack.

P in the right court serves high to the RC.

Fs will try to hit a winner or force an error.

Fs can smash, drop or attack clear to either court.

Ps must lift all replies to the RC.

Work schedule: 10 rallies.

Note: The players remain in their own side of the court except for the central area where there may be an overlap and some doubts about who hits the shuttle.

Serving and receiving the serve

In these practices the emphasis is on the receiver. It is expected that players do practise serving, although in my opinion more time and attention could be spent on serving practice. Whenever I stress serving practice I am reminded of the Indonesian player Tjun Tjun who possessed a very fine backhand serve. At the 1977 World Championships in Malmo, I was working one of the England players in practice. Tjun Tjun was practising his backhand serve on the next court for a period of two hours, trying out variations on his low serve and the flick serve. It was not surprising that many rated him as the best doubles player in the world at that time. Just as it is possible to improve the serve with practice it is also possible to improve one's skill as a receiver. Many players need to improve their receiving skill and correct practice would certainly aid this.

Receiving the serve

It is essential that you are balanced and poised to accelerate forwards or backwards as soon as the server hits the shuttle. Balance is attained with good posture, the trunk upright and carried evenly on the legs. Acceleration forwards or backwards is achieved by a rapid extension of the legs as you thrust away from the spot. Let us look at each aspect in turn, beginning with the stance.

The stance   Stand in the receiver's position in the court. Stand upright with straight legs, feet a comfortable distance apart, the front foot pointing forwards and the rear foot pointing to the side, at right-angles to the front foot (see fig. 241). Hold the racket in front of you in the attack position. Now bend your knees, keeping your trunk evenly balanced between your thighs (see fig. 242). You are centred in balance. Hold the position and then slowly sway forwards to allow your weight to move over the front foot. This is the receiving position (see fig. 243).

Getting ready to receive should become a ritual. It is similar to the sprinter getting ready to explode from the starting blocks, i.e. 'Take your marks. Set. Go!' Sprinters practise for hours on end to improve their skill in starting because it is so important to them. It is even more important to a badminton receiver, for he does not have another 100 yards or metres in which to make up for a slow start. A badminton player has about 6ft 6ins (1.98m) distance forwards to travel to hit the shuttle and about 12ft (3.65m) to travel backwards to hit the shuttle. He does not have much time if he wants to make an effective attack against a good server.

Fig. 241   *Fig. 242*   *Fig. 243*

The forward attack As the server hits the low serve, thrust down into the ground to launch yourself *forwards and upwards* to attack the shuttle as it crosses the net. Commit yourself fully (see plate 28, p.99). Practise the action slowly to feel the thrust away from the spot and the drive upwards. When you have the feel of the movement, begin to accelerate until you can launch yourself forwards. Don't worry about the landing and recovery; if you commit yourself fully your body will look after itself.

The backward attack As the server flicks the shuttle above your head, sway backwards while keeping both knees bent. In doing this you will transfer your body-weight backwards over the rear foot (see fig. 244). Now you are in position to thrust away from the spot, backwards in the direction of the shuttle. Your right leg is bent and ready to act as the take-off leg to thrust you *backwards and upwards* into the air. As you transfer your weight onto your rear foot your shoulders twist to prepare the racket for an overhead hit (see fig. 244). Practise the action slowly to get the feel of the movement. When you feel the weight transfer is smooth then quicken it up and take-off the rear foot into a backward jump to mime a smash in mid-flight. Don't worry about the landing. Let yourself 'fly' backwards to smash and allow the body to look after itself on landing (see fig. 245).

Fig. 245   *Fig. 244*

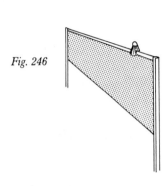

Fig. 246

Fig. 247

Practice 58

Aim: To improve skill in attacking the low serve; to develop explosive power.

Players: One player (P).

Instructions: The player places a shuttle on the net.

Note: Use an old feathered shuttle and jam it on top of the net by the feathers. The base of the shuttle is uppermost (see fig. 246).

The player positions himself to receive serve, as in fig. 243.

P concentrates and explodes *forwards and upwards* to hit the shuttle down off the top of the net.

Work schedule:

(a) 10 shuttles from right court, 5 forehand grip, 5 backhand grip.

(b) 10 shuttles from the left court, 5 each grip. Complete 3 repetitions.

Practice 59

Aim: To improve skill in leaping backwards to receive the flick serve; to develop explosive power.

Players: One player (P).

Instructions: The player positions himself to receive serve. Mimes receiving the flick serve.

Work schedule: Right court, 10 repetitions; left court, 10 repetitions.

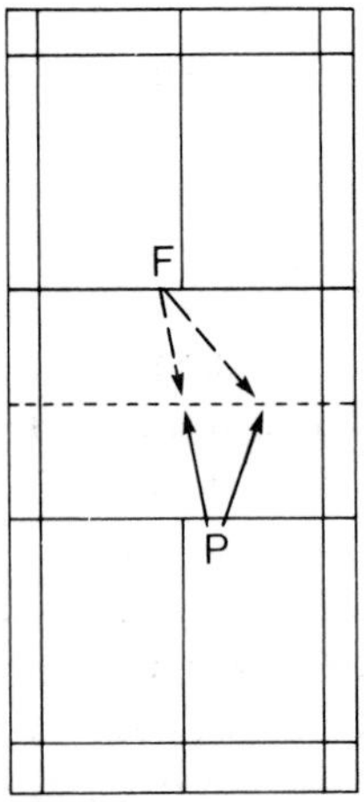

Practice 60

Aim: To improve skill in receiving the low serve.

Players: One player (P) and one feeder (F).

Instructions: The players position themselves in the serving and receiving positions (see fig. 247).

(a) Feeder in right court.

F serves low to centre or side of right court.

P leaps forwards and upwards. Tries to hit the shuttle as it crosses the net.

F allows the shuttle to hit the floor.

P recovers and gets ready to receive another serve.

Work schedule: 10 serves.

(b)   Feeder in the left court. Complete as for (a).

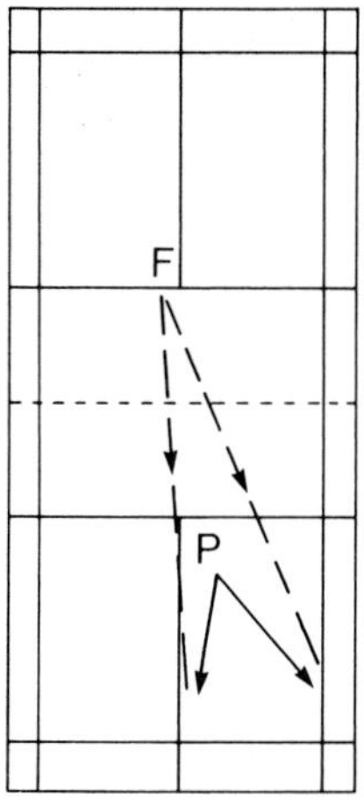

Practice 61

Aim: To improve skill in receiving the flick serve.

Players: One player (P) and one feeder (F).

Instructions: The players position themselves in the serving and receiving positions (see fig. 248).

(a)   Feeder in the right court.

F flick serves to centre or side of right court.

P leaps backwards and smashes. Lands and recovers.

F allows the shuttle to hit the floor.

P positions himself for another serve.

Work schedule: 10 serves.

(b)   Feeder in the left court. Complete as for (a).

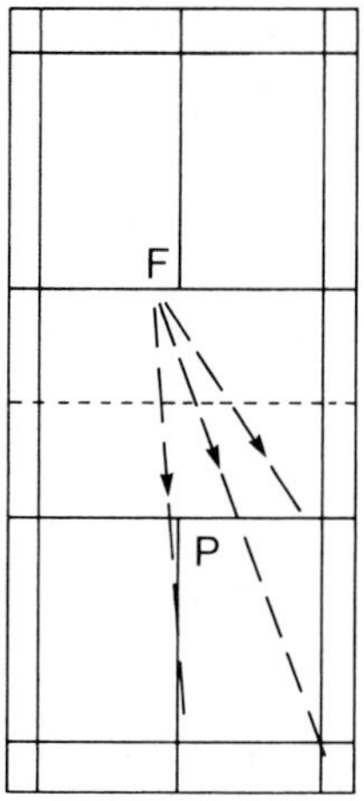

Fig. 248

Practice 62

Aim: To improve skill in receiving the low serve and the flick serve; to develop power and the explosive start.

Players: One player (P) and one feeder (F).

Instructions: Players position themselves in the serving and receiving positions (see fig. 249).

(a)   Feeder in the right court.

F can low serve or flick serve to the side or centre.

P attempts to 'kill' the low serve and smash the flick serve.

Work schedule: 10 serves.

(b)   Feeder in the left court. Complete as for (a).

Fig. 249

Tactical practices

In this group of practices the emphasis is on the positional play of the players as they travel about the court to make their stroke-moves and cover the replies. Much of this aspect of the game has been covered in Chapters 4, 5 and 6. You should be familiar with the many situations that occur during play. In addition, if you work hard at the technical practices you should be able to contend with most of the situations that arise when you play. There are times, however, when you need to practise the moves and positional play in a specific situation. It could be that you are due to play a fast attacking pair and want to speed up on your interceptions in the midcourt as front man. On another occasion you might have played a pair and been caught by their cross-court whip. You and your partner decide to work on the switch of positions as the front man travels back to the rearcourt to deal with the cross-court whip. You devise a practice routine which will help you to improve this aspect of your play together. It does not take much imagination to realise that it is possible to devise hundreds of tactical practices to cover all the situations you experience in play. It would need another book to include them all.

I have selected a few to include here. For the sake of simplicity all the practices commence with the players rallying in a sides attack situation. From that situation the game opens up to various attack and defence formations. I have chosen a few examples to show how they develop and end up with one side hitting a 'winner'. It is important that a tactical practice is simple and ends with a 'winner'. The 'winner' gives a neat, precise, meaningful end to the rally. It helps the confidence of any player if he experiences success, if he hits a winner – even in practice.

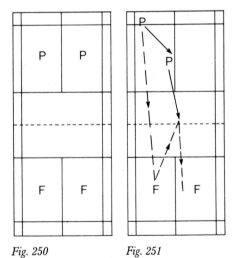

Fig. 250   *Fig. 251*

Practice 63

Aim: To develop the skill of the front man in 'going for the winner'.

Players: Two players (P) and two feeders (F). A 2 v. 2 practice.

Instructions: Players position themselves as shown (see fig. 250).

Ps an Fs rally at fast pace in the MC.

F lobs shuttle to P's right RC.

P (rear man) goes back to smash whilst P (front man) adjusts his position in the MC (see fig. 251).

Fs take up defensive positions.

P smashes straight.

F blocks straight or X-court.

P (front man) travels into FC, hits a winner and recovers.

Fs allow the shuttle to hit the floor.

Work schedule: 5 rallies. Players rotate in turn.

Practice 64

Aim: To improve the speed of the front man in getting in position; to develop skill in hitting a 'winner'.

Players: Two players (P) and two feeders (F). A 2 v. 2 practice.

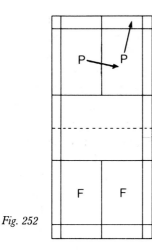

Fig. 252

Instructions: Players position themselves as shown in fig. 250.
Players rally at a fast pace in the MC.
F lobs the shuttle to P's left RC.
P (rear man) travels back to smash while P (front man) travels
into the left MC and adjusts his position relative to the shuttle
position (see fig. 252).
P smashes straight.
F blocks to the centre.
P (front man) travels forwards whilst P (rear man) travels into
position into the MC.
P (front man) hits a 'winner' and recovers into position outside
the FC.
Work schedule: 5 rallies. Players rotate in turn.

Practice 65
Aim: To improve the speed of the front man in getting into
position; to develop co-operative play between the attackers; to
develop skill in hitting a winner.
Players: Two players (P) and two feeders (F). A 2 v. 2 practice.
Instructions: Players position themselves as shown in fig. 250.
Note: This practice is similar to practice 64 except that the
attackers are forced to change from the right court to the left
court several times before the front man 'kills' the shuttle.
Players rally at a fast pace.
F lobs to the right RC.
P (rear man) travels into position in the RC while P (front man)
adjusts his position to the right MC (see fig. 253 for positions of
Ps).
Fs adopt central defence positions.
Now the main action begins:
P smashes straight. F blocks straight.
P (front man) attacks in forecourt while P (rear man) travels into
position in the midcourt (see fig. 253).
P (front man) taps straight. F lobs x-court to RC.
P (rear man) travels into the RC while P (front man) adjusts his
position in the left MC.
Fs adopt centre defence positions (see fig. 254).
P (rear man) smashes straight. F blocks straight.
P (front man) attacks in FC while players adjust their positions.
F lobs x-court to RC . . . Continue until the fifth smash and
then P (front man) hits a 'winner'.
Work schedule: 5 rallies. Players rotate in turn.

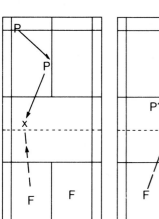

Fig. 253

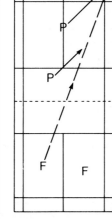

Fig. 254

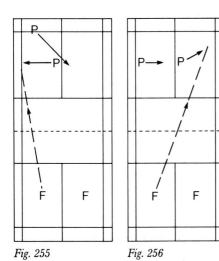

Fig. 255   *Fig. 256*

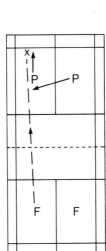

Fig. 257

Practice 66

Aim: To develop speed in changing from RC 'front and back' attack to 'sides' attack.

Players: Two players (P) and two feeders (F). A 2 v. 2 practice.

Instructions: Players position themselves as shown in fig. 250. Players rally at a fast pace.

F lobs to the right RC.

P (rear man) travels into the RC while P (front man) adjusts his position in the MC.

Fs adopt centre defence positions.

P smashes straight to the side line.

F drives the shuttle back down the line.

P (front man) dives across and slashes at the shuttle while P (rear man) sprints across to the left MC into sides attack position (see fig. 255).

P (front man) hits the shuttle straight at F and recovers quickly into sides attack.

F whips the shuttle x-court towards the left RC (see fig. 256).

P (sides attacker) leaps up, intercepts and smashes a 'winner'. End of rally.

Work schedule: 5 rallies. Players rotate in turn.

Note: This practice can commence with the lob from F in the right MC to P's left RC. Then the front man can practise jumping to hit a backhand interception.

Practice 67

Aim: To develop speed in getting into 'channel attack' formation.

Players: Two players (P) and two feeders (F). A 2 v. 2 practice.

Instructions: Players position themselves as shown in fig. 250. Players rally at a fast pace.

F lobs to right MC/RC.

P (rear man) travels quickly into position. P (front man) travels quickly into position in front of him in the right MC (see fig. 257).

Fs take up centre defence positions.

P (rear man) smashes straight – at F's body.

F blocks, pushes or drives straight.

P (front man) attacks and hits a 'winner'.

Work schedule: 5 rallies. Players rotate in turn.

Practice 68

Aim: To develop speed in getting into different attack formations – sides attack to wedge attack to channel attack.

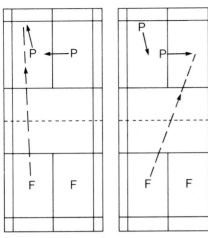

Fig. 258

Fig. 259

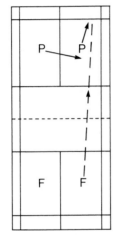

Fig. 260

Fig. 261

Players: Two players (P) and two feeders (F). A 2 v. 2 practice.

Instructions: Players position themselves as shown in fig. 250. Players rally at a fast pace.

F lobs straight–to MC/RC.

P (rear man) travels into position while P (front man) adjusts position to 'wedge attack' in the MC (see fig. 258).

P smashes straight.

F whips the shuttle x-court towards the left RC.

P (front man) travels back to attack while P (rear man) travels into position for sides attack (see fig. 259).

P (previous front man) smashes straight–from the MC–and recovers.

F lobs straight to the left MC/RC.

P travels back into position to attack as rear man while partner travels into the left court directly in front of him as front man (see fig. 260).

P (rear man) smashes straight at F's body.

F blocks, pushes or drives straight.

P (front man) leaps forwards and hits a 'winner'.

Work schedule: 5 rallies. Players rotate in turn.

Practice 69

Aim: To develop speed in adjusting position in attack; to improve the skill of the front man in MC attack.

Players: Two players (P) and two feeders (F). A 2 v. 2 practice.

Instructions: Players position themselves as shown in fig. 250. Players rally at a fast pace.

F lobs straight to right RC.

P (rear man) travels into position while P (front man) adjusts position in the MC.

P smashes.

F blocks straight to right FC.

P (front man) travels forwards to attack while P (rear man) adjusts his position in the MC.

P (front man) taps the shuttle at F and recovers.

F lobs the shuttle to the right RC.

Players adjust positions as before (see fig. 261).

P (rear man) smashes straight.

F drives straight to the side of the right MC.

P (front man) dives across and hits shuttle to the centre MC for a 'winner' as P (rear man) travels forwards into a sides attack position (see fig. 261).

Work schedule: 5 rallies. Players rotate in turn.

Appendix

Throughout the text the emphasis has been placed firmly on the tactics of the game. Tactics is the expression of the player's intelligent thinking or lack of it in a game. Even more than that, it is the expression of the player's awareness of and co-operation with another human being to achieve a particular goal: to defeat the other side and win the game. It is the *principle of attack* that determines what tactics are used and that accounts for all the activity that should occur both in the preparation for the game, if any, and in the game itself.

There are many features of the game that can be discussed with advantage. I have tried to deal with the most important features of the game, as you will have seen if you have read this far. However, there are some points that I have mentioned—and a few that I have not—which are worth considering further. Even a brief discussion of these will contribute towards your understanding of the game and your improved performance in it.

1. Attitude in competition

The competition is the test of attitude. When a contest is a close one and skill, fitness and attitude seem to be equal between the contestants, then a player must call on something extra; in some way he must intensify his efforts. This he will be able to do if he has acquired the discipline that comes from submitting himself to the work required to attain the standards of excellence within the different aspects of performance. It is no easy task to pursue and achieve some degree of excellence; it requires a great deal of sacrifice and much time and effort in the commitment to work. It is only by doing the work that a player learns that he is up to the task, and it is this knowledge that gives him the confidence required to do the job on court, however demanding and difficult it may be.

If the player has done the work he should have no doubts about his ability. He should know what he is capable of. In this way doubts are removed and he can concentrate on the task of winning. But if all things are equal between him, his partner and the opponents, something more is needed. That something is character and the will to win, which also comes through and from the work and yet is unique to each individual. It is the combination of mental toughness and spirit that enables a player to intensify his resolution and lift himself to that extra dimension of human endeavour. He raises his standards. Thus we see, and his partner and the opponents feel, that total commitment, cold determination, absolute concentration, rigid control, continual perseverence, and carefree adventurousness as chances are taken fearlessly. The player becomes totally lost in the moment, playing with controlled passion in single-minded pursuit of victory and with such relentless pressure that his partner is lifted, just as the opponents must eventually succumb.

How does a player develop such an attitude through and in his work? He does it by caring about how he does what he does. He does it by expressing concern for himself as an athlete. He does it by never allowing his standards to fall below his best in the contest. How does this happen? First, let us consider how the player shows he cares about how he does what he does. Let us take practice as an example. Practice entails continuous work on the technical/tactical aspects of skill in order to achieve control and accuracy at speed and play intelligently in the tactical situations that occur in the game. The player must care about getting things right. Any old way of performing will not do; he must work at his technique of hitting the shuttle and travelling from one situation to another to make his stroke-moves until he gets it right. And he knows when he has got it right, for then he does not have to think consciously about how to hit the shuttle, jump and land, or where to hit the shuttle in a particular situation. He does it automatically and intuitively. To do this he must practise constantly. He cannot afford to miss his practice and will work on it until he gets things right, even though he must sacrifice his time and other interests to do it.

Second, how does the player express concern for himself as an athlete? Here the highest standard is his potential maximum fitness for badminton. The rigours of training required to reach this standard rule out anything detrimental to it. Players who do not maintain regular training sessions, who do not work hard in training, who over-eat or eat the wrong sort of food, smoke or drink too much alcohol, if any, and fail to get the necessary rest, will find it more than difficult to attain the standard: they will find it impossible. The penalty for any neglect is a lower standard of fitness and consequently a lower standard of performance in the game. There are too many players who deceive themselves that they are fit. Too few test their fitness scientifically to know just how fit they are and how fit they could become. It is my opinion that badminton players, with few exceptions, only scratch the surface of fitness (and here I am writing about world class players). Too many get by on technique and experience, when more work on fitness could improve their performance to levels they could not conceive at the present time.

Any player who seriously considers full-time badminton as a career should have his fitness level tested regularly and should construct a fitness training programme specifically related to his personal needs as a player. Such a programme is progressive, not over a few months prior to the main season but over years, and related to all the major tournaments. How many players actually do this in a serious fashion? I wonder. For those players who do not aspire to full-time badminton the same applies. Although there will not be the same degree of commitment to high standards of skill and fitness, because time does not permit, there should be some commitment. If a player claims to enjoy the game I should imagine that he would want to become better at it. One might expect some care about practice and, I should hope, a great deal of enjoyment from practising even if it can be hard work. There is much satisfaction to be gained from 'getting it right', whether it is the sliced smash or a spin-jump. Similarly, we might expect all interested players to want to improve their fitness. This belief would certainly apply to younger players. It does not take up much time each day to perform 'slow stretching' exercises, complete a simple body circuit of training for strength, and jog and run for 15 minutes minimum or 30 minutes maximum four or five days each week. Training should become a habit, a daily routine like cleaning the teeth. It is enjoyable and contributes to good health and a sense of well-being. It certainly helps to improve performance in badminton.

Third, how does a player never allow his standard to fall below his best? This is a matter for all players, whatever their level, for each player has his personal best which he is constantly trying to make better. I am reminded here of a conversation I had with Rudi Hartono. I have always been an admirer of Hartono's play because he never appeared to allow his standards to fall on all the occasions I watched him play at the All England Championships. His record of singles titles would seem to confirm my view. He always won a rally in as few moves as possible. At his peak, few players scored more than nine points in a game and most scored only a few points. His opponents were submitted to constant pressure as he moved early to the shuttle with speed and applied speed and power to the shuttle. He gave the impression of always pursuing and 'coming at' the opponent. He was a great player.

I asked Hartono about his attitude in play and how he managed to maintain such constant pressure with so few mistakes at any stage in the game, for he began fast and finished fast. He told me quite simply that he played every shot as if it was match point. He did this always in practice and from the moment he stepped on the court in a competition, no matter whom he played. Now, all players are capable of doing this in singles or doubles. Of course, Rudi Hartono's best was a great deal higher than that of other players at the time, but he played no other way. He trained himself to play that way because he enjoyed the game and cared about himself as an athlete and about how he did what he did.

The responsibility for attaining the standard in the game rests with the player. If he wants to do well he must submit himself to the standards required, to the extent that he becomes the best at the level he wants to play at. Those who do will naturally acquire the discipline to maintain them in competition and thus adopt appropriate attitudes. Through the work the player learns to lift himself even when tired or bored and frustrated. In preparation, he has overloaded the work to ensure that there is nothing in the game that he cannot contend with. The disciplined player is trained like the good actor. No matter how tired, upset or fearful he feels, 'the show must go on', and accordingly he submits himself to the discipline of his craft and gives a good performance. In this way the years of training and sacrifice, in striving for standards, pay off.

2. Deception

With so much emphasis on speed in doubles there might appear to be little need for deception. Yet in fact the greater the speed of play, the greater is the need for deception. Let me explain. Deception takes the form of a pretence by a player, who tries to communicate to his opponent his intention to do one thing, by looking as if to play a specific move, when in actual fact he intends to make another move. He could, for example, look as if to drive the shuttle to the left of the opponent and then as the opponent moves to the left, hit the shuttle to the right of the opponent. The opponent has been deceived.

For deception to succeed it is important that the opponent

'reads' the body language of the player as 'he looks as if to hit the shuttle to my left' behaviour. The player presents a picture of himself which the opponent sees and interprets as being of a certain sort. His response—in this case, 'to the left'—indicates his interpretation of that picture. The players might be said to 'speak' the same body language as one communicates non-verbally his intentions to the other. However, it could be different. If the 'picture' is unclear, vague or too complex then the opponent might not be able, or have time, to interpret it and will not respond as desired. Even if correct interpretation is possible, the opponent might have insufficient time to make his response and the deception would fail.

It is most important, therefore, that the deceiver presents the opponent with a clear picture of the stroke-move (his intention), which he knows the opponent will recognise, and then allows time for him to make the desired interpretation of that picture and respond to it. If the deceiver can achieve this then he can manipulate the opponents' responses to his advantage. This is why I said earlier that deception is needed even more now to combat speed.

The speed of the opponents' response to a move poses a threat to the other side. The speed at which a player responds is dependent on two factors: (a) his reaction time, which is to do with how quickly he can transmit information through the nervous system to his muscles, and (b) speed of movement, which is determined by how quickly those muscles can contract to enable him to make his response.

The deceiver cannot do much about the speed of contraction of the opponents' muscles unless he tires him out, but he can do a great deal about the information that is passed through the nervous system to those muscles. He can, quite simply, present the wrong information. He can look as if he will do one thing and then do another. The opponent transmits the information gained from the 'picture' he sees before him to the muscles and he responds. But it was a false 'picture' he saw—he has been deceived. The deceiver can then hit the shuttle where he wants it to go with less threat of an immediate counter-attack and with the possibility of creating a situation in which he can eventually hit a winner.

Deception has a tactical basis. That, really, is the only point to it. When the opponents anticipate early, as they pre-judge the stroke-move you intend to play, then you have a problem unless you can deceive them in one of two ways: (a) cause them to anticipate too early and make the wrong response to the stroke-move you intend to make, and (b) get them to delay their response until it is too late for them to benefit from it so that the reply they make is to your advantage.

In what ways can you be deceptive?

1. Always prepare as if to play the most attacking stroke-move in any situation. As this poses a threat to the opponent you can be sure that he will get ready to receive the shuttle. Now you are free to play other moves.
2. Try to keep your preparation identical for similar groups of strokes. The preparation for overhead strokes should look the same whether you intend to play a clear, drop or smash. If this is so then the opponent cannot anticipate too early and may actually experience some doubt and uncertainty about your intention.
3. Always have the racket prepared to make the stroke-move as you approach the shuttle. In this way you can pause during the stroke with the racket held in the preparation phase and so create the illusion of 'holding the shot'. The opponent can be tempted to anticipate your move.
4. Learn from other sports. Football is full of deception as are basketball, rugby, netball and hockey. In these sports much of the deception takes the form of the use of 'body sway' as the players feint or swerve one way to wrong-foot the opponent, and then change direction to send the ball or themselves the other way.

In badminton there is much scope for body sway when serving, and body sway and feints when making the block return, the push and the drive replies to the smash or in a midcourt 'slugging' attack situation. Look at boxing and karate as the contestants feint at speed with their hands, a shrug of the shoulder, a quick body-weight transfer – sufficient to make the opponent respond in some way to give the deceiver the opening he wants to make a move to his advantage.

Learning deception

You must develop skilful use of the racket. You must learn to control the speed of the racket head; to speed it up or check the speed at any time during a stroke. You must learn to control the racket face so that you can direct the shuttle where you please with a change of position of the racket face at any time before the impact with the shuttle. You must acquire an enjoyment in cleverly outwitting the opponent, to trick him and entice him into making a futile response. You must relate what you do to the opponent as it is the deceiving of the opponent which will enhance your chances of winning the rally. You won't indulge in too much deception if you remember that its purpose is purely tactical.

Finally, learn it by practising it in the game. You might just find that it adds that extra something required to raise your practical standard in the game.

3. Team work

It should be apparent throughout the text that team work is the very essence of doubles play. It is also obvious that team work will develop if two players play regularly together. There are several ways that two players can assist in their own development as a team.

First, they should decide how they will play together. This will entail some critical analysis of each other's game and a detailed discussion about how each will operate in certain situations, e.g. as front or rear hit- or set-up player. Such discussion is a continuous ongoing process before and during a game as conditions change. The players should always be ready to modify their play and adapt it to the situations as they alter in the changing game.

Second, they should decide who does what in any situations in which both players might attempt to make a stroke-move. A typical example here is the centre of the court. A friend of mine recently asked me who should reply to the clear down the centre of the court. It appears that the shuttle was just in her court, the right court, and she was well placed to smash it. Unfortunately, her partner came across to hit the shuttle; they collided and both missed it. My friend complained to her partner who replied that the player who can hit the shuttle with a forehand stroke should play the shot. They were both right from their own point of view. The partner was following the general rule that the forehand player takes the shuttle down the centre. My friend was following the rule that the player best placed to hit the shuttle should do so. What they forgot to do was to decide what policy to adopt before they began playing.

During the rallies there will be many instances of doubt about who should travel into position to hit the shuttle. All players should adopt the policy of top class players, particularly the ladies. They talk constantly during the play, letting each other know what to do and not to do. The court echoes with sounds of, 'mine, yours, yes, no, in, out, leave it, get it, go, run, OK' and so on. If they are not passing information to each other they are encouraging each other to play well and complimenting each other after a good winning move has been made.

It is normal for one player to go through a bad patch during a game. It may be disappointing for that player and his partner but it is just one of those things. When that happens it is very important that the partner encourages him and helps him through his bad patch. Too many players become frustrated and show their annoyance when this happens. This is too negative an approach. Players must be positive and take on the responsibility for the side until the partner gets into his stride again. That is team work.

4. Analysis of opponents

It is not always necessary to analyse the opponents' game. If you and your partner are the best pair around, you can play your normal game and let the opponents analyse *your* game. Much of the analysis of the opponents, if any, in these circumstances will be ongoing during the game.

There are times when it is essential that you analyse the opponents' game. If you know you are playing a pair who are known to be or have proved themselves to be better than your side, then you should study the way they play. You must analyse their game to some extent either after playing them or beforehand. It is quite possible to analyse the play beforehand and work out what tactics to use against them and how to respond to the situations they create. There is sufficient information in the charts and the chapters on doubles play to help you to analyse any pair of doubles players.

The questions you should ask and answer are of this sort: Where does each opponent stand to receive serve? Do they stand back to cover the flick serve or forwards to attack the low serve? *(Note:* If the receiver stands back you can serve low and force a lift. If he stands forward you can use the flick serve to catch him out – if you have practised your flick serve.) Does the receiver who attacks the net use one grip only and hit one way only? If so you can serve to obtain the reply you want. Does the front man stand on the T during the rearcourt attack or in the midcourt? If he stands on the T you can drive or push the shuttle down the sides and bring the rear man in to lift it. If he stands in the midcourt you want to find out whether he is adventurous. Does he leap sideways to attack the shuttle or does he block it? Does he leap forwards to hit down from above the net or does he step forwards and play a push or a net return? In brief, is he much of a threat as the front man? Because if he is not you can return the shuttle to the forecourt without any concern that he will hit a winner.

If you work through all the different situations, it should not be too difficult to work out how the opponents play together and where you can hit the shuttle to exploit them and create situations to your advantage. If you know what you want to do but find that you lack the skill or speed to make certain stroke-moves, then devise a practice (if you cannot find one in Chapter 10), and work until you can perform the stroke-moves.

5. Thoughts for the future

I have always believed that there is room for tremendous developments within badminton. The athletic potential of the players and the speed at which the game is played provide good examples of this. Players could become much fitter, especially in Europe and North America. The eastern players, particularly the Indonesians and Chinese, are superior athletes in general, no doubt because they have a tougher time getting to the top and when they do they work in training camps under the supervision of top coaches and fitness training experts. Few European players work with the intensity of the Asian players in their fitness development and their speed of movement.

It is only by working hard on flexibility and agility, speed and strength, that a player can make that extra bit of an effort to stretch out and reach the shuttle that much earlier. Such players possess a dynamic which is exciting to watch just as it is successful in competition.

The morning of writing this part of the text I was coaching at my local sports hall. Two England singles players were practising on the adjacent court. They were working hard and covering a lot of distance on the court. They played a game and worked just as hard to finish, soaked through with perspiration. The rallies had been long ones and hard fought. But the play was dull and mediocre. They were just getting fitter with respect to their endurance, and practising their established racket skills. There was no excitement in the game. Neither player expressed any extra effort that required him to dig deep into his inner resources, to stretch himself that little bit more each time. They could play that way all day and learn nothing and improve nothing. There was no point to their work—no goal to achieve in their practice. In match play they could not hurt the opponent for they would not put any pressure on him. The point is that players at this level need guidance. They need to be stretched and to know how to stretch themselves. There are too many good players, potential contenders for the world titles in both singles and doubles, who need taking that much further towards what is possible within the game.

In both singles and doubles, racket skills are quite easy to learn. Compared with learning to play tennis, with all the difficulties entailed in hitting a bouncing ball that can spin and rebound differently on different surfaces, learning to hit a shuttlecock is easy. What is difficult in badminton, more so than any other racket game, is the ability to move well and contend with the complexity of the tactics of the game. In badminton a very high degree of gymnastic/athletic type movement skill is required. It is easy to hit the shuttle but it is very difficult to travel into position to do so – especially as the game speeds up and the skilful players begin to use deception.

I believe that players could improve in the following areas:

1. They could become stronger and learn to hit the shuttle much harder with less movement. This is particularly so in the forecourt and midcourt where 'fast hands' are required. If players could learn karate-hitting techniques, the ability to apply tremendous force quickly as they use the racket, we would see a different game. For this players need to do speed work with weights and develop greater strength in the trunk.

2. Players could learn to be more adventurous in their movement about the court. Greater leg strength can be gained from working with weights, practising power jumps, and learning to explode from a stationary position with ease. Players need to develop smooth controlled power. Work on agility and stretching are also important for fast adventurous movement – to reach that extra distance with control and recover in balance at speed.

Finally, players must learn to throw themselves about the court in situations when it is required. Such a situation happens in the midcourt when the front player has to leap to the sideline to intercept and attack the shuttle; similarly in the forecourt.

I believe that players could be even more adventurous in these situations. Often if a player cannot intercept the shuttle by leaping and reaching he lets it go by the rear man. But if the front man *dived* across the court almost horizontally he would travel quicker through the air and most probably hit the shuttle down for a winner. Will a player dive for the shuttle as a goalkeeper would in football or a player in volleyball? Not likely, for to do so could result in injury as he lands on the hard floor. Yet there is no reason why players cannot be taught to dive and land properly; goalkeepers and volleyball players do so. It is quite easy to avoid injury by wearing elbow and knee pads during the game. It is only a matter of practice in the situation until players learn how to dive and land without hurting themselves. It is only a matter of time until players get used to wearing protective clothing. Will we see this sort of development in the game? I believe so. We will have to wait and see.

6. On planning and play

The whole purpose of studying the game, training and practising, is to equip you and your partner to solve any problem in any situation that arises. It is to help you to create situations to your advantage and to free you from conscious thought during a rally. It is certainly not the intention that you should go on court with preconceived plans which you follow regardless of the way the game develops, or to theorise about the game in the middle of a match (although if you have both done the work you should be able to discuss the play and possible tactics to use at different times in the game as the need to do so arises). In general, if you have done the work you should be able to play intuitively and imaginatively in making the necessary stroke-moves.

The more you think, study and prepare yourself mentally off the court, the less mental work you have to do on the court. The more physical work you do in training, the less you need that fitness in the game. The more time you spend on technical and tactical practices, the easier it is to perform strokes and create situations to your advantage in the contest. Your game becomes simplified in competition relative to how much work you both put in developing it in practice and training. It is through the work that you acquire confidence in the knowledge that you are fully prepared as individuals and as a team. And with that you can become totally immersed in the task of trying to beat the opponents – in playing winning doubles.

Glossary

Active defence	The defenders use stroke-moves to neutralise the attack and/or regain the attack.
All-court player	A player who can operate with equal ease as a hit-player or set-up player in the RC, MC and FC.
Angle of return	The angle formed by the lines of direction of the possible returns of the shuttle to the left and right sides of the court (see fig. 270).
Attack clear	An attacking clear used to hit the shuttle on a shallow pathway to the RC behind the defenders (see fig. 263).
Attack position	The racket is held in front with the racket head above the hand, ready to be used like a weapon to attack.
Attacking stance	An upright alert stance, with knees flexed and the racket held in the attack position. The player adopts either: (a) a *forward attacking stance* with his right foot slightly forwards and his rear foot used as a pivot or push-off foot ready to attack in the FC, or (b) a *backward attacking stance* with his right foot behind him ready to attack in the RC.
Backward jump smash	A backward jump performed at speed to smash a shuttle hit on a low trajectory to the RC, e.g. the flick serve, whip, or attack clear.
Block	A stroke-move used to meet a fast shuttle in the FC or MC and return it to the FC, e.g. the midcourt block to the smash or the forecourt block to the drive (see fig. 265).
Brush-shot	A stroke-move used to meet the shuttle just as it crosses the net. The racket face is 'brushed' *across* the shuttle in a very fast action parallel to the net, to hit the shuttle down without the racket hitting the net.
Centred	Describes the state of the player when his trunk is evenly balanced between his points of support, i.e. his feet and legs.
Centre defence	Both defenders occupy a central position in the MC.

Channel attack	The attackers adopt a 'front and back' formation with the front attacker positioned directly in front of the rear player. The attack is then focused on one defender only.
Check-smash	The player begins his smash action and then abruptly checks the racket head speed to hit the shuttle softly into the FC. It is used to deceive the defender and cause him to be late getting to the shuttle.
Chopping	An exercise used to develop hand speed and flexibility.
Cross-court (x-court)	Describes the pathway of the shuttle when it is hit to travel across the centre line of the court (the line dividing the court into right and left sides – see fig. 271).
Dab	A rebound hitting action used to make the kill when the shuttle is close to the net, and to prevent the racket head hitting the net. Similar to but stronger than the 'tap'.
Diagonal defence	A defensive formation with one defender positioned either in the FC and his partner in the MC, or one defender in the MC and his partner in the RC.
Dink-smash	A steeply angled smash performed with a tapping action of the racket from outstretched arm height above the player.
Drive	A stroke-move used to hit the shuttle at speed to skim the net on a horizontal pathway.
Drive serve	To serve the shuttle horizontally at speed.
Fast drop	An overhead stroke-move similar to the smash, used to hit the shuttle downwards on a steep pathway into the FC.
Flat	A shuttle hit to travel horizontally.
Flick	A quick action of the hand used to generate racket head speed with the minimum of movement, e.g. flick serve, the whip.
FC	Forecourt.
Forward attack	The receiver springs forwards and upwards to attack the low serve.
Forward defence	The defenders take up positions near the FC.
Front defence	The defenders stand square on to the attackers, ready to defend on both sides of the body.
Front and back formation	A formation with one player operating as the rear player and the partner as the front player.

Hairpin drop	A stroke-move used when the shuttle is low and close to the net. The shuttle is hit upwards to 'crawl' over the net and fall vertically on the other side. The pathway of the shuttle is 'hairpin' in shape.
High clear	A stroke-move used to send the shuttle very high to fall vertically in the RC (see fig. 263).
High defence	The defender hits the shuttle with the racket head held up above the level of the hand.
Hit-player	An adventurous or powerful player whose main function is to attempt to hit a winner.
Kill	A strong winning hit usually performed in the MC or FC. The following strokes are used to make the kill: smash, slash, brush, dab.
Kinaesthetic awareness	The sense of knowing in the muscles the movement and spatial position of your body, e.g. when you experience the feeling of the movement in performing a drop shot or make fine adjustments in balance when you land and recover after a backward jump smash.
Lift	To hit the shuttle upwards from below net level.
Lob	To hit the shuttle from below net level up towards the RC (see fig. 266).
Low defence	The defender hits the shuttle when the racket head is below the level of the hand.
Low return	The shuttle is hit from below net level in the MC or RC and aimed to fall quickly near the FC after crossing the net (see fig. 265).
MC	Midcourt.
Move	A tactical shot.
Net reply	Any stroke-move used to hit the shuttle from the FC over the net into the opponents' forecourt.
Neutral situation	A situation when neither side is predominantly on the attack or in defence, e.g. a MC 'slugging' rally.
Passive defence	The defenders use defence for the sake of defence – that is, they return the shuttle constantly to the rearcourt and give the opponents the attack.

Power smash	The shuttle is hit with maximum force: the racket face is square on to the shuttle on impact.
Principle of attack	The underlying principle which provides the rationale for all the stroke-moves.
RC	Rearcourt.
Scissor jump smash	A backward jump 'round the head' smash. The legs change position in the air during the flight as the player takes off on his right foot and lands on his left foot.
Set-up player	An imaginative, creative player whose main task is to create the opening and set-up the chance for his partner to hit a winner.
Side-on defence	The defender turns slightly sideways to defend on one side of the body only.
Side-on jump smash	The player remains side-on to the shuttle during the jump and when he lands after the smash.
Sides attack positions	The players stand in attacking stances level with each other in the MC.
Sides defence	The defenders position themselves level with each other in relation to the attackers.
Slash	A powerful stroke-move used to hit the shuttle from above net height on the player's right side with a forehand 'slashing' action.
Slugging rally	A fast MC rally with both sides hitting the shuttle hard at each other.
Spin-jump smash	A jump smash from the forehand side. The player rotates in the air as he smashes and lands facing the net, his weight evenly balanced on both feet or on his front foot ready to accelerate forwards.
Spinner	A stroke-move used in the forecourt to strike the shuttle a glancing blow and cause it to rotate around its vertical axis.
Standard clear	A clear used simply to manoeuvre the opponent into the RC (see fig. 263).
Stroke-move	A stroke used as a tactical move.
Tap	A quick light hitting action with the racket face rebounding on impact with the shuttle.

Transition move	A stroke-move used to alter the positions of the players in the court, e.g. used by one side to manoeuvre the front hit-man to the RC, or to regain their strongest positions if already manoeuvred out of position.
Tumbler	A stroke-move used in the FC to strike the shuttle a glancing blow and cause it to rotate around its horizontal axis.
Underarm net reply	Any stroke-move used to hit the shuttle from below the net in the FC to anywhere in the opponents' forecourt, e.g. a hairpin drop.
Wedge attack	The attackers adopt a 'front and back' formation with the front player positioned to one side of the rear player ready to cover a x-court reply. The attack is focused on one defender only.
Whip	A fast lift to the RC played from the MC or near the top of the net in the FC (see figs 266, 268).

Rearcourt stroke-moves

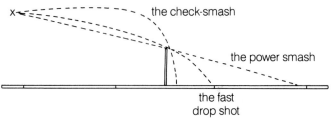

Fig. 262

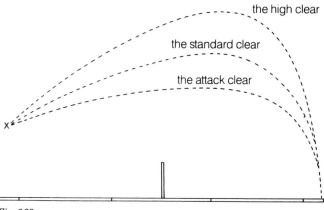

Fig. 263

Midcourt stroke-moves

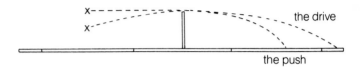

Fig. 264

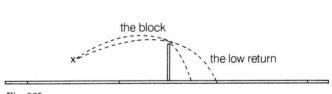

Fig. 265

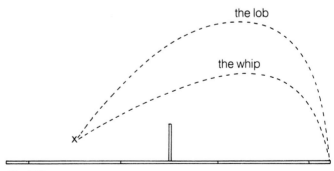

Fig. 266

Forecourt stroke-moves

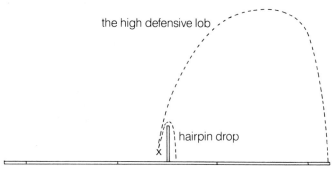

Fig. 267

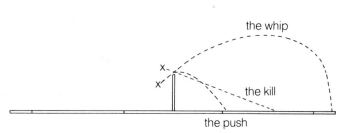

Fig. 268

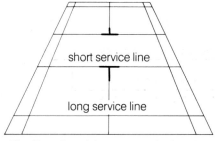

The T section of the court − the junction
of the short service line and the centre line

Fig. 269

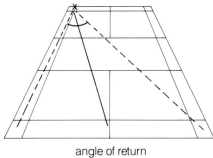

angle of return
with line dividing the angle of return

Fig. 270

The Doubles court

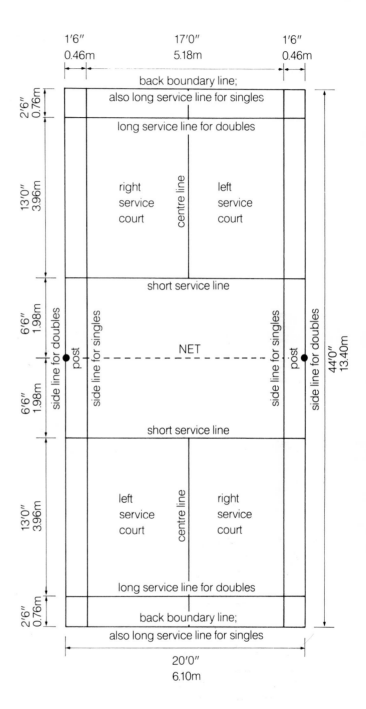

diagonal measurement of full court: 48ft 4ins (14.723m)
diagonal measurement of half court: 29ft 8¾ins (9.061m)
(from post to back boundary line)

Fig. 271
(measurements include line widths)